Glasnost' in Context

Berg European Studies Series

General Editor: Brian Nelson (Monash University, Melbourne)

Advisory Board: Michael Biddiss (University of Reading), John
Flower (University of Exeter), Paul Michael Lützeler
(Washington University, St. Louis), David Roberts (Monash
University, Melbourne), George Ross (Harvard University),
Walter Veit (Monash University, Melbourne)

David Roberts and Philip Thomson (eds.), *The Modern German
Historical Novel: Paradigms, Problems, Perspectives*

– Forthcoming –

Brian Nelson (ed.), *Naturalism in the European Novel: Modern Essays
in Criticism*

Glasnost' in Context

On the Recurrence of Liberalizations in Central and East European Literatures and Cultures

Edited by
Marko Pavlyshyn

BERG

New York / Oxford / Munich

Distributed exclusively in the US and Canada by
St. Martin's Press, New York

First published in 1990 by
Berg Publishers Limited
Editorial Offices
165 Taber Avenue, Providence R.I. 02906, USA
150 Cowley Road, Oxford OX4 IJJ, UK
Westermühlstraße 26, 8000 München 5, FRG

Library of Congress Cataloging-in-Publication Data

Glasnost' in Context: On the Recurrence of Liberalizations in
Central and East European Literatures and Cultures /
edited by Marko Pavlyshyn.
    p. cm. — (Berg European studies series)
Selected papers from an interdisciplinary conference held
at Monash University in Feb. 1988.
Includes bibliographical references.
ISBN 0–85496–598–X
1. Europe, Eastern—Intellectual life–Congresses. 2. East
European literature—History and criticism–Congresses.
I. Pavlyshyn, Marko. II. Series.
DJK24.T43 1990   89–39740
947—dc20   CIP

British Library Cataloguing in Publication Data

Glasnost' in Context: On the Recurrence of
    Liberalizations in Central and East European
    Literatures and Cultures. – (Berg European
    Studies Series).
    1. Eastern European arts. Influence of Eastern
    European political events, history.
    I. Pavlyshyn, Marko
    700'. 947
    ISBN 0–85496–598–X

Printed by Billing and Sons Ltd, Worcester

Contents

Contents

Preface

In 1954, amid the excitement and expectations released by the death of Stalin in March of the previous year, the venerable Soviet writer Il'ia Erenburg published a short novel, *Ottepel'* (The Thaw). It was a case of a term emerging simultaneously with the most typical example of the phenomenon which it designated. The metaphor rang true: after a bitter winter came warmer temperatures and the hope of a spring, the rigidity of the ice seemed no longer absolute, and seeds that had lain dormant throughout the long cold began to germinate.

Eventually it would become clear that the thaw had been merely an episode of fickle and temperamental Khrushchevian weather that had failed to melt the Siberian permafrost. It yielded, in the second half of the 1960s, to a new freeze, but not before contributing to general usage a notion that has helped shape our perception of political and cultural change – and not only in the USSR of the 1950s. As was to be expected, the term 'thaw' came to be used with reference to events in those Central and East European states which, remoulded after the Second World War in the image of the Soviet Union, followed their political master into a phase of liberalization, especially after Khrushchev's criticism of Stalin in 1956. The term was subsequently applied to the period of relaxed censorship in late eighteenth-century Austria under Joseph II and, more loosely, to the less repressive periods in Russian imperial and early Soviet history: the reform years of Alexander I, the prelude to the emancipation of the serfs in 1861, the years following the revolution of 1905, and the 1920s. Not surprisingly, the new Soviet reform initiated in 1985 by Mikhail Gorbachev was apprehended by observers on both sides of the Iron Curtain as a thaw.

The metaphor, however, is limited in its application to a narrow range of political circumstances. It has not found its way, for example, into descriptions of change in Western-style democracies or in right-wing dictatorships, even though both are susceptible to phases of liberalization or deregulation. For the metaphor to be accepted as appropriate, it seems, a number of conditions must apply. A central authority must have a monopoly of state power, which, as a rule, it exercises in an authoritarian and coercive way. The Centre must profess to derive its legitimacy, however, from a commitment to modernization, progress and human emancipation – that is, from an ideology, be it benevolent autocracy or Marxism-Leninism, that traces its genealogy to the Enlightenment. The legitimating ideals of the state must be, initially at least, acceptable to the potential opposition, whose discontent at first is focussed, not on the objectives which the state claims to pursue, but on the manner in which it does so. Any real increase in the degree of individual freedom may then be perceived by members of the incipient opposition as a convergence between the practices of the state and their own wishes, a perception which may well account for the public enthusiasm that characterizes the early phases of thaws.

Thaws may include among their salient features concessions to private enterprise and a more flexible foreign policy (both are especially typical of the Gorbachev period), but their central characteristic is enhanced freedom of expression. Censorship is relaxed; punishments for nonconformist opinion are moderated. In the post-Stalin thaw in the USSR and Eastern Europe, for example, political show trials, purges and executions ceased, the secret police were reined in, some individuals who had been persecuted for deviating from ideological orthodoxy were rehabilitated, and dissent was, to a limited extent, tolerated. All parties, however, remain aware that a thaw is in the gift of the authorities. It is granted on the initiative of the Centre in pursuit of goals which the Centre defines. Usually these goals include modernization and economic development in the interests of maintaining or achieving parity with an external competitor ('catching up with the West'), or, indeed, of politically strengthening the state by improving the economic well-being of its citizens.

The limits of a thaw are determined from above: beyond a certain pale of toleration, whose extent is unknown until tested, transgressors will be brought to heel. If, as was the case in Hungary in 1956, Czechoslovakia in 1968, Poland in 1980, and the People's Republic of China in 1989, the reform initiative passes from the authorities to some other group, especially one which may plausibly claim to represent the population at large, the model of thaw becomes less fitting than that of revolution. Climatic fine-tuning of the symbols of repression becomes an inadequate guarantee of control, and the state is obliged to call on more substantial measures, such as military intervention or martial law. Revolutionary situations are characterized by the mobilization of a large part of the population; thaws by the mobilization of a privileged minority, the intelligentsia, whom the state, by condoning their quasi-oppositional activity, at the same time co-opts as advocates of its legitimacy.

It is certainly the case that, while the objectives of thaws may be defined in political and economic terms by the powers that set them in motion, their actual manifestations reflect the intelligentsia's interest in cultural issues. Much of the energy of thaws is expended in the modification of myths. Stalin is desacralized. History is rewritten, and previously inadmissible facts and unmentionable people are brought into its orbit. In a process which Katerina Clark, following Bakhtin, calls 'reaccentuation', the cultural tradition is reviewed and new canons and sources of authority are recovered from it. The legitimacy of old sources of human identity other than those approved by the formerly all-powerful Centre is asserted; national cultures and religions effectively breach the state's cultural and ideological monopoly.

And yet, though the most prominent dimension of thaws is the cultural, they seldom correspond with breakthroughs in the aesthetic domain. Thaws are times when aesthetic issues, important though they are, seem less crucial than political ones. In consequence, the arts in times of thaw risk becoming journalistic and proclamatory. Sometimes the very techniques that had grown distasteful in the panegyrical culture of the old order are regenerated in paeans to the new. It is true that in most of the East European satellites Socialist Realism, introduced with Sovietization in the 1940s, was abandoned during the first thaw, never to return; in the USSR, however, the slow death of Socialist Realism was not visibly accelerated by the Khrushchevian and Gorbachevian thaws. Indeed, some of the most interesting changes in the Soviet literatures took place in the late 1970s, in the depths of what Soviet commentators now call Brezhnevite stagnation.

Thaws – their detailed manifestation in literature and the other arts, as well as the relationship between thaws in culture and overarching social and political phenomena – exercised the participants of an interdisciplinary conference that was held at Monash University in February 1988. Selected papers from that meeting are presented in this collection. Their scope ranges from the broad essay into cultural and literary history to the close reading of individual, but symptomatic, works. Katerina Clark proposes a description and a theory of thaws in culture which identifies as their basic feature a revision in the public perception of time in general and of the past in particular. While Clark takes the Soviet thaws as her point of departure, Leslie Bodi derives from Josephinian Austria his model of the thaw as a complex dialogue between the central power and its potential adversaries. Clark's perspective leads her to observe thaws as episodes of transition from one cultural paradigm to the next, and therefore as events in an essentially linear history. Bodi, more pessimistically, perceives thaws as part of a cyclical recurrence: as creatures of authority, they are inevitably brought to an end when they challenge their creator. Thaws in the refraction of neo-colonial situations – that of Czechoslovakia in its political dependence on the Soviet Union and that of Ukraine in the USSR's inner empire – are the subject of Pavel Petr's paper and my own.

A number of discussions focus on particular spheres of cultural activity. Aleksandar Pavković describes the demise of Marxism-Leninism as the sole authoritative doctrine in thaw-affected Yugoslav academic philosophy; Zhanna Dolgopolova surveys the thematic span of new Soviet Russian literature published in the course of 1987, a year when Gorbachev's *glasnost'* had reached full amplitude; Peter Stupples considers the Soviet visual arts, and Rosh Ireland the Soviet theatre, under thaw conditions. Amanda Metcalf and Janet Neville, using little-known materials from the history of theatre, discover a short-lived Soviet thaw that occurred in 1940.

Four contributions approach particular facets of thaws by analysing works or groups of works associated with them. Interpreting the imagery of April thaws in the poetry of Irina Ratushinskaia, Judith Armstrong discovers an antecedent of such formulations of hope for a warmer and better future in the poetry of Osip Mandel'shtam. David Wells, in another paper which considers a work wrought in hard times but in expectation of a thaw, examines the structure of encoding and concealment in Anna Akhmatova's *Poema bez geroia* (Poem Without a Hero). David Farrer, on the other hand, treats of a work which made use of thaw conditions to confront the reader with unorthodox, if protectively enciphered, arguments: *Za shyrmoiu* (Behind the Curtain), a novel by the rehabilitated Ukrainian writer Borys Antonenko-Davydovych. In his discussion of portraits of Beria in Soviet Russian literature, Kevin Windle documents the shifting definitions of what may legitimately be represented in literature at various stages of the thaw–freeze cycle.

The collection does not claim to furnish the reader with a geographically and historically complete image of Central and East European thaws. It hopes, rather, by its selection of perspectives and by its combination of the broad overview with the detailed interpretation to help the reader intuit the significant features of a process which, though universal in one half of Europe, is frequently

Preface

misunderstood in the West, where it has no tradition. The need for
such informed intuition concerning the Soviet Union and its European dependencies at the time of an unprecedented increase in their
dynamism scarcely requires justification or proof.

Marko Pavlyshyn
Monash University, Melbourne, Australia, August 1989

Rethinking the Past and the Current Thaw

KATERINA CLARK

It's 'The Return of the Thaw', or 'Thaw II' ('Thaw IV' if you accept the convention that there were three under Khrushchev). Out of the Soviet 'night' here it comes again, strange and thrilling. Of course a thaw does not really come 'out of the night'. All that the term really means is a greater degree of liberalization. It marks a transitional period, usually occasioned by a political changeover, when an agenda is thrashed out to the accompaniment of much inflated rhetoric.

It would seem that not only revolutions have a recurring structure – so do thaws. They are a component of Soviet history, a category of change that is a feature of highly centralized governments. If we look at the classic thaws of the Khrushchev era to get some sense of their typical pattern, we can see that they involve essentially two phases. The first, which marked the years 1954, 1956 and 1962, is distinguished by three features, all of them facilitated by the liberal climate. Firstly, there is a gripe list; this is what a 'thaw' largely is, and the gripe list tends to dominate all public forums during its first phase. Secondly, there is a 'shopping list'. In the case of literature, this list primarily comprises proposals for liberalizing publishing procedures and helping more young writers get into print, plus a list of authors and texts currently blacklisted but which writers want to see published. Thirdly, some of the more daring trends to be found in literature of the past five years or so emerge with greater intensity, and there is a partial clearing of the backlog of unpublished manuscripts.

A thaw, then, essentially marks a period of revaluation, a transitional period. We call it a 'thaw' if we like the kind of literature and values which are permitted freer access to public forums as a consequence of the ideological shake-up. 'Thaw' is a label we attach selectively and somewhat subjectively to such a time. Others might, for instance, have attached it to the Brezhnev years when Stalin's name could be mentioned in a positive way once again, or when certain religious thinkers could be referred to in print, and possibly even quoted – a situation which was partially reversed shortly after Brezhnev's death. From a certain point of view, also, the period immediately after the Bolshevik Revolution might be called a 'thaw' in that, in the absence of religious censorship or aesthetic and political control by the imperial bureaucracy, many works could be published, and plays produced, which previously had been impermissible – the full text of Pushkin's *Mednyi vsadnik* (The Bronze Horseman), for example.

Literature of this transitional period is highly journalistic and contentious, and in that sense ephemeral and largely of historical interest. Only in the wake of the thaw do new directions emerge and are new paradigms generated in literature. In the Khrushchev years, this second phase can be found in the reaction that set in after the Hungarian uprising of 1956 and extended to the 1962 thaw. It was during these years that the racy 'youth prose' of a new generation of writers like Vasilii Aksenov emerged. In the 1920s, we can find the second phase not during the frenzied years of War Communism, but in the more staid years of NEP (New Economic Policy) when many of the classics of Soviet literature were written and Socialist Realism emerged embryonically in works by Fedor Gladkov, Aleksandr Fadeev and Dmitrii Furmanov. Thus, we should not expect to see anything fundamentally new in Soviet literature as yet, and I am not going to attempt to find new paradigms in a putatively 'Gorbachevian' novel but will, rather, look at certain historical patterns to be seen in the current thaw.

In many respects, the current thaw takes up the unfinished business of the last ones, blithely jumping over twenty-five years of Soviet literary history to do so. Thus, this thaw's buzz word, *glasnost'* (openness), can be seen as merely a different version of the buzz word of 1956, *pravda* (truth). The series of attempts under Khrushchev at founding independent literary almanacs has developed under Gorbachev into the movement for independent cooperative publishing houses. Similarly, we can see an element of resuming the old agenda in many of the attacks on Stalinism made recently. Even the publication in 1988 of Boris Pasternak's *Doctor Zhivago* for the first time in the Soviet Union, of which so much has been made, could be construed as another instance of taking up the old agenda again: the novel was meant to come out in the Soviet Union during one of the thaws under Khrushchev, but publication was stopped in the period of reaction after the Hungarian uprising of late 1956.

It might be said that this thaw is not merely taking up the old agenda, but taking each item on it a stage further. For instance, during the last Khrushchev thaw, that of 1962, intellectuals began calling for a 'white paper' to be prepared on the purges – one which would go into who did what. The party balked at this, however; in fact some people have explained the fact that the thaws came to an end in 1962 as a consequence of the party's lack of preparedness to go further. The closest thing to this white paper can be found in Solzhenitsyn's *Arkhipelag gulag* (The Gulag Archipelago), the journal *Pamiat'* (Memory) and other such *samizdat* and *tamizdat* publications, most of which are, of necessity, based largely on oral sources rather than on official documents. But in the present thaw, authors are naming names in print. Thus Anatolii Rybakov in his *Deti Arbata* (Children of the Arbat, 1987) discusses the purges in terms of a theme popular in the earlier thaws – the detrimental effects of sectarianism on Soviet science and hence on the economy. But he does so not by inventing some fictional 'Drozdov' (I am referring here to Vladimir Dudintsev's anti-hero in one of the most sensational works of the 1956 thaw, *Ne khlebom edinym* [Not by Bread Alone], who epitomizes the corrupt Stalinist bureaucrat and whose name became a household word in that year), but by depicting and naming Stalin, Poskrebyshev, Ordzhonikidze, and so on.

Many of the outspoken attacks in recent literature can be housed under the rubric *glasnost'* in the sense that their authors could be said to be exposing – dutifully, as they are urged to do – social ills which have been swept under the rug and kept out of print in the immediately preceding 'period of stagnation' (i.e. under Brezhnev). However, literature today does not merely present object lessons in the wisdom of the new platform, as it did under Khrushchev more often than is generally recognized; it provides an independent critique of Soviet society and of its fundamental values. Thus it lacks the fundamental optimism of literature from the Khrushchev years. As is stated quite explicitly in Valentin Rasputin's *Pozhar* (Fire!), the unquestioning priority which is given to economic development (particularly to plan fulfilment) and to the Promethean ideal – without regard for spiritual and moral values – does not merely threaten the realization of the country's official goals, but has also reduced human beings to little more than beasts. Indeed, among literary intellectuals *bezdukhovnost'* (lack of spiritual values) has become a catchword more frequently used than even *glasnost'*.

One must note, however, that *Fire!* was published in 1985, while Gorbachev came to power only in March of that year. Thus it seems more than possible that the work was commenced before the thaw proper began. Many of its ideas and, in particular, its apocalyptic predictions, based on observations of the gross neglect of ecology and spiritual values, are reminiscent of those made in Iurii Bondarev's *Igra* (The Game) of 1983 and even earlier fiction. Indeed, *bezdukhovnost'* might be called *the* theme of Soviet literature from the late 1970s on.

In this sense, then, the current thaw is more a writing in larger letters of the main themes of the late Brezhnev era (the late 1970s and early 1980s) than it is a return to 1956 and all that. The pattern is like that of the first thaw under Khrushchev when, for instance, Leonid Leonov's *Russkii les* (The Russian Forest), published in 1953 but clearly written largely before Stalin's death, was regarded as an early text of the thaw. Interestingly, *The Russian Forest* can be read both as a text of the late Stalin era (it celebrates Stalin's schemes for afforestation), and as a text of the thaw (it attacks the Stalinist disregard for human life).

Thus, the present thaw – and, for a thaw, this is prototypical – derives much of its content from a build-up in the past, rather than appearing mysteriously out of the 'night'. In this sense, a thaw does not really represent a distinct period at all, nor does it make a radical break with the immediate past. And yet it does mark a break, and not merely in the sense that the climate is so much more liberal and so much more can be said and published than in the immediately preceding period.

A thaw is a highly volatile time marked by confusion in the temporal models. This aspect is particularly marked in literature. In the current instance, thaw literature typically blends the neo-Khrushchevian and the late-Brezhnevian. Also, some of the backlog of unpublished manuscripts is being cleared. The manuscripts that at long last are being published range from fiction by writers like Andrei Bitov and Vladimir Makanin, who could get little into print under Brezhnev, to texts written in the immediate pre- or post-revolutionary years. Some of these have never been published in the Soviet Union before, while others have not been published there since the 1920s or 1930s. They were written at very different times, and yet are appearing more or less simultaneously. A new, but non-coherent sense of time results.

In a thaw, then, time is out of joint. But it is confused in order that it should be reordered.

Soviet culture has always been grounded in a particular temporal model. Although the society is ostensibly future-oriented, the greatest care has, in fact, been taken to define the past and establish the society's genealogy; the society is legitimized through a myth of origins and through a line of succession (of either great men or great epochs) stretching from the moment of origin to the present. With each major political upheaval, the canonical points of temporal orientation have been reshuffled and re-evaluated, and a new gene alogy has emerged to replace the old.

What one typically finds in thaws is, in fact, similar to a phenomenon which Bakhtin analyzed in his essay 'Discourse in the Novel' of 1934–5: the phenomenon of reaccentuation which is characteristic of periods of flux. Although Bakhtin described reaccentuation primarily in the context of the evolution of the novel, he insists that the dual processes of canonization and reaccentuation are 'processes of transformation (to which every language phenomenon is subject)'.[1] Canonization means appropriation into the literary language (or literary canon) of material which was previously deemed non-literary, a process which occurs to a most marked degree 'in the most heteroglot eras, when the collision and interaction of languages is especially powerful, when heteroglossia washes over the literary language from all sides.'[2] The analogue to this in the case of a Soviet thaw would be the introduction into public discourse during times of temporal confusion of symbolic historical moments, of imagery and vocabulary not considered to be canonical in the reasonably stable and conservative preceding period. Reaccentuation, according to Bakhtin, occurs 'under changed conditions for perceiving an image [. . . .] In an era when the dialogue of languages has experienced great change, the language of an image begins to sound in a different way, or is bathed in a different light, or is perceived against a different dialogizing background [. . . .] Such conditions merely actualize in an image a potential already available to it.'[3] 'New images in literature are very often created through a reaccentuation of old images, by translating them from one accentual register to another (from the comic plane to the tragic, for instance, or the other way around).'[4] Thus, in Soviet society much of the vocabulary and many of the mythemes, images and values which are constituent parts of its cultural myths are reaccented, transvalued, recombined and thereby changed. They are the same material as has been used before, but they have been made different; above all, they have been revalued.

---

1. M. M. Bakhtin, 'Discourse in the Novel', in *The Dialogic Imagination: Four Essays by M. M. Bakhtin*, trans. Caryl Emerson and Michael Holquist, Austin and London: University of Texas Press, 1981, p. 417.
2. Ibid., p. 418.
3. Ibid., p. 420.
4. Ibid., p. 421.

Bakhtin continues:

> Every age reaccentuates in its own way the works of its most immediate past. The historical life of classic works is in fact the uninterrupted process of their social and ideological reaccentuation. Thanks to the intentional potential embedded in them, such works have proved capable of uncovering in each era and against ever new dialogizing backgrounds ever newer aspects of meaning, their semantic content literally continues to grow, to further create out of itself. Likewise their influence on subsequent creative works inevitably includes reaccentuation.[5]

A thaw, in that it represents a same-but-different time, has in a sense a figural shape, a same-but-different structure – as does a metaphor. The very term 'thaw' is, of course, also metaphoric. Its vehicle of metaphor, a thaw in nature, is a time when the winter snow and ice melt; it invites comparison with the melting of rigid restraints. A thaw, however, also seeks out metaphors in the sense that it seeks out a point, or sequence of points, of orientation in the past – without the intention that society should return to such a period literally, but rather that some canonical image of this period should illumine and serve as an exemplum for, and a point of view on, the present.

A thaw, then, represents an intensified expression of what is a normal process in the history of literature at all times. There is in culture a constant rethinking of the past, a process of constant re-evaluation which is reflected in reaccentuations in the discourse we use and in the make-up of our dominant symbols and images. There is a constant, if not always perceptible, process whereby the master-narrative which informs our very perception of reality is slightly reordered or transvalued. In the Soviet Union, where the hegemonic forces characteristically attempt to freeze history, to countervail against such flux, these fits of memory are necessary components in the struggle to master history as change.

Another fruitful, although admittedly somewhat banal analogy for the model of alternating periods of thaw and stasis which I am adducing here, would be that used by Thomas S. Kuhn in his classic work, *The Structure of Scientific Revolutions*. Kuhn analyses the history of science in terms of periods of 'normal science', when certain paradigms or canonical theories prevail and all scientific work is structured by them or in some other paradigm-confirming way. But these periods of normal science alternate with periods of what he calls 'unnatural science', when the paradigms begin to break down,

5. Ibid., p. 421.

scientific work challenges them, and there are no certainties accepted by 'science' as a whole. These interstitial periods end in a return to a new period of 'normal science', when new paradigms are adopted. There are, however, two crucial differences between the model I am proposing for Soviet culture, and Kuhn's for science. Firstly, cultural change in the Soviet Union is far from a spontaneous affair; indeed, the fact that the lid is kept on for long periods during the (only *relatively*) more spontaneous times of paradigm-challenge accounts for the highly dramatic nature of thaws. Secondly, thaws are always effects of major political changeovers.

A thaw can, indeed, be seen as merely one of the more liberal variants of the kind of cultural revolution to which the Soviet Union is intermittently subject. I can identify at least five other such moments of temporal confusion and reorientation, each of which produced its own vocabulary, symbols and language, the accentuation of which was grounded in a distinctive genealogy. The first of these can be found in the period of War Communism, the years 1917–21, which followed the radical temporal break of October. At that time, the dominant genealogy informing mass spectacles and other public rituals, and also many of the editorials and leading articles in the party press, began with ancient Greece and went through the French Revolution and the Paris Commune of 1871 to the October Revolution as the culminating link in a purported chain of historical progression. Actually, this genealogy represents in its own way an intensification of trends in the immediate pre-revolutionary years by claiming for Russia the role of the ultimate realizer of the Hellenic ideal. Thus, as has also been the pattern in later thaws, the dominant genealogy emerged from the cultural myths of the immediate past. Rather than being appropriated wholesale, however, it was reaccentuated (in this instance, to take into account the violent upheaval of revolution).

The second and most dramatic temporal reshuffling of Soviet times came with the Stalin revolution. At first, during the heady era of the first Five-Year Plan, Stalinist culture sought to annihilate history, and the new genealogy did not crystallize until the mid-1930s, after that initial phase was truly over. The new genealogy centres on the account of how Lenin passed his baton to Stalin.[6] By the Zhdanov era (the late 1940s), however, Soviet culture was already generating a third temporal model. After the dramatic upheavals of the war, the myth of origins was revived; it

6. See my book *The Soviet Novel: History as Ritual*, Chicago: University of Chicago Press, 1981.

was focussed, however, less on party figures as leaders of a communist movement than as leaders in the Russian national tradition. The medieval classic *Slovo o polku Igoreve* (The Lay of Igor's Campaign), a tragic epic telling of the heroic stand of the princes of Rus' against the advancing Pechenegs, provided a new point of orientation in interpreting the significance of the current leaders. They had, by implication, proved even more worthy successors in the heroic line inasmuch as they had allegedly succeeded in repelling much more menacing foreign aggressors.

After Stalin's death in 1953, his cultural heritage was partially dismantled. The fourth genealogy, introduced during the Khrushchev thaw, represents a deliberate reordering of the High Stalinist model. It posits a new line of succession from Lenin through the Old Bolsheviks and their supporters, but bypassing Stalin and Stalinists as usurpers and unworthy heirs of Lenin. Under Brezhnev, a new genealogy emerged in literature, a particularly significant one in that, for the first time, literature generated semi-autonomous models which were not mere subfunctions of the official platform. This new genealogy was clearly counterposed to the kind of line which had dominated cultural models not only during the period of High Stalinism, but also under Khrushchev, and which entailed a strictly male line of succession running from worthy leader figure to worthy leader figure. This new line involved extra-systemic figures who rarely held any Soviet office, let alone were leaders. Predominantly, they came from rural areas (the dominant literary school at this time was called 'village prose'). The new icons of Soviet literature under Brezhnev can be found in such larger-than-life matriarchs as Aleksandr Solzhenitsyn's Matriona, the protagonist of his *Matrionin dvor* (Matriona's House) of 1963, or Rasputin's Daria from his *Proshchanie s Matioroi* (Farewell to Matiora) of 1976. The burden of such fiction was that we have all come out of the village – that is, not necessarily literally out of the village, but out of a distinctively and uniquely Russian culture which can also be identified with pre-Muscovite Rus'.

It is not as yet absolutely clear what the temporal model will be under Gorbachev. Rather than reject previous models, however, the new fiction and films typically incorporate, but also reaccentuate, many of them. Thus, while there are both neo-Khrushchevian and late-Brezhnevian elements in the literature of the present thaw, the thaw itself represents neither a return to Khrushchev, nor a continuation of changes already perceptible in the late 1970s and early 1980s. Its dominant thrust, that which 'bathes in a new light' or reaccentuates the clichés of both periods, derives from neither.

A thaw is by its nature both iconoclastic and retrospectivist. In meeting its task of generating new paradigms, of reorienting to a different temporal figure, a thaw must be dramatically iconoclastic; fiction must question and denigrate not merely the immediate past and its leadership, but also its informing myths.

If one abstracts the gripe list from current literature, one will find that it is to an inordinate extent looking back over time to fateful moments in the national past. The element of retrospectivism which is endemic to all thaws is particularly strong in this one. Indeed, one of the intelligentsia's favourite periodicals of the moment, the re-vamped *Ogonek*, while functioning as a popular source for outspoken critiques of Soviet society, at the same time has in some of its issues been almost completely given over to retrospectivism – a curious phenomenon in a thaw whose ostensible prime aim is to save the country from stagnation and conservatism. For instance, most of the writers who have been rehabilitated in print in 1985–7 were first published in a trial-balloon sample of their work in *Ogonek*.

The central focus of this retrospectivist vogue has arguably been the 1920s. It is true that much attention has also been paid to the evils of Stalinism, as was the case *a fortiori* in the thaws under Khrushchev, but that has largely been a matter of completing unfinished business. There has, for instance, been a tendency to widen slightly the parameters of the subject by bringing in moments in the purges which had not previously been covered. Thus, the ethnic factor, which has been a major topic of the present thaw generally, has been discussed in such works about the Stalin experi-ence as Anatolii Pristavkin's *Nochevala tuchka zolotaia* (A Golden Cloud Passed the Night) of 1987. Significantly, however, most of the writers who have published on the Stalin theme recently either did so under Khrushchev as well (e.g. Vladimir Dudintsev), or are themselves victims of the purges (e.g. Chingiz Aitmatov, for whom this is far from a new subject).

The 1920s are a suitably vague concept, and have been variously interpreted. A similar situation obtained during War Communism when the dominant genealogy, which set up a line of succession from ancient Greece through the French Revolution and the Paris Com-mune to the October Revolution, proved vague, too. Then there were at least two principal interpretations of the temporal model. The non-party intelligentsia understood it as originating in 'humanistic' Hellenic Athens, whose baton was taken up by the French Revolution. It acknowledged, but downplayed, the Paris Commune as a stage in the historical progression, and proclaimed the October Revolution to be the ultimate realization of the Athenian spirit. The Bolsheviks, however, tended to understand by 'ancient Greece' not Athens but Sparta, and looked to a more regimented and militaristic version of this point of origin. Similarly, in their account of the next stage in the progression, the French Revolution, the Bolsheviks focussed on the later years of the Revolution when Marat and others were unflinching in suppressing 'counterrevolutionaries', and the Revolution had to prove strong in the face of invading foreign armies.

In popular Soviet parlance, 'the twenties' often means NEP, the time of the New Economic Policy, when limited private enterprise was allowed, and hence also more variegated cultural activity. Today several intellectuals – apparently in concert with the leadership – advocate a reorientation along the lines of the economic and cultural policies of that time which, after all, Lenin himself had so wisely advocated. One of the most prominent statements of this position can be found in Sergei Zalygin's long novel *Posle buri* (After the Storm) which began to appear in the early 1980s.

A second common approach to the meaning of 'the twenties' looks at the crucial party debates of the early part of the decade in the belief that these events have to be re-evaluated. This approach is taken primarily by party members or writers who are embroiled in re-evaluating the role of some of the major party leaders, such as, most recently, Nikolai Bukharin. The writer most closely connected with this strand is the playwright Mikhail Shatrov, allegedly the nephew of Bukharin's associate Aleksei Rykov. Shatrov's plays about the early Soviet period such as *Brestskii mir* (The Peace of Brest-Litovsk) typify the literature of political rehabilitation of the current thaw in that they name names. When I was in Moscow in December 1986 I had a great deal of difficulty in getting into Shatrov's earlier play *Tak pobedim* (Thus We Shall Triumph) because the Supreme Soviet was being taken to see it. In that play, which is set during the last occasion when Lenin recovered sufficiently from his fatal illness to return briefly to the Kremlin, much of the drama is presented as Lenin's recollections of some of the fateful moments and crucial debates of the leadership after the Revolution. The audience sees on the stage individual Bolshevik leaders who have clearly been made up to represent specific historical figures such as Trotsky and Stalin, and who enter into party debates on stage, but are not identified by name. The only figure other than Lenin who is singled out for special veneration is Iakov Sverdlov, who succumbs to illness and dies, deeply mourned by Lenin, as a martyr to the Revolution. Sverdlov is, likewise, not referred to by his last name, but in a deathbed scene Lenin addresses him by his first name and patronymic, Iakov Mikhailovich, clearly indicating that this newly recanonized revolutionary hero is Jewish, a subtle detail which implicitly challenges the widespread anti-semitism which still lingers from the Brezhnev years. Shatrov's play smoothed the way for naming the names of some other and more senior Bolshevik leaders of those years who were likewise Jewish but were later purged and had not yet been rehabilitated.

The dominant interpretation of what is meant by 'the twenties', which has informed the recent work of the creative and scholarly intelligentsia, also focuses largely on the fateful moments of the early part of that decade. Some sense of this new orientation can be found encoded in the list of writers and texts that are being rehabilitated. The new list, unlike the one cited under Khrushchev, primarily comprises writers who emigrated in the early years after the Revolution (or, in the case of Nikolai Gumilev, were shot for alleged anti-Soviet conspiracy) and who were important in the immediate pre- and post-revolutionary years, that is, at the very moment of 'origin'. The list includes, besides Gumilev, Vladimir Nabokov, Vladislav Khodasevich, Dmitrii Merezhkovskii and Aleksei Remizov, and in addition some individual texts never published in the Soviet Union but by writers who themselves have been published sporadically, such as Evgenii Zamiatin's *My* (We, 1920) and Boris Pasternak's *Doctor Zhivago*. (This novel was written much later and published in the West in the 1950s, but Pasternak was most prominent as a writer in the immediate pre- and post-revolutionary years, and *Doctor Zhivago* is, of course, an interpretation of the Revolution.)

The dominant trends in recent films and literature also share with the faction represented by Shatrov a proclivity for martyr figures. However, these martyrs are intellectuals rather than party leaders. Indeed, the image of the martyred intellectual must be one of the dominant *topoi* of culture in this thaw; it can be seen in many of the recently released films, such as Roland Bykov's *Chuchelo* (The Scarecrow) and Tengiz Abuladze's *Pokaianie* (Repentance), and is arguably at the heart of the most widely debated work of fiction as yet published in the thaw, Chingiz Aitmatov's *Plakha* (The Executioner's Block).[7] In *The Executioner's Block* the central character, Avdii, an expelled seminarian embarked on his own religious quest, dies after he is subjected to a mock trial and execution. His death is represented as a conflation of Christ's execution, a burning at the stake, and a lynching. Moreover, Aitmatov rivals Bulgakov in this novel by slotting into his narrative a fictionalized interpretation of

7. *Novyi mir*, 1986, nos. 6–8.

Christ's interrogation by Pontius Pilate and establishing parallels and points of meeting between that historical moment and Avdii's interrogation by his tormentors.[8] Many critics have fastened on these and other features of the novel to proclaim that it preaches some version of non-received Russian Orthodoxy (for instance, that Aitmatov is a close follower of the religious thinker Nikolai Berdiaev). In my view, however, Aitmatov, who has been quite outspoken in the defence of Kirghiz ethnicity against the threat of Russian cultural imperialism, is in this novel not espousing an alien Russian Orthodoxy, but rather invoking the image of the questing intellectual who comes up against the institutionalized dogmatism of temporal powers. Indeed, the conflation of the image of Christ's passion with that of a burning at the stake suggests the highly generalized context in which we are to view Aitmatov's appropriation of Russian Orthodox material.

The *topos* of the martyred intellectual is one of the many elements in this thaw which can be found strongly represented in Soviet culture of the immediate pre-thaw years. For instance, it is to be found in Bondarev's *Game* (1983), where the martyred Old Believer Avvakum is advanced as a spiritual mentor for the protagonist, himself a modern Soviet film director. During this thaw, however, the figure of the martyred intellectual has frequently been 'bathed in a different light' or 'reaccentuated', because of the thaw's new dominant point of orientation.

The intelligentsia has been obsessed with the early 1920s and with the mission of reclaiming lost, i.e. unpublishable, writers of that period. It clearly wants to be whole again, to reclaim that which considered itself (or was considered) non-Soviet, and hence broke off (or was broken off) from Soviet culture. A similar impulse can be seen in the many overtures made to former cultural leaders now in exile to return or revisit, or at least to return in the form of a Soviet publication. However, it is arguably more the ethos and orientation of those years to which the intelligentsia is most drawn.

A remarkable number of points in the literary intelligentsia's current programme are reminiscent of typical concerns of the early 1920s. For instance, *bezdukhovnost'* could well have been used as a catchword for the 1920s intelligentsia's main critique of the Bolshevik Revolution. Indeed, criticisms of Bolshevism for its lack of a spiritual dimension were then common not only in such predictable places as the lectures given at Vol'fila (the Free Philosophical Association), which put at the centre of its platform the necessity of

8. I am referring here to Mikhail Bulgakov's version of the exchange between Christ and Pontius Pilate in his novel *Master i Margarita*.

combining socialism with some spiritual or religious component, but also in the poetry of Vladimir Maiakovskii. One could go on iterating such parallels. However, it is not the parallels with the 1920s which are important to my argument, but the use of the 1920s as a symbolic point of reorientation.

A good way to get at this new point of reorientation would be to look at the intelligentsia's current guru, the academician Dmitrii Sergeevich Likhachev. Likhachev, himself a medieval scholar, has been used in the current thaw to pronounce in the press not just in his area of competence, or even on general cultural questions, but also in the area of morality. It is a sign of his extraordinary standing that, when his eightieth jubilee was celebrated in December 1986, the film director Tengiz Abuladze as a special tribute to Likhachev showed his *Repentance*, which at the time had been withdrawn and was not being screened anywhere.

Likhachev's esteem derives in part from the fact that his career as a highly respected intellectual extends back to the 1920s. In addition, he experienced the mandatory martyrdom: in the late 1920s, he was arrested and exiled and his career did not resume until the late 1930s. Moreover, he has not been loath in recent years to allude to this fact. It was to be expected that the guru of the hour would be associated with the early 1920s, but there are few intellectuals still active who go back so far in their careers. One of these few, Veniamin Kaverin, has been used as a figurehead by some groups trying to set up publishing cooperatives, but his name does not stand for that precise nexus of characteristics which today's literary intelligentsia predominantly associates with 'the twenties'.

By the late 1980s, Soviet culture having been through a series of reorientations, many different cultural models have accumulated. These are not negated in the figure of Likhachev. Rather, as an emblematic figure he distills several of them, but also reinflects them, just as a lens gathers rays of light and then redistributes them. For instance, Likhachev was actually arrested in the 1920s for being a member of underground religious discussion groups. This, together with his specialization in Medieval Russian (i.e. primarily church) literature and his avowed patriotism, gives him appeal as a potential symbol for the less xenophobic factions within the Russophile intelligentsia which came to the fore during the Brezhnev years. At the same time, inasmuch as he spent most of the Second World War in blockaded Leningrad, as well as being a noted champion of the *Slovo o polku Igoreve* and defender of its authenticity against attacks by Western scholars, he meets the criteria for a cultural hero of the 1940s.

Likhachev's recent writings have many points in common with those of the typical Russophile under Brezhnev. For instance, he is concerned with the environment, with restoring threatened cultural treasures of Russia's past, with the central importance of medieval Russian texts as part of the national treasure, and with what he calls the 'spiritual ecology' of Russia. He departs from the main Slavophile positions of those years in rejecting the excesses of Russian nationalism. Likhachev calls such recent fads among the intelligentsia as donning the peasant shirt or growing a beard 'play-acting Russianness' and contrasts them with true Russianness, which he gives a somewhat unexpected characterization as *mental'nost'* (mentality). Moreover, he counterposes to a dominant interpretation from the Brezhnev years of what Russianness means (one which might be especially associated with a Vasilii Shukshin and his cult of Stenka Razin) an interpretation which advances as central values not the wild and untrammelled – the 'Scythian', to use a term from the early 1920s – but rather 'culture' and 'mind'. Crucial to this reorientation is an expansion of the spatial horizons of what is to be deemed *echt* Russian – an expansion which takes it out of the farm, so to speak, and into the purview of general *European* culture. I emphasize European, because a corollary of this orientation is a marked anti-Americanism and a rejection of popular mass culture. Such a stance is taken, for example, by Sergei Zalygin, the new editor of the crucial literary journal *Novyi mir*; his appointment to that post was particularly striking, since he is not a party member, a fact which is without precedent for a Soviet journal editor since the 1920s.

A similar orientation can be found in much of the fiction and cinema appearing over the past few years. It informs, for instance, Aitmatov's *Executioner's Block*. Indeed, in an interview published in the journal *Druzhba narodov* in February 1987 it is clear that Aitmatov, himself a Kirghiz and therefore of a background which is Moslem and non-European, made his protagonist Avdii a Russian Orthodox and presented an interpretation of Christ's encounter with Pontius Pilate (an act of presumption which infuriated many among the Russian Orthodox intelligentsia) because he has ambitions to be recognized as a major *European* writer and the story of Christ is the dominant myth of that culture. Aitmatov told his interviewer, 'I wanted to be heard beyond the borders of Kirghizia', and used the words 'European consciousness' to characterize the informing values of the novel.[9] In a similar shift, the huge environ-

9. Chingiz Aitmatov, 'Kak slovo nashe otzovetsia'. Interview conducted by N. Astaf'ev, *Druzhba narodov*, 1987, No. 2, 237.

mentalist lobby among the literary intelligentsia is now colouring its rhetoric less in the 'Blut und Boden' terms used in the preceding period, and more to sound like a Russian expression of the pan-European Green movement.

In his recent writings, Likhachev uses Dostoevskii to make a point about Russianness. In Russian reality, he says, one can find any number of Mitya Karamazovs with their expansiveness and lack of discipline, but a culture should be defined less by a nation's reality than by its ideals. Dostoevskii's ideal, Likhachev maintains – and here we see something of a warmed-up version of the nineteenth-century critic Vissarion Belinskii – was Pushkin.

Aleksandr Pushkin, whom Maiakovskii and company wanted to throw off the steamer of modernity in late 1912, is no innocent figure in Russian cultural history. Admittedly, his example has been invoked in the service of almost every position on the political and literary spectrum. During the Soviet period (and before) he had also been used by intellectuals as a symbol for the writer's struggle with the state. Hence the recent Pushkin revival, associated partly with the celebration in 1987 of the 150th anniversary of his death, can be seen as part of the cult of the martyred intellectual. This is not, however, its main significance.

It will be noted that many of the authors recently rehabilitated have been champions of Pushkin, as well as symbols of a particular nexus of values also associated with the myth of Petersburg. Names which come to mind include Vladimir Nabokov, Gumilev, Khodasevich and Osip Mandel'shtam. Additionally, the Leningrad school, led by writers like Andrei Bitov and Boris Kushner whose work has been obsessed with Pushkin and the Petersburg myth, have been among the beneficiaries of the reordering of the literary stakes with the advent of Gorbachev. Indeed, at Bitov's triumphant fiftieth jubilee evening in 1987 he read his 'Polet s geroem' (Flight With a Hero), a story about his relationship to the Petersburg myth, as a banner statement. Moreover, as these writers have fallen into favour again and have been granted trips overseas, some of them have been reunited with their lost brother Iosif Brodskii in exile in the West.

The intelligentsia wants to be whole again to face square one anew, but of course even before the fateful emigrations and expulsions of 1921–2 the intelligentsia never really was whole. The main split in the first years after the Revolution was arguably less between Bolsheviks and non-Bolsheviks, or between those who supported the Revolution and those who became actual or internal émigrés, than it was between an iconoclastic avant-garde representing an inter-national movement (who largely supported the Bolsheviks) and retrospectivists and *Kulturträger* (who were usually not pro-Bolshevik, but with whose cultural tastes the Bolsheviks largely sympathized). These latter figures rallied around the name 'Pushkin', and in 1921 they instituted a series of Pushkin anniversaries as central activities in their missionary work of spreading a particular configuration of cultural values – values generally considered by the avant-garde to be antithetical to their own.

Historically, the public cult of Pushkin in Soviet Russia has been prosecuted by those antagonistic towards the avant-garde. Indeed, although the main celebration of a Pushkin anniversary in the Soviet period, the infamous jubilee of 1937, cannot be linked to those who organized the celebration of 1921, it is consistent that the 1937 celebration should have been accompanied by a campaign against all manner of 'Formalists'. Although during the current thaw some voices have called for rehabilitating such figures from the avant-garde of the 1920s as Daniil Kharms and Leonid Dobychin, and there have even been exhibitions of work by Vladimir Tatlin and Pavel Filonov, the main emphasis has as yet been on rehabilitating champions of Culture with a capital K. While the writers of the 1920s singled out for re-publication were usually far from anti-Western, they called for a highly selective appropriation of Western culture, and usually its highbrow, 'European' variant. It is instructive to recall that during the Khrushchev thaws a structural slot comparable to the one now filled by Likhachev was occupied by the highly cosmopolitan Il'ia Erenburg, whose *Ottepel'* (The Thaw, 1954) gave the period its name. At that time, the interest in the West and the avant-garde which he fostered proved particularly productive in generating new literary paradigms.

Thus, in terms of structure, this thaw has on the whole conformed to the pattern of its predecessors. But in terms of the dominant values, crucial changes have occurred. We cannot know when phase two will begin, or even whether it has perhaps already begun. The kind of writing which emerged during phase two of the last thaw, 'youth prose', was, despite the guise it adopted initially of being a variant on 'production fiction', essentially a Westernizing movement. It is no accident that Aksenov and most of its other practitioners have since emigrated to the West. A major question today, therefore, is what kind of new paradigms can be generated out of a thaw which has to date had a predominantly retrospectivist thrust.

Establishing a Model for *Glasnost'*: Censorship, Writers and Literary Forms in Late Eighteenth-Century Austria

LESLIE BODI

This paper is based on work in the field of eighteenth-century Austrian literature. My interest in the subject arose from experiences in Hungary in the 1950s and from research on the literature of the German Democratic Republic over the past forty years. As my discipline is literature, I have tried to understand the literary and artistic aspects of 'thaw' periods in the development of East and Central European political systems. Such issues have now become relevant again in relation to Gorbachev's Soviet Empire.

In general terms, the slogan of *glasnost'* denotes openness and transparence, especially in the specific form this 'openness' takes in closed, authoritarian or totalitarian societies in which the ruling establishment has a monopoly, or, at least, very tight control, over all forms of communication in public life. In societies where there is no machinery for democratic decision-making it is extremely difficult to bring about the restructuring and modernization which are necessary for fast economic and social development. The established political system is and remains firmly in power and has no intention whatsoever of relinquishing its dominant position. Change can only come from above, and, if it is to do so, at least some powerful groups of the establishment must favour a policy of movement and restructuring. Such change, called *perestroika* in present-day Soviet terminology, has become necessary because of economic mismanagement and stagnation. There is a perception of backwardness vis-à-vis other competing countries, including also a fear of falling behind in the field of military power.

In such situations there is a need to activate broad layers of the public in the interests of innovation, change and development, and to mobilize the intelligentsia for improvements in technology, science, administration and education. There is a need to attack ideologies frozen into sanctified authoritative canons in order to make such movement possible. Within the enlightenment project, there is increased emphasis on rationality, justice and sincerity, with an ever-present belief in the possibility of a better life in a realizable secular utopia. Eastern and Central European societies have a long-standing tradition of seeing artists, and particularly writers, as the most important articulators of social and political programmes, as often no other possibilities for their expression exist. Thus, in periods of fast change and modernization the role of artists, writers and intellectuals is strongly emphasized.

The accepted metaphor for the cultural and literary aspects of such a policy is that of a 'thaw', in reference to Il'ia Erenburg's novel *Ottepel'* (The Thaw, 1954).[1] This nature metaphor is suitable in many ways. It has connotations of warming sunshine from above, from the centre of the solar system, bringing flux and movement to a frozen world. It implies the instability of April weather and the tenuous nature of a change in which thaw and frost might alternate in a circular movement. This model of 'thaw' does not indicate a revolutionary situation. All the forces involved know very well that the regime is stable, the majority of the population largely passive, and the forces of opposition weak and unorganized. Nevertheless, there is a widespread subliminal feeling that the 'thawing' of frozen prescriptions and taboos might develop a dynamic of its own and grow to a point where it could go beyond purely artistic, ideological criticism and unleash real revolutionary forces endangering the very existence of the system. In such situations, the fears of the established powers may rise to a point where they might see the necessity of putting an end to the 'thawing' process and introduce a new 'frost' to prevent a revolutionary explosion. Such dangers are especially strong in constellations where a seemingly monolithic system consisting of a number of easily identifiable subsystems wants to intro-

1. For descriptions of thaws in Soviet literature I have used Marc Slonim, *Soviet Russian Literature: Writers and Problems, 1917–77*, 2nd, rev. ed., Oxford, New York: Oxford University Press, 1977; Deming Brown, *Soviet Russian Literature since Stalin*, Cambridge: Cambridge University Press, 1978; and Dina R. Spechler, *Permitted Dissent in the U.S.S.R.: '? mir and the Soviet Regime*, New York: Praeger, 1982. General definitions are attempted in Leslie Bodi, 'Tauwetter', in *A Glossary of German Literary Terms*, ed. E. W. Herd and August Obermayer, Dunedin: University of Otago, 1983, p. 219, and Agnes Heller and Ferenc Fehér, '"Thaw" as Promesse de Bonheur', in *Antipodische Aufklärungen. Antipodean Enlightenments: Festschrift für Leslie Bodi*, ed. Walter Veit et al., Frankfurt: Lang, 1988, pp. 133–9. On the eighteenth-century thaw in Austria, see Leslie Bodi, *Tauwetter in Wien: Zur Prosa der österreichischen Aufklärung 1781–95*, Frankfurt: Fischer, 1977, henceforth *TW*.

duce a period of thaw to achieve development and restructuring. This is the case in multinational empires where the thaw situation in the centre has an increasingly strong impact on the periphery; liberalization here means an increased possibility for oppressed nationalities to formulate their own needs and demands, and endanger the cohesion of the whole system. In the first European case of such a development – the Habsburg Empire in the late eighteenth century – the thaw led to a clash between 'enlightened modernization' and nationalist interests, both of which had been awakened and fostered by one and the same reformist policy.

The manipulation of thaws and frosts is the product of a policy of 'guided literature' in which, in a 'closed' society, the handling of censorship has a prominent place. Censorship, however liberalized, interferes with the communication between writer and reader. The author, as the sender, has to encode his message in such a way that the reader as receiver should be able to decode it without the censor being able to do the same. The censor is meant to understand only the overt, surface level meaning. The real message, however, lies in the totality of the text. This is increasingly the case in industrial and post-industrial societies with undemocratic systems of political control, where a broad reading public expects truth and honesty from the censored writer. In 'thaw' periods this problem becomes ever more acute. Writing simultaneously for the reader and the censor, the author is placed in an almost schizophrenic situation and must exert continuous self-censorship. Further complexities can arise from a complicity between author and censor (who might well be an artist or a member of the reformist intelligentsia), from the confusion of ever-changing political prescriptions, from tactical moves that might be caused by infights between groupings within the establishment and, in a period of thaw, from doubts about the seriousness and reliability of signals received from the highest echelons of the leadership. All these complexities may also have an impact on the structure of the literary text, as Lev Loseff has lucidly shown in his book on 'Aesopian language'.[2]

I would distinguish between two phases within the process of a single period of thaw, which I take as beginning once a clear indication has been given 'from above' that a new era of liberalization of censorship, of expanded freedom of expression, of greater openness and tolerance is now to set in. In the first stage, writers are enthusiastic about the new possibilities of communication which are

---

2. Lev Loseff, *On the Beneficence of Censorship: Aesopian Language in Modern Russian Literature*, Munich: Otto Sagner, 1984.

opened up for them. There is an atmosphere of optimism brought about by the prospects of greater freedom and permissiveness. An information explosion may occur in pamphlets, journals and periodicals. These are aimed at the broadest public, which is now becoming interested in reading about a much widened range of subjects. The sheer fact of being able to obtain and to disseminate large quantities of information of whatever kind is itself felt to be a sign of the coming of a new and better age. Violent attacks are mounted against the forces which are seen to have perpetuated the 'old system' of tutelage and repression and which still might endanger the new situation of openness. Linear, one-dimensional satires are written against all past and present enemies of the thaw, basically in support of new government policies. The critical 'line' of these writings is largely 'constructive', fully supporting the reformist aims of the established authorities by attacking and debunking the enemies of change and 'progress'.

At the second stage of the thaw, writers become aware of the limits of permissiveness. They see that the old machinery of control has remained virtually intact, and they begin attacking the process of liberalization as insufficient, false and ultimately repressive. There is increasing criticism of the attitude described by the slogan 'everything for the people, nothing by the people'. Demands for democratic change from below instead of the unquestioning acceptance of authoritative change from above are more and more clearly articulated. Linear satire and the dissemination of plain, explicit information are replaced by ambivalent, ironic and parodic forms which give voice to 'destructive criticism' and question not only the symptoms, but also the essentials, of the system. There is a strengthening feeling of working under pressure of time, with a constant fear of the revocation of the thaw, together with an awareness that a further extension and sharpening of criticism, a utilization in full of the chances given by the more open atmosphere, might well precipitate the coming of a renewed frost. This highly critical literary situation is often expressed in such concise, trenchant and pointed forms as epigrams, jokes and anecdotes. The literary atmosphere may now become ripe for the development of strong elements of playfulness and sensualism, of the grotesque and the absurd, as counterpoints to the puritanical rigidity of earlier norms and prescriptions and their continued presence in the new situation. By quoting and refunctioning the language of their adversaries, new forms of parody are used by the writers in this period as signs of protest and dissent. There is a chance for the creation of artistic works of high complexity and polyphony which are able to express the bewildering contradictions of a social and political situation of heightened hopes and fears, euphoria and anxiety. Characteristic of this second phase of the thaw is a paradoxical attitude that arises on the one hand from the wish to enjoy fully the newly won freedom of expression while fearing the consequences of overstepping the borders of permitted dissent, and on the other from fighting simultaneously against the old forces of repression and the wavering givers of the new freedom.

Understanding the totality of thaw processes helps us comprehend such literary phenomena as censored texts – a task often difficult for readers and critics in open societies. In periods of thaw, an extensive consensus has developed between the writers and their public; the readers are conditioned to understand all references and allusions based on a common political and artistic experience. In the elaborate system of Aesopian language, the carefully encoded political message might sometimes seem to be trivial; it might want to impart political facts which are common knowledge – as, for instance, in modern East European societies the barbarous traits of a Stalinist regime, the existence of political prisoners or the privileges of the party elite. Why make enormous efforts to state the obvious? This happens because in situations of full censorship the medium has become the message in an extreme way. As the process of liberalization takes place, added pleasure is derived by both reader and writer from the knowledge that stating the obvious even in an encoded form is a victory over the forces of restriction, despotism, stupidity and insensitivity. Pleasure comes not only, indeed not mainly, from what is said, but from the way in which it is said, and from the fact that it now can be said at all. Many things can be verbalized more openly in periods of thaw, but many still have to remain in encoded form, giving rise to increased and ever more radicalized demands for the right to speak openly about everything.

In this situation, substantial enjoyment is gained by the public from watching the interplay between ritualized norms generated by repression and censorship, and the new permissiveness expressed in an equally ritualized overstepping of norms and prohibitions; it is an enjoyment closely related to watching a tightrope artist or animal tamer daringly taking calculated risks. A carnivalistic element of liberation is evident on both ends of the political spectrum: dissenting artists, writers, editors, publishers and critics are bravely and cheerfully fighting against censors, functionaries, policemen and conservative critics who doggedly want to maintain restrictive norms. It should be noted that this game is only possible if, within the confines of the authoritarian state, the initiators of the thaw are also aware of the calculated risk they are taking and thus consciously become players in this game of liberalization and repression. This, I believe, was the case with Joseph II.[3]

Eighteenth-century Austrian literary history provides an early example of the process of thaw.[4] Evidently this process is not fully comparable with developments in pre- and post-revolutionary Russia and the present situation in the Soviet Union; it may, nevertheless, provide some interesting parallels. To a certain extent it might even serve as a model for later thaw processes. The history of the decade of the personal rule of Joseph II and its immediate aftermath – the period between 1781 and 1795 – is a history of the rapid modernization of a Central European absolutist state, helped by the opening up of information channels in the name of the Enlightenment. The model character of this process is determined by its short duration and clear delimitation: it starts with a radical liberalization of censorship rules in 1781 and ends with political trials at the onset of a new frost in 1794–5. It is a period of utmost acceleration and concentration at a historical watershed which is also marked by the birth of modern Western democracy and the advent of modern nationalism in the American War of Independence and the French Revolution.

In the 1750s, the Habsburg Monarchy was an amorphous entity, still the central part of the Holy Roman Empire, but also a well-defined absolutist state which had grown into an important European power after the defeat in 1683 of the Turks, who had been perceived for centuries as the arch-enemy of Europe. It contained within its borders a dozen ethnic groups at different stages of their national development and self-identification. The ruling establishment of the Monarchy, shocked by the defeats suffered at the hands of Prussia in the struggle over Silesia, realized that the Habsburg State was backward and needed to catch up with the more developed countries of Western Europe and Protestant Germany, which had far surpassed Austria since the seventeenth-century victory of

3. The only full scholarly biography of Joseph II is that of the Russian historian Pavel Mitrofanov, published in 1907 and translated into German as *Joseph II. Seine politische und kulturelle Tätigkeit*, 2 vols., Vienna and Leipzig: C. W. Stern, 1910. This project is being continued by Derek Beales in his biography, of which one volume has appeared: *Joseph II*, Vol. 1: *In the Shadow of Maria Theresa, 1741–1780*, Cambridge: Cambridge University Press, 1987.
4. The most extensive description of eighteenth-century Austrian literature and literary life is still J. W. Nagl, J. Zeidler and E. Castle, *Deutsch-österreichische Literaturgeschichte*, Vol. 2, Vienna: C. Fromme, 1914. The Austrian theatre of the period is treated in Roger Bauer, *La réalité, royaume de Dieu*, Munich: Hueber, 1965, the prose literature in Bodi, *TW*.

the forces of the Counter-Reformation. A policy of change and reform was initiated, at first cautiously and then ever more resolutely, during the reign of Maria Theresa (1740–80); it became a fast and concentrated process in Joseph II's decade (1780–90). Joseph's aim was the creation of a modern, centralized absolutist state; the main emphasis was on restructuring in the service of efficiency and higher productivity. This could only be achieved by reducing the power of feudal institutions, estates, and regional interests. The power of the Church had to be broken and its organization subjected to the state, even if the tenets of the Catholic faith were not to be openly attacked. Serfdom was abolished and the state tried to limit the rights of feudal landlords and restrictive privileged corporations. The regime promoted industry and technology and set out to improve agricultural production and propagate a new work ethic. All this could only be achieved by extending literacy and numeracy; primary schooling was reformed under Maria Theresa, while Joseph II reorganized the whole education system and strongly restricted the Church's influence on it. In many areas such as health care and the support of infants and the aged, the groundwork was laid for the future secularized welfare state. All these reforms were, however, also introduced with the intention of strengthening the military potential of the Monarchy.

The activity of Joseph II stood clearly within the enlightenment project. It was based on an optimistic, rationalist belief in human perfectibility and a fully realizable utopia. The tenets of the European Enlightenment, interpreted as a demand for the extension of knowledge and science coupled with a struggle against the power of the Church and all forms of mysticism and irrationality in the name of progress, were virtually adopted as the legitimizing principles of a new state ideology.[5] The programme stood for religious toleration and rational methods of economy – first on a mercantilist basis, but increasingly incorporating ideas of the physiocrats. The whole programme was highly pragmatic; it was basically different from the designs of the French or English Enlightenment in that it was neither formulated nor carried out by a strong urban middle class. It also lacked the theoretical sophistication and utopian

5. T. C. Blanning repeatedly emphasizes that it would be wrong to deny Joseph's sincere belief in the tenets of the Enlightenment and to see his reforms as based only on pragmatic considerations (*Joseph II and Enlightened Despotism*, London: Longman, 1970). It should probably be said, however, that an honest belief in the tenets of the Enlightenment in the late eighteenth century could well coexist with an equally honest belief in the absolute supremacy of the state. This paradoxical double-think was fiercely attacked by the critics of enlightened absolutism in the second part of Joseph's rule.

dimension of eighteenth-century German thought, as the programme of reform was to be realized within an existing powerful
absolutist state which did not promote dreams and visions beyond
purely instrumental considerations. Vienna was very different from
Weimar.

It has often been noted that the rule of Joseph II probably was
the most radical manifestation of 'enlightened absolutism'. (The
English term 'enlightened despotism' is somewhat misleading due to
its pejorative connotations.) The reforms were based on a genuine
belief in 'enlightenment' on the part of the ruler and his supporters
in government, even though most of them still belonged to the old
establishment of confessional dynastic absolutism. New layers, however, needed to be recruited to strengthen and support the modernization of the state. Bureaucrats, teachers, professionals, students
and military officers combined with members of the old gentry and
aristocracy to form the nucleus of a new intelligentsia, helping the
propagation and implementation of a policy of instrumental enlightenment understood as social and economic progress. The new ideas
of universalist humanism and tolerance were discussed in private
circles, in the masonic lodges of metropolitan Vienna and the urban
centres of the Monarchy. It was generally understood that, in the
Austrian situation, change and reform could only come from above.
The journalist Johann Friedel in 1785 propagated his belief in an
'enlightenment *a posteriori*', an ideology of enlightenment which
would only bear fruit once the state had opened the way for more
modern thinking through its policy of reform and restructuring.[6]
Throughout the whole period of radical innovation in Joseph II's
time, the government never intended to change the basic power
structure of society or the form of absolutist government. Already in
1771, the writer, reformer and public servant Josef von Sonnenfels
had described the supporters of Maria Theresa's reformist policies
as waging a war on two fronts, simultaneously warding off the
attacks 'of Fanaticism from one side, and Libertinism and Anarchy
from the other'.[7] Fighting both the resilience of the old forces of
fundamentalist religious zealotry and the impact of radical atheist
enlightenment remained, to the end, the task of the Emperor and his
closest advisers.

In this situation, a unique experiment was initiated. It was in
keeping with the aims and concepts of the European Enlightenment,

6. Johann Friedel, *Briefe aus Wien . . . Theil II*, Vienna, 1785, pp. 151–63; *TW*, pp.
   173–5.
7. Quoted in F. Kopetzky, *Josef und Franz von Sonnenfels*, Vienna: 1882, p. 189; *TW*,
   p. 43.

but its main intention was to create an articulate public opinion and mobilize it in support of the reformist restructuring of the Empire. By the time of the death of Maria Theresa, censorship needed urgent reform.[8] Since the victory of the Counter-Reformation it had been dominated by the Jesuits, and attempts at its secularization and reorganization after the abolition of the Order in 1773 could only proceed with great difficulty. Censorship was costly, cumbersome and inefficient, and led Joseph to remark to his mother as early as 1765 that its only use was to make every forbidden book easily available in Vienna. It can be seen as a total admission of the collapse of the system that in 1777 the immensely inflated *Catalogus librorum prohibitorum* was itself forbidden, in order to prevent the reading public from gaining access to the titles of the most interesting censored works which then could be easily acquired.

On his accession to the throne in 1780, Joseph had his discussion paper on the 'basic rules for defining a future orderly censorship of books' circulated among high government officials and commissions. It proposed an extensive liberalization of censorship rules and was based on an assumption formulated by Joseph as early as 1765: 'Permit everything as long as it does not harm the common good, forbid everything that might harm it.'[9] The paper contained clauses against openly atheistic and pornographic publications, stressed considerations of foreign policy, diplomacy and military matters, and was more permissive in regard to expensive scholarly books, which only the upper classes could afford, than to cheap reading matter for the general public. Its most important and frequently quoted passage proclaimed that,

> because the lover of truth must rejoice when he finds it, however it was attained; there will be no ban on works containing criticism of personalities whether they are directed at the sovereign or the humblest subject, unless the attacks are libellous. This will be especially the case if the author appends his name to the piece, as a guarantee of the accuracy of the contents.[10]

After lengthy debates and against strong resistance from some of the more conservative State Councillors the discussion paper was promulgated as law in June 1781. On publication, this censorship

---

8. See Grete Klingenstein, *Staatsverwaltung und kirchliche Autorität im 18. Jahrhundert*, Vienna: Verlag für Geschichte und Politik, 1970, and Oskar Sashegyi, *Zensur und Geistesfreiheit unter Joseph II*, Budapest: Akadémíai Kiadó, 1958.
9. Quoted in Sashegyi, *Zensur und Geistesfreiheit*, p. 17.
10. Quoted in translation by Blanning, *Joseph II and Enlightened Despotism*, p. 142.

decree was hailed by intellectuals throughout the Empire and in the whole of Europe as a great achievement of the Enlightenment. The censorship law did, however, clearly not mean the full liberation of the press, as it was never intended to allow more than an 'extended freedom of the press' ('erweiterte Pressfreiheit'), even though its tone was unique in the absolutist monarchies of Europe. The Censorship Committee was made more efficient. It was secularized and its working streamlined to cover the whole Monarchy. It showed great permissiveness, but its activities were also marred by petty bureaucratic practices, such as the provision for having more daring books or pamphlets published only on condition of the use of pseudonyms or fictitious imprints. The members of the Committee were high-ranking public servants, university professors and even writers. Most of them also belonged to masonic lodges. There were constant differences of opinion between the conservative and more liberal members of the Committee, and it was impossible to maintain full secrecy about its deliberations in the circles of Viennese intellectuals.

The liberalization of censorship rules created a state of euphoria among the intelligentsia of the Monarchy, particularly in metropolitan Vienna. It was immediately followed by a 'deluge of pamphlets' ('Broschürenflut'), resulting in the publication between mid-1781 and September 1782 of about 1,200 pamphlets in Vienna alone.[11] The development of a new reading public for secular publications was based on the general spread of literacy as a result of Maria Theresa's educational reforms in the 1760s; this public increasingly included women readers. The pamphlets covered a broad range of topics from the plainest description of social customs and mores to questions of economy and technology, and also included purely entertaining, whimsically humorous pieces. In their bulk these pamphlets supported the Emperor's policies. They were filled with optimism about the marvellous prospects of enlightened ideas and attacked the establishment of the Catholic Church as the greatest and most dangerous enemy of reform and modernization. They helped to build the image of Joseph II as an enlightened ruler and were even used by government agencies to promote or defend their policies. The pamphleteers were instrumental in creating a veritable Josephinian myth, which also had an impact on public opinion in the rest of Europe.

The pamphleteers, fully convinced of the rightness of Joseph's

---

11. Aloys Blumauer, *Beobachtungen über Österreichs Aufklärung und Litteratur*, Vienna, 1782, pp. 36–9.

policies, were sometimes even willing to take over the functions of censorship. Thus, a group of young 'Aufklärer' set itself the task of publishing a weekly critical commentary on the sermons held in the churches of Vienna, denouncing all deviations from the phraseology of 'enlightened religion'. Their lively reports, which almost read like shorthand transcripts, were, for a time, best-sellers in the city. In this first phase of the thaw, the dominant literary prose forms were those of the linear, not too sophisticated satire, often in the tradition of Voltaire's writings. Such a work was Johann Pezzl's *Faustin* (1783). Local interest novels with unsophisticated plots developed, which also had a satirical slant against the enemies of the Enlightenment. The poet Aloys Blumauer wrote *Die Abentheuer des Helden Aeneas . . .* (The Adventures of the Hero Aeneas, 1782), which contained a sharp attack on the aspirations of the Catholic Church. Although censorship of 'high theatre' remained relatively stringent, popular comedy had survived in Vienna – as in some other great European cities – and the comical figures of Hanswurst and Kasperl became much more open in their criticism of the ills of society.

From the outset, Joseph's literary policies were strongly based on economic considerations; they tried to establish an indigenous Austrian printing and publishing industry in defiance of the almost total control of the German-language book market by Protestant Germany. A start had already been made under Maria Theresa. Two factors had given Austria's printing industry a boost: an anticipated increase in demand for textbooks in the new, extended system of primary schools throughout the Monarchy, and the promotion of pirated editions of books from more advanced German territories. The liberalization of censorship in 1781 then brought an explosive development of the Austrian book market. The reform created new strata of the intelligentsia, who became writers and readers of printed material. Lively debates about copyright developed among the literati, who now competed on an open book market which had never previously existed in Habsburg lands. Between 1773 and 1792 the value of Austrian book exports increased from 135,000 to 3,260,000 Thalers.[12] All this, obviously, turned writers, booksellers and publishers into enthusiastic supporters of the policy of enlightened reform.

In the years 1784–5, however, an ever-increasing feeling of doubt and dissatisfaction became dominant in Austria. The impact of the general economic and social crisis of the *ancien régime* in Europe

---

12. Johann Goldfriedrich, *Geschichte des deutschen Buchhandels*, Vol. II, quoted in Sashegyi, *Zensur und Geistesfreiheit*, p. 89.

also made itself felt in the Habsburg lands. Internal opposition to the policy of reforms from the old establishment, the Church and the nobility strengthened. The new system had not brought the expected improvements in living standards, and there was increasing discontent with the secularization of everyday life, as well as its strict regimentation and bureaucratization. The resentment against modernization became more vocal in the provinces, and the regional estates put up growing opposition against the policy of centralization.

The strongest resistance came from the non-German nationalities of the Empire, mainly from the ethnic groups which had long-established traditions of independent statehood. In the wake of the reforms they also shared in the broadening of education, the development of literacy, the extension of the literary market, the permissiveness of censorship, and the general impact of the European Enlightenment. Some of the smaller ethnic groups now had their first chance of developing a literary language and publishing facilities of their own.[13] The policy of restructuring encouraged the development of an indigenous intelligentsia. All this meant the growth or, in some cases, the first awakening of national self-consciousness, and led to ever-increasing demands for greater independence. In 1784, the Emperor declared German the official language of the Monarchy. This was meant as a pragmatic, practical and rational measure, and the Emperor and his councillors were surprised at the deep resentment it caused in the Hungarian estates and among all strata of ethnic Magyars, in the Habsburgs' Italian territories, and in the Netherlands, where it even helped to trigger off and strengthen a revolution against Habsburg rule. The complexities of the national question also became apparent when Rumanian peasants revolted against their Hungarian landlords in the firm belief that they acted in the true spirit of Joseph's reforms. These dramatic demonstrations of the force of awakening nationalism in Central and Eastern Europe were the first open manifestations of a conflict which has remained a constant in the history of this region: the rift between enlightened, rationalist reform policies of modernization on the one hand, and the contrasting interests of national groups in search of their political and cultural identity on the other. In the case of the Habsburg Empire, this development also forced

13. Good summaries of the impact of Josephinism on the nationalities of the Empire are contained in Eduard Winter, *Barock, Absolutismus und Aufklärung in der Donaumonarchie*, Vienna: Europa, 1971, and Robert A. Kann, *A History of the Habsburg Empire*, 2nd ed., Berkeley: University of California Press, 1977, pp. 367–405.

the dominant ethnic group of German speakers to become aware of the need for their own linguistic and cultural self-definition.

In this situation, the government became increasingly nervous about the policy of reform, and conservative councillors now often gained the upper hand in the decision-making process. Fears were growing about the subversive function of secret societies, especially after the Society of the Illuminati had introduced a strong political element into its activities. Late in 1785 an imperial decree was issued with the aim of reorganizing and centralizing the work of the masonic lodges and submitting them to greater government control (the 'Freimaurerpatent'). In 1786, a secret police service was established for the strict supervision of all subjects of the Empire.

These moves strengthened the new intelligentsia's feeling of distrust concerning the process of thaw. The fears and uncertainties that now developed were typical of a situation of this kind. Writers, publishers and other 'enlightened' intellectuals raised anxious questions about the duration of the thaw. They were afraid of a full reversal of the policy of liberalization and realized that a new ruler might immediately initiate a new period of frost. These uncertainties were expressed in a feeling of urgency and in a wish to utilize what remaining period of openness might still be available. The Censorship Committee, whose deliberations very well illustrate this atmosphere of uncertainty, further encouraged radical reformers through the inconstancy of its decisions. In 1784, the censors rejected plans for a stamp duty aimed at reducing the extent of pamphleteering and journalism; in April 1786 they even abolished the censoring of manuscripts prior to printing and thus opened the way for extreme radicalization. The actions of government agencies, no less than those of writers and publishers, were motivated not only by ideological convictions, but also by economic considerations. The Emperor and his advisers wanted to increase the activities of a profitable branch of local industry, while the freeing of the book market gave writers and publishers a chance to profit from the increasing public interest in critical literature.

This is the situation in which, I suggest, the period of thaw entered its second stage. By now, a more articulate and sensitive literary public had developed in the urban centres of the Empire. The economic position of publishers and booksellers had greatly improved. More efficient and cheaper brands of paper and new printing technologies were introduced. 'Foreign' literature was now much more readily available than before. The public was conscious of the wavering of censorship between repression and permissiveness, feeling that censorship was 'changeable as April weather'. One

of the leading journals stated: 'It is easy to cheat censorship, because
it probably wants to be cheated. Yet the whole handling of censorship [. . .] remains a nuisance and an annoying bother.'[14] Writers
and publishers were constantly engaged in testing the limits of
liberalism, while the Censorship Committee and the police authorities kept watching how far writers would dare to go. The Emperor
himself participated in the game; his sarcastic remarks and disre-
spectful witty sayings were often leaked and discussed in the bookshops, salons, masonic lodges and coffee houses of Vienna. The
absurdities of censorship decisions were evident. When Beaumarchais'
Marriage of Figaro was banned, Da Ponte and Mozart were, nevertheless, permitted to write, compose and, in May 1786, perform
their opera. One of the leading Viennese journals ironically commented, 'what nowadays may not be verbalized, can nevertheless be
sung!'[15]

A greater awareness had developed in Austria of changes in the
intellectual and political climate in Western Europe, especially in
the more advanced territories of Northern and Central Germany.
The discussion of Enlightenment as a critique of all forms of oppression and injustice and as the overcoming of humankind's 'self-
imposed tutelage', as Kant had put it in his essay on Enlightenment
in 1784,[16] necessarily had a great impact in the Habsburg Monarchy. There was a noticeable radicalization in the tone of Viennese
pamphleteers and journalists. Criticism went far beyond the limits
envisaged by the government's 'tutelage' and breached its intention
of using the written word to promote an instrumentalized enlightenment understood as the motor of technological and economic ration-
alization, progress and development. Many of the pamphleteers
emphasized that, ultimately, enlightenment was incompatible with
absolutism, and that writing and thinking had to be emancipated
from government intervention and manipulation. Writers were willing to accept the role of the 'conscience of the people'. They not only
felt increasingly committed to act as a corrective for all the necessary
mistakes and misjudgements of an absolute monarch, but proceeded
to demand a full 'publicity of public affairs'.[17] Even a writer like

14. Anonymous letter from Vienna, dated 27 April 1784, *Allgemeine deutsche Bibliothek*
    (Berlin), 57 (1784), No. 1, 297.
15. Quoted from the *Realzeitung* for 1786 in Moritz Csáky, 'Mozarts Figaro nach
    zweihundert Jahren', *Pannonia*, 14 (1986), No. 4, 11.
16. Immanuel Kant, 'Beantwortung der Frage: Was ist Aufklärung?' *Berlinische
    Monatsschrift*, 4 (1784), No. 6, 452–65.
17. [Johann Friedel], *Historisch-philosophische und statistische Fragmente*, Leipzig and
    Klagenfurt, 1786, pp. 28–58. See also *TW*, pp. 249–53.

Amand Berghofer, whose early Rousseauism had been manifest mainly in idyllic nature poetry, came to the conclusion in 1787 that the double-think and double-speak of authors who 'lauded the despots while secretly despising them' would completely destroy their artistic abilities.[18] Raising doubts about the belief that a ruler can only make his people happy by adopting a system of instrumental enlightenment, the playwright, novelist and publicist Johann Friedel said in 1786, 'however that may be, I would rather sacrifice the system for the individual than the individual for the system'.[19] The pamphleteers now demanded the total abolition of censorship instead of accepting official manipulation of the 'enlarged freedom of the press', and emphasized the repressive nature of a concept of 'tolerance' which still implied the existence of absolutely binding religious norms, relaxed only out of economic and military considerations. It was a tolerance, it was claimed, that was in constant danger of revocation by the ruling powers.

The mercantilist measures of Joseph II culminated in August 1784 in a decree on emigration from Habsburg lands, which stated categorically that, 'in general, no person is permitted either to emigrate himself, or to send to foreign countries any of his children or any person under his power and supervision [. . .]'[20] This radical restriction of freedom of movement became for the pamphleteers one of the strongest arguments against the system of enlightened absolutism. They argued that an enlightened government should keep its citizens from emigrating, not by erecting walls around the country, but by improving conditions to a degree which would make such measures unnecessary. In 1785, Jean-Pierre Brissot formulated the aphorism, 'a decree against emigration is a decree of slavery.'[21] Statements of this kind often recur in other pamphlets which openly accuse the Emperor of 'tyranny' and, in some cases, explicitly go beyond the concept of enlightenment and reform from above by voicing the need for democratic changes from below. 'Constructive criticism' in the service of the regime now turns into 'destructive criticism'.

In this situation, satire is formulated in a sharper, more pointed, more concrete way than before; instead of vague and generalized attacks on repression, the writers have become bold enough to name

18. Amand Berghofer, *Schriften*, 2nd ed., Vienna, 1787, p. 196.
19. Friedel, *Historisch-philosophische*, p. 24.
20. Joseph Kropatschek, ed., *Handbuch aller . . . Verordnungen und Gesetze* in 18 vols., Vol. 6, Vienna: 1784, p. 281.
21. [Jean-Pierre Brissot], *Ein Vertheidiger des Volks an den Kaiser Joseph II . . .*, Dublin [i.e., Vienna], 1785, p. 4.

the powerful persons responsible for the maintenance of oppressive political measures. The pamphlets now sometimes show a more refined, pointed and epigrammatic structure, working with increasingly sophisticated modes of ambivalence and irony. Such are the attacks on Josephinism by Josef Grossing, Johann Jakob Fezer and Friedrich Zilmer, which have such titles as 'Probabilities' and 'Improbabilities'.[22] In the last years of Joseph's reign, parody gains significance. By contrasting the style of official texts to the realities of contemporary life and the lofty ideas of enlightenment to the practices of the emerging police state, writers became increasingly able to demonstrate, by means of language art, that the system had not really changed. These parodies indicate that the 'enlightened' enemies of past 'obscurantism' now in power have themselves turned into obstacles to enlightenment. Parody serves to demonstrate the complexity of the fight between 'true' (i.e. critical) and 'false' (i.e. instrumental, officially perpetuated) enlightenment in a situation further aggravated by strategies used by deeply conservative writers professing to be guardians of 'true' (i.e. orthodox religious) enlightenment while denouncing as 'false' all secularization, modernization and critical reasoning.

Austrian literature had at that time reached a stage where, as a preliminary to the modern novel, highly polyphonic Menippean satires could be written, which made good use of the stylistic devices of Aesopian language. These included Franz Xaver Huber's whimsical fairy-tale animal satire *Der blaue Esel* (The Blue Ass, 1786), as well as his parodic satires on the legal system in which he confronts the enlightened phraseology of natural law with surviving practices of brutal medieval forms of punishment. The best texts of these years exhibit desperate pessimism, nihilism and confusion. They express their authors' fading hopes for the future of the state-sponsored enlightenment project. This is evident in Friedrich Wilhelm von Meyern's *Abdul Erzerum's neue persische Briefe* (Abdul Erzerum's New Persian Letters, 1787) and Paul Weidmann's brilliant history of an enlightened prince-turned-ruthless-despot in *Der Eroberer* (The Conqueror, 1786), a unique work broken up into more than 120 pieces which parody all known literary forms and genres of the time.

The political and economic situation of the Empire became increasingly hopeless by 1787–8. A war against the Ottoman Empire drained the resources of the state, necessitated the introduction of special taxation, and even led to hunger riots in Vienna. There was growing resistance by feudal landlords to the Emperor's proposed

22. See Bodi, *TW*, pp. 257–79.

radical agrarian reform and disquiet in the provinces among peasants dissatisfied with the slowness of the improvement of their lot. Revolutions against Joseph's reforms broke out in the Austrian Netherlands, and dangers of further national uprisings and a Prussian intervention had to be envisaged. The first victories of the French Revolution made 'enlightened despotism' seem an untenable illusion.

In the second half of 1789 a liberal policy toward literature had become impossible. The introduction of a long-planned stamp duty decisively restricted the number of pamphlets and journals. Georg Philipp Wucherer, the publisher of the most daring pamphlets, was arrested in October, and preventive censorship was reintroduced in November. Joseph II died in February 1790. His successor, Leopold II, tried to save some of Joseph's achievements by compromising with the rebellious nationalities and trying to appease the restive estates of the provinces. He attempted to reactivate some of the intellectual potential of Joseph II's adherents in the service of his own very advanced ideas of a more 'constitutional' structure for the Habsburg Monarchy. Leopold even used the services of some of the Josephinian era's best publicists to threaten conservative Hungarian landlords with the dangers of the revolution which they would face unless they supported his reformist policies. This skilful manipulator of public opinion died, however, in 1792, after having secured the participation of Austria in the Wars of Coalition against revolutionary France.[23]

By the time of the accession to the throne of Leopold's successor, Francis I, the French Revolution had swung towards Republicanism. The emergence of Jacobin terror, as well as the trial and execution of Louis XVI and Marie Antoinette in 1793, made a continuation of reformist enlightened policies in the Habsburg Empire impossible. The end of the thaw and the introduction of a new period of frost was signalled to the general public by a series of trials against members of the Josephinian intelligentsia in Austria and Hungary who were accused of Jacobinism, revolutionary plotting and subversive activities.[24] The materials used for the verdicts in these trials were, to a large extent, provided by agents provocateurs and the secret police. The court cases of 1794–5 had a largely symbolic function: they were meant to communicate to the vocal

23. See Denis Silagi, *Ungarn und der geheime Mitarbeiterkreis Leopolds II*, Munich: R. Oldenbourg, 1961; Adam Wandruszka, *Leopold II*, 2 vols., Vienna and Munich: Herold, 1963–4; and Gerda Lettner, *Das Rückzugsgefecht der Aufklärung in Wien 1790–92*, Frankfurt and New York: Campus, 1988.
24. Ernst Wangermann, *From Joseph II to the Jacobin Trials*, 2nd ed., Oxford: Oxford University Press, 1969.

intellectuals of both the German-speaking lands and the other territories of the Empire that the thaw had come to an end and that things had gone back to the *status quo ante*. We know from the records of the trials that the prosecution viewed Aesopian language, and especially the ambivalence, irony and parody which had character-ized the writings of the second phase of the thaw period, as a grave offence and an aggravating factor in meting out verdicts. These were especially savage in the case of Hungarian writers and intellectuals, and led to executions and long prison sentences. Many writers of the period went into exile or made uneasy compromises with the new repressive government.

In February 1795, new censorship rules were decreed with the aim of creating a watertight system of supervision throughout the Monarchy. They made the printing and distribution of uncensored manuscripts a capital offence and prohibited the possession of typographic equipment by any private person without a printing licence. The printing of manuscripts in foreign countries or 'secretly in obscure institutions' was to be severely punished, and the import-ation of proscribed books from abroad strictly prohibited: 'pretend-ing that [the culprit] had lost the manuscript and that the foreign printed matter was published abroad without his knowledge and permission is especially unacceptable, as nobody must pass on a forbidden censored manuscript or keep such a manuscript if there is any danger of its further distribution.'[25] Bookshops as well as public and private libraries were searched for publications of the thaw period, and many books and pamphlets were destroyed by govern-ment agencies and by intimidated readers. In 1795 new rules for theatre censorship strictly reduced all traits of earlier permissive-ness: they prohibited extemporization and emphasized the moral-izing and educational functions of the theatre. In response to the dangers created by the French Revolution and the Josephinian thaw, all depictions of revolutions, rebellions and conspiracies against a legitimate ruler were now forbidden, as well as any reference to the 'oppression of subjects' or the elevation of burghers and peasants over the higher estates in a 'disparaging way'. In an explicit con-demnation of the tenets of Josephinism, the blueprint for theatre censorship also stipulated that 'on stage, the word "enlightenment" is to be mentioned just as sparingly as the terms "freedom" and "equality"'.[26]

25. Quoted in Julius Marx, *Die österreichische Zensur im Vormärz*, Munich: R. Olden-bourg, [1959], p. 71.
26. Carl Glossy, 'Zur Geschichte der Wiener Theaterzensur', *Jahrbuch der Grillparzer-Gesellschaft*, 7 (1897), 328.

The political and social measures taken to secure the victory of the new frost included closing the masonic lodges, re-establishing the dominance of the Church in the field of education, and entrusting censorship to the police in a newly established Ministry for Police and Censorship. Attempts were made to reduce the urban population in order to limit the development of a new critical intelligentsia in the Monarchy. These reactionary measures were first accompanied by intensive debates about 'enlightenment' and 'obscurantism' in series of pamphlets which were, however, quickly forbidden. There were desperate complaints in private letters: the poet Johann Baptist von Alxinger, for instance, writing to his friend Friedrich Nicolai in Berlin in 1796 concerning the 'state of enlightenment in Vienna', lamented 'that its thermometer, alas, has almost reached freezing point. Bans on books and clericalism are the only dams intended to be erected here against a feared revolution, even though these fears are completely unfounded.'[27]

This new era of frost, though interrupted by a short period of renewed thaw around 1809, had the effect of setting back Austrian literary and intellectual life for more than a generation. It could only catch up again with German and world literature as late as the 1830s. An Austrian tradition dating from the Counter-Reformation was renewed: music and the performing arts again came to be regarded as less dangerous than the verbalization of critical ideas.

Up to the present day, memories of the thaw of the late eighteenth century, of the explosive enthusiasm which it released, and of its brutal extinction have been an important, though largely suppressed, factor of the Austrian tradition. It has remained especially difficult in later eras to talk about this period, as its memory was traumatized by the inner contradictions of the process. As the political parties of the left and the right crystallized and polarized from the 1860s onward, Joseph II came to be seen as an absolutist autocrat by liberals and the labour movement, while his radical reforms, relentless methods and 'enlightened' rhetoric led the forces of conservatism and clericalism to see him as one of their worst enemies. Within the multinational empire, too, he was cast in the contradictory roles of a ruthless colonizer and Germanizer on the one hand, and a liberal, modernizing reformer on the other.

In the further development of Austria the era of Josephinism, in spite of all its contradictions, has remained an important factor in

27. Johann Baptist von Alxinger, 'Briefe', ed. Gustav Wilhelm, in *Sitzungsberichte der Philologisch-Historischen Klasse der . . . Akademie der Wissenschaften, Wien*, 140 (1899), Part II, p. 88.

establishing a rationalist enlightened tradition in a deeply religious and conservative society where reform could only be initiated 'from above' by the power of the state. Traditions of tolerance and human responsibility were established, as well as a belief in the importance of secular education and literacy. Even if only subliminally, they have greatly helped the further development of the country. The Josephinian thaw had a lasting impact because it was more than the result of reform and restructuring from above: it was also the fruit of increasing pressure for change from below by the forces which an interlude of permissiveness enabled to develop. It was an important feature of this brief transitional period that a vocal and literate layer of self-conscious, imaginative intellectuals could rapidly emerge in a stagnant, repressive and backward society. In the second phase of the Josephinian thaw, writers were able to articulate a situation of high complexity, fighting simultaneously for the acceptance and realization of the values of critical enlightenment and against the political system which had opened up the avenues for the promotion of these values, but still wanted to maintain old restrictive power structures. In its confrontation between critical and instrumental enlightenment and between concepts of change from below and from above, the Josephinian era already shows similarities to thaw periods of the twentieth century, especially insofar as it was enacted in a historical situation characterized by the clash between policies of enlightenment and the forces of nascent nineteenth-century nationalism.

Even though the Josephinian thaw was largely repressed in the following decades, it had created a lively literary market and a new reading public in the lands of the Habsburg Empire. Little research has yet been done to help our understanding of the impact of this explosive period of innovation on the greatest achievement of Austrian culture, the development of music. In the field of literature, the complexity of the thaw situation gave birth to new attitudes of artistic expression and sophisticated forms and genres which developed the polyphony inherent in Aesopian language. It gave rise not only to straightforward satirical attacks on the enemies of social, political and artistic freedom, but to an increasing dominance of modes of ambivalence in the structuring of literary works by the use of parody and irony. This has remained an important identity marker of a specifically Austrian literature as it has developed to the present day.

-3-

Winter, Thaw, Spring: The Czech Perspective

PAVEL PETR

The concepts of thaw and spring originate in an area of human experience where the subjective needs, wishes and actions of groups and individuals matter very little. Seasonal weather changes are governed by forces outside the subject: they occur due to the workings of higher powers, by divine authority, as a consequence of the laws of nature. The pleasant end to frost and winter must be expected with patience. If it arrives early, its onset is to be acknowledged with gratitude and the humble hope that the frost will not return. After some time, another winter must be expected: such is the working of the objective forces.

The metaphor of thaw in its most influential version goes back to a Soviet source, namely Il'ia Erenburg's novel of the same name, published in 1954. Its plot involves two painters, one a true artist, the other a political opportunist and a fake. In the frosty rigidity of the political winter, the sincere artist suffers, while the fake is successful. Ultimately, however, the frost comes to an end thanks to the intervention of highly placed party officials who act in parallel with the objective laws of nature.

A narrative constructed in this way expresses the following logic: Marxism-Leninism knows the objective laws of history, which, in Stalin's version of dialectics, function in the same manner as the laws of nature. These laws direct human history towards communism and are executed by the avant-garde of the proletariat, represented by the leadership of the Soviet Communist Party. Any deviations from the ideal road to goodness can only be temporary: they may be caused by individual officials, but the objective forces will prevail in the long run. Thus, in Erenburg's novel, high party leaders set things right. What used to be known as *deus ex machina* – the intervention of a god or of an enlightened despot – appears now in the form of personifications of the objective laws of history.

Stalinist philosophy replaced the dialectic of subject and object with the dialectic of nature, for obvious political reasons: if the laws of human history behave in the same way as the laws of nature, then they can be discovered only once, and can only be applied either correctly or incorrectly – any pluralism is out of the question, and the leading role of the Soviet Union is thereby given a scientific foundation.

This centralist and authoritarian system of thinking has become characteristic not only of the establishment, but also of many expressions of dissent within the Soviet Union. Erenburg's nature symbol implies that change can only come from the highest authorities, and the harmonizing solution of the novel is a natural result of their initiative. A closer look at Solzhenitsyn will reveal a considerable dose of Russian-centred messianism. And Mikhail Gorbachev's new establishment? His reforms do not appear as teamwork, nor are there any attempts to present them as such. His steps towards a benevolent dictatorship are many: they include the unification of the leadership of party and state, the elevation of the Presidency to new importance, the plan to deprive both the KGB and the Internal Affairs Ministry of their private armies and join them under the direct control of the party, and electoral reforms which will result in the fusion of the Soviets with the party organizations.

In a recent interview with Milovan Djilas, George Urban quoted an article from *Izvestiia* which said that 'Soviet people are accustomed to thinking that whatever a journalist writes in this paper is inspired by Authority. Now we are told that this is no longer so. How can people understand this?' Djilas' reaction: 'The Soviet people have never felt free to say "Here is what I know – and here is what I conclude from that knowledge." No, they put their information aside and wait to hear what Authority expects them to believe.'[1] The traditions created by uninterrupted oppressive centralized rule, in combination with what must still be termed a war economy, make a thaw – a temporary liberalization and relaxation of censorship – easier to absorb than a real structural change towards independence and plurality.

In Czechoslovakia, a historical background very different from that of the Soviet Union led to a significantly different understanding of communism and its philosophy and policies. When communist ideas became influential in the culture (strongly) and parliamentary politics (much less strongly) of newly born Czechoslovakia after the First World War, they were accepted as a product of

1. Milovan Djilas on Gorbachev's future, *The New York Times*, 3 December 1988, 15.

Western thinking and as part of a broad democratic spectrum of opinion. It is hardly necessary to emphasize that empire building was not an ambition present in the collective national mind of the time: it was more important to find ways of maintaining some independence, and the ideas of communism were frequently understood to represent a stance in favour of social justice and freedom for the oppressed, not without implicit reference to freedom for this much oppressed and threatened nation.

Another feature of the Czech historical tradition which distinguishes it from the Russian is the absence of a national ruling elite. The Czech aristocracy was wiped out as a result of a battle lost in 1620: it was executed, exiled or Germanized. The national awakening, which did not take shape until 1800, had to rely on plebeian elements and was centred on a romantic revival of language and poetry. In the absence of aristocrats with some power base and leadership experience, the perceived representatives of the nation were its poets, linguists and philosophers. Whilst the real rulers spoke German, the Czechs concentrated their ambitions and their pride on their culture, especially literary culture. However unhelpful such priorities may have been for acquiring real power, they were important in establishing a national identity. In the First World War, lack of identification with the interests of the Monarchy resulted in mass desertions and 'švejkism', a seemingly naive, but efficiently destructive, literal obedience to instructions – a practice which both showed up the absurdity of the instructions and provided the pleasure of laughter at the expense of those in power. An independent state was established in 1918, with a professor of philosophy as its first president. The traditional attitudes of non-participation in the shaping of political structures, however, showed little sign of receding. Neither in 1938 nor during the Hitler occupation was there decisive political action on a national scale. Ordinary people neither identified with, nor fought against, the governing forces, tacitly accepting, on the whole, the dominance of the Austrian emperor or the Western Allies who donated their country to Hitler, and again of Hitler or the post-1948 rulers with their obedience towards Moscow.

The Second World War was perceived as a mere interruption of the continuity of Czechoslovakia, which renewed itself in 1945 under the same president and with a democratic system of elections. In fact, however, as Otto Ulč observes, 'prewar political practices were not restored. Only a handful of political parties were licensed, all of which were at least rhetorically sympathetic to socialism and the Soviet Union. Any political participation outside this circle was prohibited.'[2] On the other hand, the Soviet army which liberated Czechoslovakia was welcomed with a panslavically tinted nationalist euphoria. In the 1946 elections, the Communist Party obtained more votes than any other party which was permitted to stand candidates. It secured 114 of the 300 seats in the National Assembly, and was given the prime ministership and several key portfolios. The euphoric willingness to embrace things Russian was such that even if other parties had been admitted, their likelihood of winning would have been insignificant. The 1946 elections were generally felt to have been democratic.

Against this background and within this system, the Communist Party maintained, until 1948, a degree of tolerance very different from Soviet practice. It embraced writers who had been pre-war communist sympathizers even if they had criticized Soviet policies (mainly the show trials); it accommodated the transition to communism of people associated with structuralism (Jan Mukařovský), Masarykism, phenomenology, plebeian democracy and even surrealism (Vítězslav Nezval, Konstantin Biebl). It was only after the takeover in 1948 that Stalin and his followers insisted that the party utilize its now unrestricted power to copy the Soviet system. Although Czechoslovakia was to remain a democratic society in name, essential characteristics of democracy had to be removed: the division between the legislative, executive and judicial powers was abandoned, the administrative court was abolished, regular courts had to adopt the principle of 'class justice' and explicitly reject equality before the law. These newly imposed structures were in line with Soviet conventions, but contradicted the local traditions of a country which had experienced Renaissance and Humanism as well as democracy. The heritage of Western European thinking, in which many influential Czech communists had their intellectual roots, was rejected as decadent, formalist and cosmopolitan. Many writers and artists tried to follow the required principles, with very mixed results: jailed poets and early deaths by suicide and attrition became common (Jan Zahradníček, Jan Drda, Václav Řezáč, E. F. Burian).

On the surface, this society now had many characteristics in common with its Soviet master. In some respects, the Czech traditions were suited to the new Russian order. One example was deference to the central authority in economic, military and political terms, which defied economic sense and led to an unprecedented decline in the position of the country relative to other industrialized states. Another was the ideologically motivated terror carried out by

2. Otto Ulč, *Politics in Czechoslovakia*, San Francisco: W. H. Freeman, 1974, p. 25.

ruling groups, first in 1945–6 (against the Germans), and then in 1952, when more party officials of the highest rank were executed in Czechoslovakia than in any other Soviet-dominated country. But many differences remained. Brutality and eagerness in following orders did not result from a 'tradition of despotism and of the veneration of Tsars and dogmas,'[3] but from a tradition which is specific to Bohemia: to accept foreign dominance without directly resisting any orders or even questioning them. The foreignness of these orders was regarded as the consequence of the customary foreignness of the masters, who could not be expected to understand the Czech language or the Czech situation, whatever their names might be – Franz Josef, Hitler, Chamberlain, Daladier, or Stalin. Traditionally, the Czech nation did not look to its politicians for a confirmation of its own strength, superiority or influence. In open conflicts, it expected to remain powerless: the decisions about the length of its leash would be made by foreign powers in Versailles, Munich or Yalta, or on the hotline between Washington and Moscow. For its own room to move, it turned to areas which were inaccessible to the mighty foreigners: the metaphoric language of the poets and the esoteric discourse of the philosophers. The open struggle for political change receded behind the struggle for free political expression, and this, in a further reduction, concentrated on finding freedom for literary expression. A direct political statement inevitably fell victim to political censorship; a cryptic statement in a literary context might succeed in passing through the censor's net. The political system with its pseudo-parliament and pseudo-elections provided neither a genuine political forum nor genuine political representation; the arena of the nation's political life moved to the literary journals and cultural organizations, while writers, poets and intellectuals became political representatives. The readership of literary journals and novels and the audience of the theatre and film became the political public, watching the progress achieved by its intellectuals.

Under wintry conditions, political satisfaction is typically limited to the coding and decoding of political messages. Metaphors and multi-layered ironies, intelligently deciphered and creatively completed by readers and audiences, provide the public with a feeling of superiority over the authorities and the censors, who had either not noticed or had been worn down. The fight for more elbow-room continues; metaphoric criticism may be combined with direct criticism, and the relationship between the two may change. As Lev

---

3. Otto Ulč, 'Koestler revisited', *Survey*, Summer 1969, 121.

Pavel Petr

Loseff puts it, 'Aesopian writers and the ideological censorship are drawn into a never-ending game which has the character of a ritual [. . .]. Catharsis is the inner content of an Aesopian literary work, a catharsis which the reader experiences as a victory over repressive authority.'[4] Needless to say, the repressive authority is not necessarily too stupid to notice: the game of relaxing and tightening the censorship works in favour of the establishment by providing a safety valve effect on the one hand and a reminder of its efficient authority on the other. The position of literary creators in this situation is complex and contradictory. Their identity is normally determined by factors far removed from the requirements of pragmatic political activity and their statements are not primarily focussed on the political side of human communication. When they find themselves in a position of political authority – a position denied to writers in the contemporary Western world – their statements acquire an aura of importance beyond the world of the mind and equip them with a semblance of real power. As the actual results inevitably prove the absence of such real power, the validity of their ideals and of their chosen methods (and their morality) appears in a dubious light, leading to a loss of self-respect as well. Milan Kundera, in an interview with Antonín J. Liehm in the mid-1960s, gave an interesting personal view of such a position. According to Kundera, Stalinism had been based originally on a humanitarian movement which could then be seen to change progressively, step by step, into its very opposite. While witnessing this change, writers experienced a growing feeling of insecurity concerning values and virtues. This brought about a scepticism in whose light all statements had a tendency to change into questions. As a counterexample, Kundera cited the French novelist Henry de Montherlant, who was able to be ironical about anything except himself and who asserted that he would never want to be anybody but Montherlant, with whom he was generally very happy. 'Hardly anyone from my generation', said Kundera, 'would be able to say this. We tend not to live in much harmony with ourselves; I do not like myself very much.'[5] Attitudes displayed by Czech intellectuals, even after many years of absence from their homeland – constant self-irony, evasion in everyday communication, metaphorical ways of expression and utterances filled with complex ironies – may find

4. Lev Loseff, *On the Beneficence of Censorship: Aesopian Language in Modern Russian Literature*, Munich: Otto Sagner, 1984, p. 230.
5. A. J. Liehm, *Gespräch an der Moldau*, Vienna, Munich and Zurich: Molden, 1968, pp. 125–6.

some explanation in such circumstances.

When comparing the post-Stalin thaw in the Soviet Union with the Czechoslovakian version of political defrosting which took place more or less at the same time, the historical differences can be clearly pinpointed. The decisive phase of the Soviet thaw began at the political level with Khrushchev's speech of 25 February 1956. This thaw brought some lasting results, most notably the release of political prisoners and a moderation of Stalinist inhumanity toward political dissenters. In most other respects, it remained true to the meaning of the image which gave it its name: more warmth, and a softening within an existing framework. The critical formula of the 'personality cult' served to focus attention on the 'deformation' of an otherwise valid system which could be set right again with the help of a few leadership changes, thus leaving all the main structures intact and ready for a subsequent refrosting. On the literary scene, the thaw had its parallel in the publication of works by Erenburg and Solzhenitsyn, but neither the initiative, nor the results in political terms, were ever in the hands of the literary intelligentsia. Aleksandr Tvardovskii's *Novyi mir* did not have the function of a political forum of central importance. In line with the traditions of Russian and, subsequently, Soviet history, the almighty central powers, in a system without inbuilt controls, decided to initiate a thaw – by an open and direct speech, yet within the closed confines of the ruling political body.

In Czechoslovakia, the initiatives emanated from the writers and their forums. The thaw manifested itself in the fact that the political power centre allowed enough space for the forces pushing the policy of thaw to formulate the conflict in the context of culture. The congresses and conferences of the Writers' Union became political battlefields, while literary journals served as a lively and widely utilized political forum. Towards the end of 1955, Milan Kundera questioned one of the central ideological policies of the time, the rejection of the 'bourgeois' cultural heritage.[6] At the second congress of the Writers' Union, a few weeks after Khrushchev's anti-Stalin speech, the poet Jaroslav Seifert called on writers to be the conscience of the nation. The leading literary weekly, *Literární noviny*, gradually became a journal of social criticism, discussing not only artistic problems but increasingly including features and debates on anthropological, sociological, economic, ethical and openly political

---

6. *Nový život*, 1955, No. 12. For further details, see K. Chvatík, 'Metamorfózy vztahu ideologie a literatury', *Listy*, 1986, No. 5, 62.

problems and demonstratively displaying a far-reaching tolerance of opposing views.

This thaw, however, achieved practically nothing in terms of political change, beyond the fact that dissenting opinions could be voiced and publicized without resulting in the arrest of their authors. In the field of politics, the climatic conditions did not show many signs of improvement. Stalinist policies continued to be pursued for some ten years after Stalin's death. Antonín Novotný, whose ascent to the leadership group had been a direct consequence of the eleven political executions carried out four months earlier, was given the post of First Secretary of the party when Klement Gottwald died one week after Stalin. The new person at the top did not mean new policies. The year 1954 brought the last execution resulting from a political trial, as well as the jailing of Gustav Husák and others on charges of bourgeois nationalism. In May 1955, a monstrous Stalin monument was unveiled in Prague on a dominant spot above the Vltava River. H. Gordon Skilling is correct in observing that

> the economic measures introduced in 1953 and early 1954 were on the whole shifts in emphasis rather than basic changes of direction, and were not broadened or deepened in the subsequent two years. [. . .] Collective leadership was proclaimed, and the cult of personality was condemned, although without censure of its Czech embodiment, Klement Gottwald. [. . .] Nor was there any admission that the party's line had been in any respect mistaken.[7]

At a party conference in June 1956, Novotný and other party leaders justified the unchanged party line and said that there was no need to rehabilitate Rudolf Slánský, the former Secretary General who had been executed in 1952. Reiterating Stalin's views, they affirmed the continuance and intensification of the class struggle and rejected abstract bourgeois concepts of freedom. In the economic sphere, the conference approved the directives of a new five-year plan which emphasized the need to expand heavy industry even further and to complete the collectivization of agriculture. 'It was clear', as Skilling concludes, 'that Czechoslovakia was not to be permitted even a shadow of the liberalization that was taking place in Poland and Hungary.'[8]

Of the neighbouring countries, the German Democratic Republic

---

7. H. Gordon Skilling, *Czechoslovakia's Interrupted Revolution*, Princeton: Princeton University Press, 1976, p. 31.
8. Ibid., p. 33.

experienced a similar absence of real political reform. Hans Mayer spoke convincingly of 'A Thaw Which Was No Thaw' in an account which highlights the suppression of the popular uprising of 17 June 1953, the arrests and trials of the philosopher Wolfgang Harich and the publisher Walter Janka (by which a very tentative lessening of cultural pressures was brought to a speedy end), the attacks on Ernst Bloch and himself, and finally the building of the Berlin Wall.[9]

The situation of Poland and Hungary differed in two major respects from that of Czechoslovakia. Firstly, the living standard in those countries was markedly lower than in Czechoslovakia and the GDR at that time. Secondly, both countries harboured very strong anti-Russian sentiments (for different reasons), in contrast to the Russophile attitudes of the Czechs. As a consequence, the year 1956 brought strong protests from the working populations, with powerful overtones of nationalism. In both countries, these movements reached a stage of mass political action which was suppressed by force. A visible thaw was brought visibly to an end. Meanwhile, developments in Czechoslovakia continued to follow their much less dramatic multifaceted course.

Novotný had stalled even where Khrushchev took some decisive measures. In the wake of the execution of Beria, some other Soviet instigators of political trials were arrested and shot, amongst them the 'adviser' Abakumov who was responsible for the Slánský affair. When Novotný stated in 1956 that there was no need to rehabilitate Slánský, he must have known that the accusations had been false – the relevant information had been given to him in December 1953 and personally by Khrushchev on two occasions in 1954.[10] His criticism of the 'personality cult' was not only accompanied by the unveiling of the Stalin monument, but also soon followed by his adding the post of President of the Republic to his continuing role as First Secretary. As in the Soviet Union, there was little change in the rigid attitude toward any attempted questioning of the established Stalinist dogmas: although the name of Stalin was eliminated, Stalinism was largely maintained as the heritage of Lenin. At both the party conference in December 1956 and the Slovak party congress in April 1957, Novotný repeatedly warned of the danger that de-Stalinization could be used to oppose socialism and the alliance

9. Hans Mayer, 'Ein Tauwetter, das keines war', *Frankfurter Hefte*, 1976, No. 11, 15–23 and No. 12, 29–38.
10. Cf. Jiří Pelikán, 'Das Echo des XX. Parteitages der KPdSU in der Tschechoslowakei', in *Entstalinisierung. Der XX. Parteitag der KPdSU und seine Folgen*, Frankfurt: Suhrkamp, 1977, p. 166.

with the Soviet Union.[11] The distinction made in Stalin's time between constructive criticism (from socialist positions, to eliminate minor faults) and destructive criticism (from counter-revolutionary positions, to destroy the system) remained in force. Arbitrary shifts of the borderline between the two forms of criticism and the accompanying voluntarism of the party's punitive policy continued, together with other Stalinist policy elements, until 1963, when Novotný for the first time opted for reforms in the style of Khrushchev.[12]

It can be argued that the thaw in Czechoslovakia occurred in two stages. The first stage, in the first years after Stalin's death, brought some tolerance towards previously forbidden topics in the cultural sphere (psychoanalysis, phenomenology, cybernetics and sociology, for example), but left the sphere of politics practically untouched. The second stage was initiated as a consequence of the Twelfth Party Congress, which was convened at the end of 1962, again conforming to the imagery of an elemental change due to the workings of higher powers. The real reason behind this second relaxation must be seen in the dismal economic failure of the Five-Year Plan, which had to be abandoned after only eighteen months. The Stalinist reorganization of formerly strong and efficient industrial structures was about to bring the country's economy to the verge of economic disaster, and some members of the party intelligentsia insisted on a change of direction. They were encouraged by the Moscow conference of eighty-one Communist Parties in 1960, which proclaimed the right of individual parties to march towards communism with due respect for local conditions.[13] The Czechoslovakian communists embarked upon a programme of solid research in the social sciences. An important book by Karel Kosík, arguing against the dialectic of nature and for a subject–object dialectic, was able to be published, and, in 1963, a conference on the work of Franz Kafka could take place – two events which were the first milestones on the way to the later Dubček reforms.

The year 1968 and its aftermath will not be discussed here, except to make one point: within the Czech tradition, a plurality of opinions would not appear to endanger the status quo, as a democratic variety of political programmes authored mainly by intellectuals and writers is customarily part of a game independent of real

11. Skilling, *Czechoslovakia's Interrupted Revolution*, p. 35.
12. Cf. Zdeněk Mlynář, 'Praha–leden 1968', *Listy*, 1988, No. 1, 4.
13. A good summary can be found in Peter Hruby, *Fools and Heroes*, Oxford: Pergamon Press, 1980, pp. 98–100 and 136–43.

political power struggles. Therefore, newspaper articles which follow a line different from the official party programme can be understood as harmless in a society used to a certain width in the media spectrum. The same phenomenon, however, may appear as a danger to communist power when transposed into the Soviet context, where every printed opinion is an expression of the party programme. Similarly, democratic demands, including the principle of democratic control over the Communist Party by society, were not seen by the communist reformists of 1968 as inviting counter-revolution. As Zdeněk Mlynář reflects,

> they knew from their own experience that, even without Soviet tanks, the party could successfully compete for political leadership within the democratic system and that democratic control by the people does not mean that street mobs will begin to hang communists. This, however, was precisely the picture which emerged in the heads of communist leaders in countries where the circumstances were essentially different from those in Czechoslovakia.[14]

As far as the post-Stalin thaw in Czechoslovakia is concerned, it must be said that it never got off the ground. It was a mere loosening of a rigidly homogeneous set of dogmas in the cultural sphere, but it stopped short of allowing any real counterpositions of a politically effective nature. This cultural thaw created an illusion of independence without touching the existing Soviet dominance. It could be interpreted as a political ploy: allowed from above and kept under firm control by the unthreatened rulers, it deflected attention from the real issues of political power by helping to make the citizens believe that the key to change is to be found through literature and culture. Whenever a statement managed to pass through the censor's net, it was considered a political victory – which it was not. When writers were attacked, the suggestion offered itself that it was they who were in possession of the main means of change. Even the punishment of cultural transgressors served the same purpose, by creating the impression that their protest was relevant. This was further supported by official party declarations that art is a form of ideology, that ideology is political power, and that an unorthodox literary work is a counter-revolutionary action. Literature as a replacement for politics served reasonably well to give the helpless an illusion of influence and power; it served even better to help shield those in power.

14. Zdeněk Mlynář, 'Bilance politiky Pražského jara po dvaceti létech', *Listy*, 1988, No. 5, 6.

-4-

Thaws, Literature and the Nationalities Discussion in Ukraine: The Prose of Valerii Shevchuk

MARKO PAVLYSHYN

The purpose of this paper is twofold. First, it seeks to interpret some features of literature and the literary discussion during two thaws in Ukraine – one under Khrushchev in the late 1950s and early 1960s, the other under Gorbachev in the second half of the 1980s. Second, the paper traces the development, through the alternation of thaw and freeze, of a major Ukrainian writer who is an exemplary, if by no means typical, figure of his generation: Valerii Shevchuk.

A cultural and political thaw in Moscow and Leningrad is not the same as a thaw in the Republics of the Soviet Union. There are, of course, similarities of chronology and rhetoric. For example, many of the demands under Gorbachev – for more morality in public life, for honesty about the state's past crimes, for respect toward the environment – are voiced in Kiev no less than in Moscow. But the difference of context imposes a difference of substance. In the capital, the oppositionally inclined identify the central problem of their polity as excessive authoritarianism. In the Republics, their counterparts experience the same authoritarianism both as exacerbated by, and as a consequence of, colonialism.[1] At the centre, thaws make possible the ventilation of demands for a more democratic society. In the Republics, the unifying agenda of thaws – sometimes more explicit, as in the Baltic states from 1988 onward, sometimes less – is the preservation of national identity and the restoration of auton-

---

1. For a discussion of colonial features in the development of culture, the economy and the class structure in Ukraine, see Bohdan Krawchenko, *Social Change and National Consciousness in Twentieth-Century Ukraine*, Houndmills: Macmillan, 1985, esp. pp. 202–41. The political aspects of the question are treated in John N. Hazard, 'The Status of the Ukrainian Republic Under the Soviet Federation', in *Ukraine in the Seventies*, ed. Peter J. Potichnyj, Oakville, Ontario: Mosaic Press, 1975, pp. 221–33.

omy in as many spheres of national life as possible.[2]

It is in the sphere of literature that such platforms are often first constructed: in literary works themselves, but also in criticism, in literary discussion and in the extra-literary utterances and symbolic acts of *litterateurs*. That this should be the case is not surprising. Even under strict censorship, literature in the Soviet Union, no less than in the Russian Empire, has been a vehicle for contraband ideas. It is in keeping with this traditional role that literature should be quick to respond to a relaxation of ideological control, or, in the case of Gorbachev's thaw, to an open and official invitation to participate in the critical discussion of a greatly increased range of public issues.

After Stalin's death in 1953, and especially after the Twentieth Party Congress in 1956, a thaw was experienced in Ukraine with a slight delay vis-à-vis its counterpart in Moscow and Leningrad.[3] Demands for a restoration of the rightful role of the Ukrainian language were advanced in public, the legitimate sphere of Ukrainian historical research was expanded, and open criticism of Russification, particularly in the system of education, became possible. Some, though by no means all, repressed writers and Ukrainian communist activists of the 1920s and 1930s were rehabilitated, most of them posthumously. The leading Ukrainian inter-war dramatist, Mykola Kulish, who had perished in a labour camp in 1942, was a case in point: a one-volume edition of his works, lacking the controversial plays that dealt with Ukrainian–Russian relations, appeared in 1958. His contemporary, Mykola Khvyl'ovyi, the uncrowned king of post-revolutionary Ukrainian prose, who had committed suicide in 1933 after a campaign of vilification and harassment, remained *persona non grata* until the thaw of the mid-1980s, which also brought to light the remaining plays by Kulish.

In the 1950s, a thaw in Ukrainian literature itself, as distinct from literary journalism, was slow in coming. Its first harbinger was

---

2. For overviews of the progress of the thaw in the Republics of the USSR, see the journal *Soviet Nationality Survey* (London), 2(1985) ff., and in Ukraine – *Soviet Ukrainian Affairs* (London), 1(1987) ff.

3. For a detailed study of the first thaw and its aftermath in Ukraine, see Boris Lewytzkyj, *Politics and Society in Soviet Ukraine 1953–80*, Edmonton: Canadian Institute of Ukrainian Studies, 1984. English-language discussions of the literature of the period include George S. N. Luckyj, 'Literary Ferment in the Ukraine', *Problems of Communism*, 11(1962), No. 6, 51–7; A. de Vinzenz, 'Recent Ukrainian Writing', *Survey*, No. 46(1963), 143–50; Jaroslaw Pelenski, 'Recent Ukrainian Writing', *Survey*, No. 59(1966), 102–12; George S. N. Luckyj, 'The Ukrainian Literary Scene Today', *Slavic Review*, 31(1972), 863–75; and Myroslav Shkandrij, 'Literary Politics and Literary Debates in Ukraine 1971–81', in *Ukraine After Shelest*, ed. Bohdan Krawchenko, Edmonton: Canadian Institute of Ukrainian Studies, 1983, pp. 55–72.

Oleksandr Dovzhenko, one of the leading Soviet film-makers of the 1920s and by the 1950s a patriarchal figure in Ukrainian culture. His call for an 'expansion of the creative limits of Socialist Realism'[4] is generally regarded in the West as one of the two starting-points of the Ukrainian thaw; the other is the publication of his lyrical and semi-autobiographical *Zacharovana Desna* (The Enchanted River Desna, 1956), a narrative of childhood in a pre-revolutionary village. The work set the tone for much 1960s prose.

Dovzhenko died in 1956, and for a number of years his last works seemed to be the lone swallow that had failed to make a spring. Paradoxically, it was only during the partial political freeze of 1958–61 that a sudden qualitative change in literary output occurred. A number of gifted young poets emerged, all of them born in the 1930s: Lina Kostenko, Ivan Drach, Vasyl' Symonenko, Mykola Vinhranovs'kyi and Vitalii Korotych. (Some were to play a leading role in the thaw of the 1980s: in 1986, for example, Korotych would become editor of the Union-wide biweekly *Ogonek*, one of the leading organs of *glasnost'*.)

The new poets came to be known as *shistdesiatnyky* (people of the 1960s). Their poetry, individual in tone and imbued with the pathos of sincerity, appeared to symbolize the emergence, after years of Stalinist suspicion and fear, of a new sense of trust and hope. It is true that, from a Western perspective, their lyrical subjectivism might sometimes appear sentimental, their polemical anger – an unpoetic rhetoricism, and Drach's much admired formal experimentation – a reinvention of the modernist wheel.[5] Against the background of the approved poetry of Stalinism, however, they provided their readers with the excitement of the new in a way that had been unheard-of since the 1920s. They rebelled against the generation of the Stalinist 'Fathers', claiming for themselves a sincerity and an innocence which the Fathers had lost through their collaboration with Stalin.[6] 'Art is clean when it is made with clean hands and thoughts', proclaimed the 25-year-old Korotych.[7] The rebellion against the hypocritical internationalism (a euphemism for Russian

4. Dovzhenko, 'Iskusstvo zhivopisi i sovremennost'', *Literaturnaia gazeta*, 21 June 1955.
5. See, e.g., Jonathan Galassi's review of Ivan Drach, *Orchard Lamps*, trans. Daniel Halpern et al., ed. and introd. by Stanley Kunitz, New York: Sheep Meadow Press, 1978, in *The New York Times Review of Books*, 11 March 1979, and the discussion in M[arco] C[arynnyk], 'Traduced Again', *Journal of Ukrainian Studies*, 4(1979), No. 1, 104–8.
6. See Ivan Koshelivets', 'Shestydesiatnyky', in his *Suchasna Literatura v URSR*, New York: Prolog, 1964, pp. 275–334.
7. In the poem 'Chyste mystetstvo', *Literaturna hazeta* (Kiev), 5 May 1961.

cultural chauvinism) of the Stalinist era legitimated a revival of romantic nationalism, with its cult hero, the nineteenth-century national bard Taras Shevchenko, and its canonical text, Volodymyr Sosiura's 'Liubit' Ukrainu' (Love Ukraine!, 1944), a poem written to nurture patriotic fervour during the Second World War, denounced for bourgeois nationalism in 1951, and rehabilitated in 1956.

The prose of the 1960s did not break with the past as radically as did poetry. The *cause célèbre* of 1968 was *Sobor* (The Cathedral), a novel by the doyen of officially approved writers, Oles' Honchar, who at that time was head of the Ukrainian Writers' Union. As Ivan Koshelivets' has pointed out, the work is formally a Socialist Realist novel with a positive hero and the usual master-narrative (the struggle for success in the achievement of some public goal), except that the goal is new: not a production target, but the protection of the Dnieper environment from industrial pollution and the conservation of an old cathedral, symbol of the national spiritual heritage.[8] It was for its content, and not for any breach of aesthetic orthodoxy, that the novel suffered remorseless critical attack and passed from public view until its triumphant rehabilitation eighteen years later.

In so far as the 1960s produced innovative Ukrainian prose, it was mainly in the shorter genres. Young writers of the same generation as the poets – Ievhen Hutsalo, Volodymyr Drozd, Hryhir Tiutiunnyk and Iurii Shcherbak – opted out of the big public themes of war and production, and selected a subjective and idyllic mode, concentrating frequently on the inwardness of childhood and the setting of the countryside. While this privatism produced a harvest of undeniable gems, it also provided a formula for politically safe, but sentimental and uninspired, country prose, which later led many writers and critics pessimistically to associate their own literature with irredeemable provincialism, reinforcing from within the marginality imposed upon Ukrainian culture by its colonial status.

Valerii Shevchuk was one of the recognized new talents of the 1960s. Born in 1939 in the mid-western Ukrainian city of Zhytomyr,

---

8. Koshelivets', 'Pro *Sobor* Olesia Honchara', *Suchasnist'* 8(1968), No. 8, 62–74, esp. p. 72. *Cathedral* served as a stimulus to one of the major texts of dissident Ukrainian criticism, Ivan Sverstiuk's 'Sobor u ryshtovanni', trans. as 'A Cathedral in Scaffolding', in Sverstiuk, *Clandestine Essays*, ed. George S. N. Luckyj, Littleton, Colorado: Harvard Ukrainian Research Institute, 1976, pp. 17–68. See also my article, 'Honchar's *Sobor* and Rudenko's *Orlova balka*: Environmental Conservation as Theme and Argument in Two Recent Ukrainian Novels', in *Slavic Themes: Papers from Two Hemispheres*, ed. Boris Christa et al., Neuried: Hieronymus, 1988, pp. 271–88.

he obtained, like many writers of his generation, a higher education in philology at Kiev University. Between 1967 and 1969, he published three books, *Sered tyzhnia* (On a Week Day), *Naberezhna, 12* (12, The Esplanade) and *Vechir sviatoi oseni* (An Evening of Blessed Autumn), which, in their subjective focus and their psychologism, well fitted the paradigm of young 1960s prose. There followed a ten year break, during which Shevchuk researched and translated Ukrainian renaissance and baroque texts; in 1979 came the collection *Kryk pivnia na svitanku* (Cock Crow at Dawn), then *Dolyna dzherel* (Valley of Springs, 1981), *Na poli smyrennomu* (Upon a Submissive Field, 1983), the novel *Dim na hori* (The House on the Hill, 1983), *Malen'ke vechirnie intermetstso* (A Little Evening Intermezzo, 1984) and *Try lystky za viknom* (Three Leaves Beyond the Window, 1986). Among his most recent works is a collection of short novels, *Kaminna luna* (Stone Echo, 1987). This is not, by Soviet standards, a large opus; the inducements to write much and quickly that ruined his contemporary, Ievhen Hutsalo, left Shevchuk unmoved.

The arrest of some two dozen Ukrainian intellectuals in 1965 signalled the beginning of the end of the thaw in Ukraine. Although Shevchuk's works of the 1960s were published after this date, they nevertheless reflected the enthusiasm of that earlier period and its belief in the possibility of a more humane society. *12, The Esplanade* took up a structural motif which Shevchuk would utilize in several later works: the lives of several groups of characters, here linked by their living in the one house, are treated in succession. Fates that seem isolated prove to be interconnected. In *Esplanade* the lives of each household are, initially, marred by a social problem: Pavlo the shoemaker is an alcoholic, Sashko is neglected by a narcissistic mother, Liusia is pregnant before marriage, and the Accountant is disturbed by guilt: he informed on one of his neighbours, who went to Siberia as a result. The movement that evolves, however, is one of healing: each of the problems gradually resolves itself, and the house celebrates its own renewal at the wedding of Liusia and her lover. The work is a carefully crafted model of a development from social illness to health and a vindication of faith, hope and charity. It is one of the most coherent acts of faith in the possibility of social and human improvement that Ukrainian thaw-influenced literature has produced.

Published in the same volume as *Esplanade* was *Seredokhrestia* (The Crossing), a short novel much more obviously inspired by the first thaw's values: it is a sympathetic portrayal of a loner – a student who refuses to compromise with the system, refuses to join Komsomol, stands firm against the 'constructive criticism' of his peers, and in consequence is labelled an inveterate eccentric. The satirical point of the narrative is directed against the budding careerists who already at university display the philistinism and materialism that characterize the adult world. The work is an example of the system-critical realistic prose that later became characteristic of the thaw of the 1980s, but which Shevchuk himself outgrew.

By 1969, in *An Evening of Blessed Autumn*, Shevchuk was taking a more melancholy line, depicting irresolvable human problems. The promise of thaw had proved a failure. This observation was not, of course, formulated in political terms, but was reflected in pessimistic judgements concerning the potential of the human situation.

While it is not known precisely why Shevchuk was unable to publish between 1969 and 1979, it is clear that his silence was the result of official disfavour – like that of the poet Lina Kostenko, with which it overlapped. Mykhailo Osadchyi, a communist intellectual first imprisoned for nationalist deviations in 1965, noted that among the few people who corresponded with the political inmates of his Mordovian labour camp were the poet Vasyl' Stus, who would be twice arrested in the 1970s and would die in the camps in 1985, and Valerii Shevchuk. 'Shevchuk's letters', wrote Osadchyi, 'are like polished short stories. They are read to pieces.'[9] Acts of solidarity with political prisoners could scarcely have endeared Shevchuk to the authorities. He was not among the victims of 1965, nor of the wave of arrests and house-searches of 1972 which confirmed the arrival of a new political winter in Ukraine.[10] However, unlike many among the frightened survivors – Drach, Drozd, Hutsalo, Korotych and others who managed to advance their careers during the 1970s – he did not compromise for the sake of publication. Shevchuk's work during these ten years, however, proved to have a potential for cultural subversion of the established centre–province hierarchy beyond that of anything which he had previously created. His translations and editions of Ukrainian sixteenth-, seventeenth- and eighteenth-century writers, once they were published in the early 1980s, recaptured for the Ukrainian intelligentsia an episode of Ukrainian cultural history that had previously been ignored and inaccessible. Shevchuk was not the sole author of this project, but the lion's share of the translations in the collection *Apollonova liutnia*

9. Mykhailo Osadchi, *Cataract* [1968], trans., ed. and annotated by Marco Carynnyk, New York and London: Harcourt Brace Jovanovich, 1976, p. 112.
10. For analyses of the political freeze of the 1970s, see Roman Solchanyk, 'Politics and the National Question in the Post-Shelest Period', and Bohdan Nahaylo, 'Ukrainian Dissent and Opposition After Shelest', both in *Ukraine After Shelest*, pp. 1–29 and 30–54 respectively.

(Apollo's Lute, 1982) and in the first volume of the new anthology of Ukrainian verse in six volumes (1984) were his, as was the pain-stakingly annotated translation of the seventeenth-century Cossack chronicle of Samiilo Velychko that appeared in the journal *Kyiv* in 1986–7.

The symbolic importance of this recovery of the baroque for the Ukrainian national consciousness was considerable. The baroque period of the seventeenth and eighteenth centuries was the last in which Ukraine had an autonomous, full-scale or, to use Čyževs'kyj's term, 'complete' culture of its own,[11] ranging from aristocratic to popular, manifesting itself in a wide range of the arts – especially music, literature and architecture – and in specific local styles, and possessing a native intellectual leadership in the Kiev Academy and its remarkable elite of churchmen. It was also the last period of extended political autonomy enjoyed by Ukraine prior to the com-pletion of its absorption into the Russian Empire by the fourth quarter of the eighteenth century.[12]

Shevchuk, of course, also recaptured this cultural wealth for himself. When he began writing again, it was with a new historical sophistication and with a philosophical backing for his melancholy at the failure of the thaw. His authority for the hopelessness of reform projects was now the eighteenth-century philosopher Hry-horii Skovoroda, his favoured virtues – stoic courage and endur-ance. In the title story of *Cock Crow at Dawn*, for example, the central symbol of the flux and transience of the world is the river in which the boy hero daily bathes. He experiences the vanity of love and even of art, but comes to understand that the glory of eternity may be perceived in an instant – as when, for example, the cock crows at dawn.

The tacit edict of toleration extended to Shevchuk at the end of the 1970s came a good six years before the Gorbachevian thaw, in a period which belongs to what subsequently came to be known in the Soviet press as 'Brezhnevist–Suslovist stagnation'. Yet Shevchuk's return to relative grace was not an isolated phenomenon in 1978–9. As Roman Solchanyk has pointed out, it was at this time that, without much fanfare, changes in the cultural sphere took place as part of a new accommodation with the Ukrainian intelligentsia.[13]

11. Dmytro Čyževs'kyj, *A History of Ukrainian Literature*, trans. Dolly Ferguson et al., ed. George S. N. Luckyj, Littleton, Colorado: Ukrainian Academic Press, 1975, p. 374.
12. See Zenon F. Kohut, *Russian Centralism and Ukrainian Autonomy: Imperial Absorption of the Hetmanate, 1760s–1830s*, Cambridge, Massachusetts: Harvard University Press, 1988.
13. Solchanyk, in *Ukraine After Shelest*, pp. 11–17.

Marko Pavlyshyn

Evidence of such 'cultural detente' became visible in literature. The so-called 'whimsical novel', which traced its genealogy to Rabelais and Sterne and was undoubtedly nourished by new translations of Latin American prose, especially that of Gabriel García Márquez, offered the possibility of humorous and ironic treatments of reality, although it never developed a subversive dimension.[14] The fantastic and the grotesque joined the sphere of possibilities open to writers like Roman Ivanychuk and, most importantly, Valerii Shevchuk himself. It was as though a rapprochement had been reached: writers were at liberty to innovate in form and theme, provided that they broke no ideological rules. The new state of affairs made possible the appearance of the least objectionable officially sanctioned prose for a decade. Iurii Mushketyk, soon to be head of the Ukrainian Writers' Union, wrote two novels, both on irreproachable topics (collective farms and their problems), which, however, represented Socialist Realism at its most analytic and plausible. Indeed, in many respects *Pozytsiia* (Standpoint, 1979) and *Rubizh* (The Boundary, 1984) adumbrated the critical tenor required of literature under *glasnost'*. Pavlo Zahrebel'nyi, Mushketyk's predecessor at the helm of the Writers' Union and previously the author of a voluminous and less than remarkable *oeuvre*, came forth with the ironic and playful *Levyne sertse* (Lion Heart, 1977) and the formally sophisticated historical novel *Ia, Bohdan* (I, Bohdan, 1983). The latter work illustrates the nature of the new social contract for literature. Zahrebel'nyi's hero, the Cossack leader Bohdan Khmel'nyts'kyi, is presented through the inner monologues of three narrators: the historical seventeenth-century personage, the bronze equestrian statue of Khmel'nyts'kyi erected in Kiev in the nineteenth century, and the timeless spirit of Bohdan that hovers over Ukraine. This experimentation with point of view, unthinkable under the former Socialist Realist monopoly, was, however, balanced by Zahrebel'nyi's scrupulous orthodoxy in the novel's ideological thesis: the emphatic approval of Khmel'nyts'kyi's transfer of Ukraine from hard-won independence of Poland to Russian suzerainty.[15]

It was in this ambiguous pre-thaw period, then, that Shevchuk

14. Two collections of Latin American poetry and prose in Ukrainian translation appeared in Kiev in 1978, and García Márquez' second visit to the USSR in 1979 was accompanied by a spate of translations of his works into Ukrainian and Russian. On the whimsical novel see my article, 'National Idioms in Soviet Literature? The Case of the Ukrainian Whimsical Novel', in *Literature and National Cultures*, ed. Brian Edwards, [Geelong]: Centre for Studies in Literary Education, Deakin University, 1988, pp. 109–16.
15. Under *glasnost'*, criticism would attack Zahrebel'nyi for this. See e.g. Iu. Burlai as reported in *Literaturna Ukraina* (Literary Ukraine, henceforth abridged as *LU*), 25

re-entered Ukrainian literature. He was not welcomed with open arms: prior to his receiving, in March 1988, the Shevchenko State Prize for literature, critics noted his 'obvious marginality' and pointed out 'mistakes' in his 'artistic realization of the principle of historicism'.[16] The works which now appeared had been in the making for a long time: *The House on the Hill* was written, according to the author, between 1966 and 1980, and *Three Leaves Beyond the Window* in 1968–81. The first of these adhered to the social contract only in that it did not explicitly contradict official dogmas: it was too esoteric to do so in any obvious way. And yet, the novel does admit of an oppositional interlinear reading. *The House on the Hill* is a work of great complexity which I have discussed more fully elsewhere;[17] suffice it to say here that it sets up an opposition between an archaic, mythical, cyclical conception of time which locates human satisfaction in inner repose, and the progressive, hectic, uncanny modern world whose narrative equivalent lies in the twists and surprises of the genre of the 'Novelle'. The two are contrasted and the latter is found wanting. But this argument in favour of the archaic – a belatedly romantic argument, and as such not new – is embedded in a plea for the authenticity and legitimacy of Ukrainian culture. The novel is constructed of those elements – the folkloric grotesque, the fantastic, the uncanny, and the rural – which since Nikolai Gogol' have been the defining symbols of Ukraine as an ethnographic, comic and provincial place.[18] Shevchuk reshapes these elements in such a way that the novel remains affirmatively Ukrainian, but is liberated of stereotypical self-dismissive gestures and thus marks its resistance to one of the main stratagems of Russian cultural imperialism.

When, in 1986, the impact of the Gorbachevian thaw began to be felt in earnest in Ukraine, resistance to Russian cultural imperialism emerged as its leading theme. If it is true that the central motivation for a new tolerance of criticism was the Centre's desire to promote a vigorous exchange of ideas as a prerequisite for *perestroika'* (restructuring) in the interests of modernization, efficiency and improved economic performance, then this intention was, if not subverted, at least relegated to secondary importance by the development of

September 1986, p. 2. See also my review, '"Ia, Bohdan (spovid' u slavi)" Pavla Zahrebel'noho', *Suchasnist'*, 25(1985), No. 9, 17–35.

16. Mykola Riabchuk, 'Te, shcho vyvyshchuie liudynu', *Ukraina*, 1984, No. 45, p. 11, and Mykhailo Naienko, 'Na bystryni chasu', *Radians'ke literaturoznavstvo*, 1983, No. 8, 28–36, here p. 31.

17. '"Dim na hori" Valeriia Shevchuka', *Suchasnist'*, 27(1987), No. 11, 28–41.

18. See George S. N. Luckyj, *Between Gogol' and Ševčenko: Polarity in the Literary Ukraine, 1798–1847*, Munich: Fink, 1971.

events. The energies of the new movement were released primarily
into the cultural sphere: into setting right the historical record by
exposing past crimes of the regime and into recovering alienated
cultural treasures. Nowhere was this more the case than in Ukraine,
where writers, not least those who had been frightened into com-
pliance in the 1970s, resumed the public role which they had held in
the 1960s. It was at the Ninth Congress of the Ukrainian Writers'
Union and the Eighth of the Soviet Writers' Union, both held in
June 1986, that the main complaint *topoi* of the Ukrainian intelligentsia were articulated; many of them were more forceful restate-
ments of themes from the 1950s and 1960s. The poets Dmytro
Pavlychko and Borys Oliinyk rose to prominence through their bold
proclamation of universally known, but previously unutterable,
truths. Writers and, indeed, whole periods of Ukrainian cultural
history, especially the 1920s and 1930s, it was pointed out, had been
placed under taboo: they could be neither published nor studied.
During the era of stagnation, individual writers (Drozd, Honchar,
Hryhir Tiutiunnyk) were unfairly harassed; literary criticism had
become a vehicle for denunciation; historical monuments had been
wantonly destroyed; the country's natural and cultural heritage had
been neglected through excesses of bureaucratism and corruption. A
second field of complaint *topoi* was specifically concerned with the
parlous state of Ukrainian culture: there had been a collapse in the
official use of the Ukrainian language; there had been a sharp decline
in the number of schools with Ukrainian as the chief language of
instruction; children in Russian-language schools were to a growing
extent exempted from tuition in Ukrainian; the numbers of titles and
the sizes of editions of Ukrainian books and journals were dwin-
dling; the Ukrainian film industry had all but ceased making
Ukrainian-language films. Writers pioneered a corresponding set of
demand *topoi*: there should be more research into ignored cultural
periods, and the writers and activists of the 1920s and 1930s should
be republished – Valer''ian Polishchuk, Mykola Zerov, the futur-
ists, even Mykola Khvyl'ovyi, the proponent of the orientation of
Ukrainian literature upon 'psychological Europe' and the author of
the enduringly controversial slogan, 'away from Moscow'. The
chronicles of Kievan Rus' and of the Cossack seventeenth and
eighteenth centuries should be translated into modern Ukrainian
and published.[19] Among the greatest surprises for Western observers were demands for research into the state-engineered famine

---

19. For details, see Marko Pavlyshyn, '"Openness" and the Contemporary Literary
Discussion in Ukraine', *Soviet Ukrainian Affairs*, 1(1987), No. 2, 7–10.

of 1932–3, whose very existence officialdom had previously denied. (In the course of 1988 the famine became an increasingly legitimate topic for both journalism and literature.)[20] There were repeated calls, including highly official ones by the Ukrainian Writers' Union itself, to make Ukrainian a compulsory subject of study in all schools in Ukraine, and to enshrine Ukrainian, alongside Russian, as the state language of the Ukrainian SSR by constitutional amendment.

Many of these complaint and demand *topoi* had as their unifying feature a common commitment to conserve the identity markers of Ukrainian culture, especially the Ukrainian language. The master metaphor for this preoccupation was cultural ecology, a notion introduced to Ukrainian literature (and perhaps to the USSR as a whole) by Oles' Honchar in *The Cathedral*. As the degradation of the natural environment is a tragedy for humankind – thus runs Honchar's argument – so too is the disappearance of any product of the human spirit, not to mention a culture or a language. It is not surprising that the issues of ecological survival and the survival of the national culture came to be twinned in a country on whose territory the Chernobyl disaster had occurred and where a new nuclear reactor was planned for Chyhyryn, the capital of the seven-teenth-century Cossack state and one of Ukraine's most cherished historical sites. The nexus of culture and ecology was no less a part of the platform of the radical Culturological Club in Kiev (a group harassed into silence by the authorities, *glasnost'* notwithstanding), than of many campaign speeches prior to the multi-candidate elections of March 1989 to the Congress of People's Deputies.

As the new thaw re-politicized the issue of Ukrainian culture, so the leading representatives of that culture, its writers, were cata-pulted into the role of politicians. Twenty-six stood as candidates at the 1989 election, many of them nominated, not by the Writers' Union, but by constituencies of factory workers. Seven, including Honchar and Oliinyk, leading spokesmen of re-Ukrainization, were elected. The weekly newspaper of the Writers' Union, *Literaturna Ukraina* (Literary Ukraine), took on an increasingly overt political role, publishing the draft constitutions of the new Ukrainian Language Society and the Ukrainian People's Movement, the latter against strong conservative opposition.

20. See V. Pakharenko in *LU*, 10 November 1988, 7; in the same month, the Party Committee of the Kiev branch of the Ukrainian Writers' Union decided to publish a commemorative volume entitled *1933-i: holod* (1933: Famine) (*LU*, 1 December 1988, 1). Sviatoslav Kul'chyts'kyi's '1933: trahediia holodu' ran in *LU*, 1989, Nos. 2–5. Anatolii Dimarov's short novel, *Trydtsiati* (The 'Thirties, written in 1966), which takes the famine as its theme, appeared in *Prapor*, 1988, No. 6, 9–70.

Marko Pavlyshyn

The eruption of activism by *litterateurs* spilled into literary texts themselves. Immediate literary responses to significant events or issues became almost obligatory for writers. The theme of the Chernobyl accident, for example, was used by Svitlana Iovenko, Volodymyr Iavorivs'kyi, Iurii Shcherbak and Ivan Drach, to mention only the best-known literary identities. Official demands for criticism of the system, reinforced by the new freedom to tell the truth about the past, gave rise to a documentary realism that minimized the distinction between literature and reportage. The experimental prose writers of the 1960s – Shcherbak, the author of the archly playful *Khronika mista Iaropolia* (Chronicle of the City of Iaropil', 1968), and Volodymyr Drozd, whose formally ambitious *Katastrofa* (Catastrophe, 1968) was republished in 1988 after a twenty-year ban – elected to compose in a soberly realistic style. Drozd reflected in his introductory remarks to his novel *Novosillia* (House-warming, 1986–7): 'I would define the genre of my new work as a publicistic novel. [. . .] It has not been my aim to astonish the reader with all manner of aesthetic innovations. I have placed before myself a single goal: to grasp, reproduce and reflect an instant in our fast-moving life, and everything new that is today being born'.[21]

The primary appeal of *House-warming*, and of other works often listed by critics as exemplary – Shcherbak's *Prychyny i naslidky* (Causes and Effects, 1988) and Anatolii Dimarov's *Trydtsiati* (The Thirties, written in 1966 and published in 1988), for example – was their topicality. Were it not for the publication of long-repressed works written by Khvyl'ovyi and Valer''ian Pidmohyl'nyi in the 1920s, or at the turn of the century by Volodymyr Vynnychenko, the Ukrainian reader might have found the Gorbachevian thaw, on the whole, aesthetically less interesting than the Khrushchevian. It remained the case, too, that, rehabilitations of fifty-year-old works notwithstanding, the most original and innovative writing of the 1960s, 1970s and even 1980s – the poetry of Ihor Kalynets' and Vasyl' Stus (the latter perished in a prison camp when the thaw was already in train) – remained unpublishable and only barely mentionable, as did Osadchyi's *Bil'mo* (Cataract), a memoir of prison and camp life written in the idiom of the modernist novel, and the sophisticated cultural and literary criticism of Ievhen Sverstiuk, Ivan Svitlychnyi and Valentyn Moroz.

In its first three years, then, the Gorbachevian thaw did not give birth to a new aesthetic vision. On the contrary, it renewed the

21. *Novosillia* was published in *Dnipro*, 1986, Nos. 2 and 3, and 1987, Nos. 1 and 2. The quotation is from 1986, No. 2, 9.

legitimacy of the unreflective realism and the partisan pathos which, in the late 1970s, were being allowed quietly to die alongside the dogmatic interpretation of Socialist Realism.[22] The thaw did not even produce a change in the personnel: Kostenko, Drach, Drozd, Shcherbak and Shevchuk, all now in their fifties, were still the major names, with whose reputations only Volodymyr Iavorivs'kyi – a newcomer, not of the second thaw, but of the late 1970s – could compete. The absence of a new wave of literati, brave, bold and resolute as their predecessors of the 1960s, became a conventional critical complaint. The prose works regarded as exemplary were either old (*The Cathedral*), or, like *The Cathedral*, were innovative only thematically. Such was Drozd's *Spektakl'* (The Play, 1984), a satire on the author as a faithful servant of the state and of his own material self-interest. Nevertheless, because of its accommodation to the new reformist political objectives, prose was largely immune from critical attack. Perhaps in compensation, critics vented their dissatisfaction on the new poets, who, inevitably judged by the standards of the sensational early 1960s, were found to be wanting.[23]

Despite the fact that the demands articulated in the thaw of the 1980s were more ambitious than those that were heard in the 1950s and 1960s, there was a sense of caution and calculation about the Gorbachevian thaw which had not been characteristic of its predecessor. As Vitalii Korotych put it, 'for a long while yet, we shall be learning democracy while casting uneasy glances over our shoulder.'[24] The Ukrainian actors in the drama of *glasnost'* were undoubtedly aware of their tragic flaw: at the slightest cooling of the political climate, their activity in defence of national culture could be interpreted as challenging the core value of the one and indivisible Soviet Union and could reactivate the charge of bourgeois nationalism. Cultural demands, therefore, were made, but almost always in an elaborately inoffensive way. Calls for Ukrainian cultural concessions were embedded in requests that similar provision be made for Russian culture in Ukraine: Ukrainian *and* Russian should be promoted in schools, Ukrainian *and* Russian must be the

22. Leonid Novychenko wrote of the imperative of uniting a 'perfection of mimesis' with a 'desire to persuade' in *LU*, 16 April 1987, 1.
23. On this, at least, the dissidents agreed with the establishment: see, e.g., Mykola Il'nyts'kyi, 'Perehuk cherez pokolinnia', *Kyiv*, 1986, No. 4, 133–42, here p. 134, and Iurii Mushketyk's speech at the June 1987 Plenum of the Ukrainian Writers' Union, reported in *LU*, 9 July 1987, 3, but also the response to Il'nyts'kyi's article by Mykhailo Horyn' in the unofficial journal *Ukrains'kyi visnyk*, No. 7, August 1987, rep. [Munich]: Suchasnist', 1988, pp. 26–31.
24. *Kommunist*, 1987, No. 4, 74.

Marko Pavlyshyn

state languages. Even Dmytro Pavlychko's sensational speech at the June 1987 Plenum of the Ukrainian Writers' Union, in which he warned that closures of schools with Ukrainian as the language of instruction could result in Ukrainian schools surviving only in Canada, began with praise of the Russian language and contained the qualification that the central organs in Moscow were not to blame.[25] In part, this caution was strategic, motivated by anxiety lest too much outspokenness too soon should release an official backlash and imperil the concessions already won. In part, it was the result of the personal experiences of the thaw's main protagonists – fifty-year-olds who had been angry young men in 1960. All of them had been once burnt, and, if not arrested, at least pilloried in the press and for a time ignored by the publishing houses. Ivan Dziuba, for example, after writing his celebrated analysis *Internatsionalizm chy rusyfikatsiia?* (Internationalism or Russification?) in 1965, had been harassed and humiliated until his arrest in 1972;[26] he recanted in the following year.

There was caution, too, in literary journalism, especially on issues that touched the national question. Critics, challenged to provide an agenda for a new literature, were at a loss what to suggest, in spite of the acres of often uninspired prose in *Literary Ukraine's* column on 'Literature in the Time of Restructuring'. That literature should be guided by the overarching aims of the state, however, remained an immutable principle. Leonid Novychenko, the apparently indestructible spokesman on cultural policy ever-so-slightly tinged with liberalism, voiced not merely official, but also majority, opinion when he claimed that, in the 'new literary epoch' which had just begun, the foremost question to be answered by writers was, 'how is literature to assist in the cardinal processes of restructuring?'[27] Another venerable critical thesis that at first escaped challenge was the exemplary status vis-à-vis Ukrainian literature of 'Soviet multinational literature'. One of the common critical complaints of 1986–7 was that works as sensational as Aitmatov's *Plakha* (The Executioner's Block) or Astaf'ev's *Pechal'nyi detektiv* (The Sad Detective) did not appear first in Ukrainian literature: the notion that, as a matter of prestige, Ukrainian literature needed to duplicate developments that were attracting attention at the all-Union level was accepted as self-

25. *LU*, 9 July 1987, 3.
26. Victor Swoboda, 'Cat and Mouse in the Ukraine', *Index*, 2(1973), No. 1, 81–9. Dziuba's critique was translated into English as *Internationalism or Russification? A Study in the Soviet Nationalities Problem*, London: Weidenfeld and Nicolson, 1968.
27. 'Nasha s'ohodnishnia poshukova dumka', *LU*, 16 April 1987, p. 1.

evident.[28] Later, some Ukrainian critics and writers sought to combat these symptoms of cultural cringe, most notably through a mobilization of literary public opinion against their former compatriot Vitalii Korotych, who had used his Union-wide prominence as editor of *Ogonek* to launch an attack on aesthetic standards in Ukrainian literature.[29] The resentment felt toward Korotych was a response to the central problem of contemporary Ukrainian culture: its colonial status. This status, while it cannot be acknowledged in public, imposes upon the creative intelligentsia a choice between identification with a culture that is tarred with the brush of provincialism on the one hand, and co-optation by the dominant culture of the metropolis on the other – to the even further detriment of the native culture.

It is Valerii Shevchuk's resolution of this issue in his mature works that justifies our describing him, at the beginning of this essay, as an exemplary, but not typical, writer of his time. Shevchuk was not politicized by *glasnost'*. Unlike his contemporaries, Shcherbak or Drach, he seldom made stirring speeches or engaged in public activism. Yet, in one of his few press interviews, he described the colonial malaise of Ukrainian culture with a clarity and courage that escaped other commentators:

It has become fashionable to compare the state of affairs in Russian and Ukrainian literature without drawing attention to a number of important factors:

    a) Ukrainian literature, if it is to be an autonomous, rather than imitative or provincial phenomenon, must not duplicate another, more powerful culture, otherwise it will lose its identity;

    b) the publishing base of Russian literature is incomparably broader and larger than that of Ukrainian literature;

    c) social and political conditions in the two republics are different. Therefore the same processes – a movement toward more humanism in literature and more democracy in life – take different forms in each. In Russia the literary process had not been blocked or truncated to the same extent as in Ukraine, where literature was dealt with by police methods. Recollect the political arrests of 1965 and 1972; recollect that the post-'sixties generation was deliberately prevented from going into literature

28. The critic Mykola Riabchuk was especially given to such unfavourable comparisons. See, e.g., *LU*, 22 January 1987, p. 2, and his discussion with Iurii Shcherbak in *Sotsialistychna kul'tura*, 1987, No. 1, 2–5; but see also Ivan Dziuba, *LU*, 19 February 1987, 6, and Leonid Novychenko, *LU*, 25 June 1988, p. 1.

29. A collective letter of protest appeared in *LU*, 17 December 1987, p. 8, Vladimir Drozd added his voice in *LU*, 11 February 1988, p. 2, and P. Kononenko's well-argued rebuttal of charges of inferiority, 'U konteksti', was published in *LU*, 10 March 1988, p. 7.

Marko Pavlyshyn

and that normal literary development was thereby disrupted; that some of the people of the 'sixties [. . .] were thrown out of the literary process and others ended up behind bars [. . .]. You see, Ukrainian literature was in a state, not of stagnation, as was the Russian, but of rout.[30]

With similar freedom from euphemism, Shevchuk spoke of the identification of Russian culture as the culture of the Soviet Union which renders Ukrainian literature practically invisible: 'the [central] journals are not at all interested in Ukrainian literature. This is not surprising: in essence they are not Union-wide, but Russian. [. . .] A real "friendship of literatures" does not exist – at the moment this is still one of the official fictions.'[31]

It was not Shevchuk who adjusted the manner and content of his writing to the new thaw, but rather the thaw which discovered that Shevchuk had pre-empted many of its features when it was still perilous to do so. *Three Leaves Beyond the Window*, when it appeared in 1986, was seen as a book of its time – a view that was confirmed by the award to Shevchuk of the 1988 Shevchenko State Prize, the Ukrainian SSR's highest mark of recognition for achievement in the cultural sphere. It was symptomatic of critics' perceptions of the relative value of rehabilitated and new literature that, in the following year, no living writer was deemed worthy of the award. It was bestowed, posthumously, on Hryhir Tiutiunnyk (1931–80), like Shevchuk, a writer who had made no compromises in the 1970s.

The panegyrics leading up to the award of the prize represented *Three Leaves Beyond the Window* more or less as a work embodying Gorbachev's critiques of bureaucratism and of a society bereft of initiative and responsibility.[32] While such elements are, indeed, part of the satirical design of the novel, what renders the work exemplary is its Aesopian reflection on the issue of nationality. The novel is in three parts, set in Ukraine in, respectively, the seventeenth, eighteenth and nineteenth centuries – the three during which the transformation of the country from an independent Cossack republic to a cluster of Russian provinces was accomplished. The three narratives illustrate, through three fictional autobiographies, a decay in the aspirations of the human spirit which is shown to parallel the loss of national autonomy. In the first narrative, a 'Bildungsroman', the hero, Il'ia Turchynovs'kyi, journeys into the world on a Skovorodinian search. At every step the world is hostile and hurtful;

30. *Kyiv*, 1988, No. 11, 5.
31. Ibid., p. 10.
32. See, e.g., Hryhorii Klochek, 'Hospodar u "lisi liudei"', *LU*, 19 February 1987, p. 3.

he is accompanied throughout by personified Fear; and yet he achieves personal wisdom and peace. In the second narrative, Petro, a descendant of Il'ia's and a figure of the Enlightenment, is also involved in a search. He is, however, a forensic investigator in the service of the state, and his obligation is to discover rational chains of cause and effect that would explain a series of mysterious crimes. The central figure of the final narrative, Kyriak Avtomonovych Satanovs'kyi, is a grotesque Schlemihl with the power, unseen, to accompany other people's shadows. Though by profession he is a teacher, his interest is not in Il'ias wisdom, nor even in Petro's objective and instrumental knowledge, but in the constant and obsessive observation of the worst in human nature. It was this last narrative which critics, seeking to mainstream Shevchuk's novel into the legitimate discourse of *glasnost'*, read as a straightforward social satire unmasking the creature of the bureaucracy.

But the book admits interpretation as a far more subversive critique than that: it may be read as a critique of enlightenment run wild in the centralized imperial state. The ideals of efficiency and the well-ordered society – the legitimating virtues, not only of the Russian Empire after the reforms of Peter I, but of the reform plan of Mikhail Gorbachev – are exposed as subject to inhumane perversion. In order to present these observations as self-evident, almost as commonplaces that have been familiar to European culture for two centuries, Shevchuk employs for his critique a favoured metaphor of nineteenth-century romantic cultural criticism, the automaton. (The word is echoed in Satanovs'kyi's patronymic, 'Avtomon-ovych'.) The teacher defines himself as both an implement and a victim of the construction of society, as a lifeless, soulless mechanism. 'We are preparing these children', he reflects, 'to become cogs in the gigantic human machine that is our empire, but are we not cogs ourselves? Do I not become a mechanical doll as I sit on this dais . . . ?'[33] The more complete the integration of the human being into the pseudorational order ordained by the state, the reader might conclude, the more limited the possibilities of an autonomous life of the spirit.

Shevchuk takes up another romantic theme that has special relevance for the colonial context: the rejection of the Enlightenment's claim to transcend cultural difference in the common experience of the simply human. In the figure of Satanovs'kyi, such purported transcendence is represented as a denial of self, a nihilist abdication of the right to identity: 'I am a Little Russian', Satanovs'-

---

33. Shevchuk, *Try lystky za viknom*, Kiev: Radians'kyi pys'mennyk, 1986, p. 400.

kyi claims at a job interview, using the ethnic tag which most vividly symbolizes the imperial subordination of the Ukrainians, 'but not one who would regard them as a separate tribe.'[34] This statement is part of his successful strategy to endear himself to his superiors in the government service by studying and fulfilling their desires. His national self-denial is part of that self-effacement as an individual which is necessary for the adaptation of his person to his place in the imperial hierarchy; it confirms his dehumanization.

Certainly, no Soviet critic placed such a construction upon *Three Leaves*, nor must the argument which here has been abstracted from the novel necessarily reflect the conscious intentions of the author. In creating a complex work open to such a political reading, however, Shevchuk has gone beyond any of his contemporaries (with the exception of those who, like Viacheslav Chornovil or Mykhailo Horyn', have no public voice beyond the organs of *samizdat*). Shevchuk has allowed his criticism to penetrate – or, more precisely, he has allowed the attuned reader to *perceive* his criticism as penetrating – beneath the symptoms of bureaucratized imperialism to identify and condemn the imperial disease itself.

This, clearly, is not one of the sanctioned uses of *glasnost'*. *Three Leaves* can function in the manner described because it retains that Aesopian quality of ambiguity which we might term 'plausible deniability' – a feature with which Ukrainian literature, thaw or no thaw, may not yet safely dispense.

It is a general feature of thaws – indeed, *a priori* a part of their structure – that they threaten to subvert the authority which released them. Hence their tendency, often attested to in Eastern Europe since the Second World War, to end amid crackdowns and renewed repressions. Thaws in the non-Russian areas of the Soviet Union pose a particular problem to the central authorities. They are perceived, not merely as promising to modify the outward manifestations of the state, but as threatening to challenge its sovereignty and its territorial integrity. The anti-colonial tenor of thaws at the margins of the USSR strikes at one of the Centre's cherished myths, inherited from the Russian Empire: that of benignly absorbed, and now inalienable, frontier territories.[35] In Ukraine, as a result, liberalization even under Gorbachev was less far-reaching than elsewhere. The political survival of the Brezhnevite Volodymyr

34. Ibid., p. 348.
35. The system of Soviet historical legitimation myths is described in Lowell Tillett, *The Great Friendship: Soviet Historians on the Non-Russian Nationalities*, Chapel Hill: University of North Carolina Press, 1969.

Shcherbyts'kyi at the head of the Communist Party of Ukraine – only superficially an anachronism – had corollaries in the cultural sphere: changes in education, historical conservation policy and language policy were made painfully slowly, if at all, and critical analysis of the cultural situation in Ukraine beyond the mere enumeration of symptoms almost remained impossible, except with the hedge of plausible deniability in a literary work.

The exemplary quality of Valerii Shevchuk lies in his rendering visible these limitations of the Ukrainian thaw and addressing the issues that it fails to resolve or even to name. The problem unfolded by Shevchuk is deeper than a prohibition of certain autonomist demands. Shevchuk understands that even the demands that thaws admit into the public arena serve merely to demonstrate the impasse which confronts Soviet Ukrainian culture. Any thaw in Ukraine, experience now suggests, releases forces which crystallize as traditional, romantic, nineteenth-century nationalism: they champion language, history, folklore and nature as the threatened symbols of national identity in opposition to a universalism identified as the pernicious ideology of a dominant power. Implicit in Ukrainian thaw discourse is a sense that, before these issues are satisfactorily resolved, there can be no proceeding to new problems and no addressing of new cultural goals. But there can be no such resolution while the empire remains intact. Shevchuk reflected the situation of impasse symbolically in the third part of *Three Leaves*, where the middle of the nineteenth century – the moment of the genesis of a Ukrainian nationalist agenda – is simultaneously the end of history: the world which Satanovs'kyi inhabits is, in keeping with his speaking name, the Russian Empire as hell, a place that is not only unpleasant, but also eternal.

The special problems of a culture thus burdened with the unresolved problems of the nineteenth century are not widely known or understood outside the borders of the empire. Within the empire the chief advocates of Ukrainian culture, its writers, seldom receive a sympathetic hearing. Not only do they risk being labelled as antiregime; they risk being interpreted, in a society accustomed to defining motivations in terms of class interests, as a small and specialized pressure group struggling to protect its privileges and, consequently, Ukrainian culture as its *raison d'être*: Ukrainian culture is the defining attribute of the Ukrainian reader, who is the sole consumer of their anachronistic product, Ukrainian literature. In pursuit of this sectional interest they are prepared to play a Luddite and obscurantist role, opposing the rationality of a transition to a monolingual and monocultural state.

The thaws in Ukraine have not inhibited hostile commentary of this kind, but they have, at least, made possible the formulation of the alternative view. They have revealed the struggle of the weak periphery not to cede even more of its vitality to the powerful Centre. They have brought into view the coercive cultural hierarchies within the professedly multicultural state, but without being able to change them.

–5–

Two Thaws in Yugoslav Philosophy

ALEKSANDAR PAVKOVIĆ

The very word 'thaw' implies a loss of rigidity by unfreezing. A thaw in philosophy should, by this token, imply the loss of rigidity in a philosophical view or doctrine. The doctrine, or rather the doctrines, I shall be concerned with are those of Marxism. The first thaw I shall discuss did indeed involve a loss of rigidity by the doctrine of Marxism-Leninism; the second involved more than the loss of rigidity – it involved the loosening of the grip which Marxism had held over philosophical thought in Yugoslavia. I say 'loosening' instead of 'breaking', because in a country ruled by a Communist party (however unorthodox it may be) it seems impossible to break the grip of Marxism: the Marxism on which the ideology of the ruling party is based requires that any other approach to philosophy be subjugated to, or incorporated into, Marxism. Marxism in the form of an official ideology does not allow for any philosophical approach which does not acknowledge Marxism's superiority. As we shall see, even so unorthodox a Communist party as the Yugoslav never officially condoned work by Yugoslav philosophers in analytic philosophy which was not carried out within a general Marxist framework.

In discussing the first thaw, one should start from the doctrine to be thawed: the Marxist-Leninist doctrine of dialectical and historical materialism. The doctrine is rigid in at least two respects. First, it contains statements which, in spite of protestations to the contrary, are not open to revision. An unrevisable statement of this kind is, for example, that history is a progression of class struggles which will end in a classless society. Second, the doctrine prescribes a number of immutable general methods of enquiry – the methods of dialectics. Crudely put, in any phenomenon one should be able to distinguish a stage of thesis, its opposite – antithesis – and, finally, the reconciliation and transcendence of the two – synthesis. In the eyes of the authors and adherents of this doctrine (among whom may be numbered Stalin himself), this rigidity constitutes its major virtue. For the primary use to which the doctrine was put was that of a standard of ideological and, consequently, of political purity and loyalty; the acceptance of this doctrine was a necessary condition for being a Marxist-Leninist and thus a good Communist. Those who expressed any doubt as to any of its aspects could safely be thrown out of the select group; and even those who did not, but were to be thrown out in any case, could be accused of having 'objectively' abandoned the doctrine and thus of having deserted the ranks. For these purposes a certain degree of rigidity is necessary: without rigidity the doctrine could not have been applied as a standard of any kind.

The exact degree and scope of rigidity were never precisely defined. Such a lack of definition facilitated the use of the doctrine as a standard for the evaluation of ideological purity: when the appropriate authorities decided that some view was ideologically incorrect or impure, they could always find a suitable interpretation of the ruling doctrine to back up their decision. Furthermore, because Marxist-Leninist doctrine functions as an (allegedly) rigid standard for ideological evaluation, any attempt intentionally to loosen its rigidity becomes a deviation from the doctrine: if the doctrine is rigid, an attempt to modify any of its tenets or methodological principles is an abandonment of the doctrine. The most dangerous deviation is that which advocates revision of the doctrine: openly to advocate revision is to question the main purpose and use of the doctrine as an incontrovertible standard of ideological purity. But not all deviation need be revision. One can deviate from the doctrine by an incorrect selection of the sacred, unrevisable tenets and principles. This is still dogmatism; it errs merely in locating rigidity in the wrong place. As a form of deviation, it has always been less dangerous, because it recognizes the role of the doctrine as the supreme standard of ideological evaluation.

For a thaw of the first kind, then, it is not sufficient that there should be a deviation from the current version of dialectical and historical materialism, because a deviation need not always involve a thaw's characteristic loss of rigidity. However, a considerable loss of rigidity – and, therefore, a thaw – did attend the deviation from Marxism-Leninism promoted by a group of Yugoslav philosophers from the early 1950s onward.

The Philosophy of Praxis and the First Thaw

The Communist victory in Yugoslavia in 1945 was also a victory of the 'Dia-Mat', the Soviet version of dialectical and historical materi-

alism, over any other approach to philosophy. The victors in philosophy set about cleansing this discipline of any bourgeois and
non-dialectical thought. This task was carried out with great vigour
by two pre-war Communist philosophers who immediately after the
war were appointed to chairs of philosophy: Dušan Nedeljković in
Beograd and Boris Ziherl in Ljubljana. Both were academic philosophers in the pre-war years, and both fought with the partisans.
As true Communists, untainted by Trotskyism and revisionism of
any kind, they wholeheartedly espoused Dia-Mat as propounded,
for example, by G. F. Aleksandrov and M. B. Mitin in the Soviet
textbooks of the day. Philosophers who did not agree with these
views were often proclaimed enemies of the people and accused of
'objective' (and 'subjective') collaboration with the Nazis. This type
of argument yielded immediate results, especially since Dušan
Nedeljković was a presiding judge in a court dealing with cases of
alleged collaboration. For example, Nikola Popović, a professor of
the history of philosophy and a translator of Kant, was sentenced to
prison and after his release in 1950 died of malnutrition and mal-
treatment. Professor Branislav Petronijević, regarded by many as
the greatest Serbian metaphysician, was forcibly retired from his
post in the Serbian Academy of Sciences. Docent Kajica Milanov,
the first Serbian analytic philosopher, was summarily dismissed
from his post at the University of Beograd and forced to leave the
country. By 1948 there was no active philosopher left in Beograd
who was not an adherent of the Dia-Mat. Indeed, there were not
many qualified philosophers left at all, and Professor Nedeljković
lectured in all philosophical disciplines. Whatever educational disadvantages might result from this, Nedeljković wanted to make sure
that the young Communists who were sent to him from their Army,
Party and youth organization posts received the best grounding in
the Dia-Mat and became ideologically upright leaders and academics.

In Ljubljana, Boris Ziherl did not have to contend with so many
philosophers, but the purge he instituted was as thorough as
Nedeljković's: soon after his appointment there was no one teaching
philosophy in Slovenia who was not a Marxist-Leninist. The University of Zagreb for some unknown reason was spared such a
thorough purge of bourgeois elements; a few pre-war lecturers whose
main interests were in the history of philosophy were retained, but
did not publish anything which could be viewed as a deviation from
the ruling doctrine. They were even spared the public conversion to
Marxism-Leninism which some philosophers in Beograd were subjected to. For example, Bogdan Šešić, whose interests, before the

war, were in phenomenology, was sent to the provinces by Nedeljković, only to return to Beograd a fully converted hard-core Marxist-Leninist; he did not abandon the doctrine even after the fall of Nedeljković, when it would have been quite safe for him to do so.

There is nothing unusual about these purges and occasional public conversions: they were a common experience of philosophers in all the countries of Eastern Europe in which Communists took power. It was only the manner of Dušan Nedeljković's removal from his post of professor of philosophy at the University of Beograd that was unusual. The first step was an attack on Nedeljković's style – in particular his long-windedness and unintelligibility – by Milovan Djilas, the then chief ideologue of the Party, in the new journal *Nova Misao* (The New Thought), which Djilas had founded himself. It is not clear why Djilas chose to notice these qualities of Nedeljković's approach only in 1953, when they were obvious in Nedeljković's pre-war philosophical writings. Djilas's fall from power in 1954 did not bring Nedeljković any reprieve: his best students organized a boycott of his lectures. This protest – the first of its kind since the war and not to be repeated until 1968 – was clearly approved by high Party authorities. Since even this would not move Nedeljković, the Minister of Education issued an order dismissing him instantly from his chair. He was obliged to leave without finishing the oral examination he was conducting, never to return to his chair again.

The doctoral students and assistants who prepared his removal were not led to do so only by their ambition to take his place: in Nedeljković's philosophy they saw a stultifying dogmatic deviation from authentic Marxism. For in the course of their research they had come upon a work of the early Marx – his *Economic and Philosophical Manuscripts* – which differed greatly from the Dia-Mat taught by Nedeljković. The most notable difference was the absence of historical determinism: the early Marx did not mention the iron laws of history which are to usher in communism. Instead, the emphasis is on individual human action – the action of self-conscious individuals leading to revolutionary change. Moreover, such revolutionary action is viewed in the broadest terms, and is not limited to action leading to the violent overthrow of the capitalist system. The justification for revolutionary action so broadly conceived comes not from the immutable laws of history but from the nature of humankind itself. And instead of the general dialectical laws which rule nature, in the early works of Marx one finds the concept of praxis – practical activity – which provides the basis for our knowledge of both nature and society. It is through praxis that we come to understand natural and social phenomena; but there is no set of laws which we are bound to discover or to follow in the process of discovery.

In fact, this concept of praxis seemed to provide a tool for philosophical analysis and a standard for the evaluation of philosophical or ideological doctrines. For a doctrine to be authentically Marxist, it has to show how its theoretical statements relate to and are based on praxis: a Marxist doctrine is not neutral on the issue of practical action. Such a doctrine should point a way to the emancipation of humanity through practical activity. But even when used as a standard of evaluation, the concept of praxis is much less rigid than the concept of immutable dialectical and historical laws. For the immutable historical laws demanded of a true Marxist that he or she side with the proletariat on every issue; which is the side of the proletariat only the highest organs of the Party can tell. On the other hand, the criterion of correct Marxist views based on the concept of praxis is intentionally underdetermined; on this criterion various doctrines may all be truly Marxist, although each of them offers different advice as to the course of practical action leading to the emancipation of humanity. The courses of action may be different but lead to the same general goal; the goal, one should note, is no longer defined in terms of a specific class. And not only could one differ on the course of action to be taken and yet remain a good Marxist: one could also differ on the interpretation of the very concept of praxis. The Yugoslav philosophers who endorsed the praxis version of Marxism still differed in their interpretation of the concept without throwing doubt on each other's Marxist credentials.[1]

Their deviation from the Dia-Mat was radical. Not only were some of the unrevisable statements and principles of Dia-Mat implicitly (and often explicitly) abandoned, but some of the concepts which replaced them, such as that of praxis or of the essence of humanity, were intentionally underdetermined and flexible. And not only were the concepts of the constant class struggle and of the inevitability of the violent overthrow of capitalism abandoned, but no corresponding historical concepts were introduced. For these concepts of class struggle and the violent socialist revolution were, in

---

1. See, for example, one of the early collections, *Problemi filosofije marksizma*, Beograd: Rad, 1967, in which the concept of praxis is viewed by some as exhibiting the essence of humanity in mankind and by others only as a criterion of truth with a limited application in the discussion of the problem of knowledge. For a similar variety of views on praxis, see the collection, *Praxis: Yugoslav Essays in the Philosophy and Methodology of the Social Sciences*, ed. by Mihailo Marković and Gajo Petrović, Boston Studies in the Philosophy of Science, Vol. 36., Dordrecht: D. Reidel, 1979.

the view of Praxis philosophers, empirical descriptions applicable only to some periods of history; in their view, these descriptions had no universal validity and could not be criteria for assessing the ideological purity of a doctrine or a view. So radical was their departure, not only from the tenets of Dia-Mat but from its aims, that one could easily regard their doctrine not as a deviation but as a doctrine of a different kind.

Whatever its relation to the philosophy of praxis, Dia-Mat did not survive the scathing attack launched on it by Gajo Petrović from Zagreb and Mihailo Marković and Svetozar Stojanović from Beograd at the philosophical conference at Bled in 1960. The very basis of Dia-Mat – the copy theory of knowledge according to which knowledge is a subjective copy of objective reality – was, according to these philosophers, un-Marxist and incorrect. Marx certainly had never held it, and it was not clear that Lenin had held it in this simplistic form either. Since the authority of Soviet philosophers had been undermined by the official break with Stalin, neither Nedeljković nor Ziherl could find an appropriate response to this. Dia-Mat finally disposed of, Praxis Marxism dominated Yugoslav philosophy until the middle 1970s.

As we have seen, the Praxis approach to Marxism certainly involved a considerable loss of rigidity, and in this respect its replacement of Dia-Mat certainly constituted a thaw. The Praxis approach allowed for a variety of views on the same issue, provided that all the views employed some of the key Marxist concepts, such as that of praxis. But what of the views which avoid the use of any such concepts? Some non-Marxist views, according to Praxis philosophers, may be of some use in philosophical discussion but are essentially incomplete and flawed: only authentic Marxism can lead to a comprehensive view of the essential questions of human existence. Further, non-Marxist doctrines, unlike Marxist ones, cannot handle urgent moral issues, because they do not aim for the radical transformation of the world, whereas Marxist doctrines aim to change the world so as to satisfy the demands of our human nature.

However simplified, this account of what Gajo Petrović, Svetozar Stojanović and Mihailo Marković held in the early 1960s in the heyday of Praxis philosophy[2] clearly indicates that non-Marxist

---

2. A similar simplified account of their views can be found in Mihailo Marković and Robert S. Cohen, *Yugoslavia: The Rise and Fall of Socialist Humanism (A History of the Praxis Group)*, Nottingham: Spokesman Books, 1975. A more detailed account is given in David A. Crocker, *Praxis and Democratic Socialism: The Critical Social Theory of Marković and Stojanović*, Brighton: Harvester Press, 1983.

doctrines were not held to be on a par with Marxist ones. The superiority of Marxism was held to be conceptual and moral, and this time its superiority did not rest on its historical role as the ideology of the winning side. Yet, in evaluating other doctrines from both the theoretical and the practical point of view, the Praxis philosophers seemed not to notice that their standards of evaluation were precisely those of the creed whose superiority they wanted to establish. Like their Dia-Mat predecessors, they believed that their own standards were universal; to change the world to fit the demands of human nature as disclosed by the most comprehensive theory was, in their view, simply the universal aim of any progressive social and philosophical theory. Failure to recognize the universality of this aim was itself a sign of a moral or intellectual inadequacy.

The official party ideologues in the mid-1950s fully endorsed the work of the Praxis philosophers, praising them for their consistent and original Marxist approach. Some of the philosophers and social theorists from the Praxis group were members of party committees and commissions on ideology. The first signs of tension between them and the official party ideology appeared in 1965, when at a philosophers' conference Mihailo Marković offered a critique of the then current party programme of economic reform. His main objection was to the increased role assigned to market forces in the Yugoslav economy. For him this meant abandoning humanist Marxist ideals and returning to an earlier stage in which the 'blind' forces of the market were allowed to shape human destinies. But the full confrontation with the party came in 1968 when Beograd students, like their colleagues in Paris, Berlin and elsewhere, took to the streets and clashed with the police. The Praxis philosophers joined the students in their occupation of the Faculty of Philosophy in protest against police brutality and succeeded in exerting considerable influence on the demands put forward by the students to the party and state leadership. Least acceptable to the Party leadership was a demand that the party confine itself to the role of an advising body and abandon its assumed right to control and direct every aspect of political, social and cultural life in the country. The party leadership regarded this not only as a sign of ideological deviation but, more importantly, as an indication that the Praxis philosophers had put themselves on a par with, and even above, the party and its leadership. In consequence, the Praxis philosophers and social theorists at the Beograd Faculty of Philosophy were expelled from the party in 1968 for anarcho-liberal tendencies, and a campaign was launched to relieve them of their university posts. In order to accomplish this, the authorities were forced in early 1975 to pass a special law in the Serbian Parliament: ministerial orders, apparently, were no longer deemed legally effective for the dismissal of philosophers.[3]

But as the ministerial order dismissing Dušan Nedeljković brought in the first thaw, so the special law of the Serbian Parliament suspending the Praxis philosophers inaugurated the second, which differed considerably from the first.

The Second Thaw Comes by Default

Praxis Marxism was the dominant approach to philosophy in Yugoslavia from the mid-1950s to the mid-1970s. A cursory look at the two leading philosophical journals of this period, *Filozofija* in Beograd and *Praxis* in Zagreb, would confirm this. Apart from articles on historical topics, most of the contributions employed or discussed such concepts as self-emancipation, alienation, the essence of human beings, self-management and the true freedom of a human being. University courses on philosophy and Marxism, extra-mural lectures and radio broadcasts on Marxism, sociology and philosophy, as well as secondary school textbooks in these disciplines, reflected these interests too. Although non-Marxist approaches to philosophy were not banned outright, it was clear that they were tolerated only if incorporated into a broader neo-Marxist framework. Works on areas of philosophy remote from central neo-Marxist interests, and even studies of other philosophical approaches, usually included an endorsement of the neo-Marxist approach.[4] Philosophers who systematically refused to conform to this convention and showed indifference to neo-Marxist topics were prevented from teaching at universities and publishing their work in philosophical journals.[5]

3. The dismissed members of the Beograd Praxis group were Mihailo Marković, Svetozar Stojanović, Miladin Životić, Zagorka Pešić-Golubović, Dragoljub Mićunović, Nebojša Popov, Trivo Indjić and Ljubomir Tadić. In 1982, under intense and prolonged pressure from various leftist groups and individuals from abroad, the authorities appointed seven of these academics to research posts in the Institute for Social Sciences and allowed them to establish a separate department, the Centre for Philosophy and Social Theory. Most of the original appointees still hold jobs there, and their department has expanded to include some postgraduate teaching.
4. For example, Staniša Novaković's *Problem metafizike u savremenoj analitickoj filozofiji* (Diss. 1964), Beograd.: Institut društvenih nauka. Odeljenje za filozofiju, 1967; and Nenad Mišćević's *Filozofija jezika*, Zagreb.: Naprijed 1981.
5. The best examples are two highly talented philosophers, Jovan Ćulum and Jovan

This implicit ban on blatant non-Marxism (as opposed to a mere lack of interest in the central themes of neo-Marxism) was slowly lifted even before the Beograd Praxis philosophers lost their university posts. Already in the early 1970s, a group of younger philosophers with a strong interest in analytic philosophy who started publishing articles without the obligatory obeisances toward neo-Marxism nevertheless secured appointments in the Praxis-dominated departments of philosophy.[6]

The official campaign against the Praxis Marxists, in addition to the dismissal of the Beograd group, led to other changes in the philosophical life of Beograd and Zagreb. In 1975, the main journal *Praxis* was forced by the authorities to suspend publication. *Filozofska Istraživanja* (Philosophical Investigations), started a few years later in Zagreb, has a broadly based editorial board and publishes articles exemplifying a wide variety of methodologies including that of the Praxis neo-Marxists. In protest against the discontinuation of *Praxis*, the Beograd philosophical journal *Filozofija* changed its name in 1976 to *Theoria*; the first editor of the renamed journal was a logician who had no particular interest in Marxism. In consequence, *Theoria*, which remained under his editorship until 1980, opened its pages to diverse philosophical approaches, the Praxis approach included.

Deprived of their institutional base and constantly in conflict with the authorities, the Praxis neo-Marxists lost much of their influence. From time to time, the authorities prohibited their public appearances (as extra-mural lecturers, for example), and pressure was brought to bear on philosophical societies in Zagreb and Beograd to curb their still considerable influence in these bodies. The main publishing houses under party control would no longer publish their works.

All these changes meant that the domination by Praxis neo-Marxists of philosophical life in Beograd, Zagreb and Ljubljana was

---

Hristić. The first was fired from his post at the University of Beograd for his blatant non-Marxism and the second was refused employment at the Department of Philosophy for the same reason. For a discussion of their work see my Introduction to *Contemporary Yugoslav Philosophy: The Analytic Approach*, Dordrecht: Kluwer Academic Publishers, 1988.

6. The personal loyalty of some of the analytic philosophers, however, was never in doubt: for example, Igor Primorac and Vojislav Stojanović, whose main interests were in analytic philosophy, were members of the Communist Party cell at the Faculty of Philosophy, which the Praxis philosophers dominated and which, on order from above, was disbanded in 1968. Like their Praxis colleagues, these two philosophers never applied for readmission to the party.

at an end. Sarajevo remained a bastion of Marxism: philosophers at the University of Sarajevo wholeheartedly supported the party line and excelled in their attacks on their Praxis colleagues. From 1975 until 1987 Praxis philosophers had to confine their activities to philosophical circles and dissident groups in both Zagreb and Beograd. After their recent (1987–8) return to fully fledged public life, they have started to give interviews in the mainline press, making pronouncements, as they did before, on a great variety of social and political issues. Although their philosophical approach seems to have changed little,[7] some of them have adopted a more nationalist outlook than before. Ljubomir Tadić and Mihailo Marković came out in defence of Serbian national rights and in support of the current Serbian Party leader, and seem, thus, to have abandoned their previous internationalist and dissident stance. Their willingness to modify their positions may, in fact, have contributed to the lifting of the ban on their public appearances.

Apart from the rule of Marxism in Sarajevo, from 1975 up to the time of writing no philosophical approach had achieved dominance in any of the Yugoslav philosophical centres. The two non-Marxist traditions which have achieved the greatest prominence are the analytic and the phenomenological, in particular in its Heideggerian variant. In 1981 a group of philosophers in Beograd formed a Section for Analytic Investigation in Philosophy within the Philosophical Society of Serbia. A few years later a similar section was formed in Ljubljana. The Ljubljana section now publishes a journal in English entitled *Acta Analytica*. Although the phenomenologists have no separate organization, their works are published by the largest publishing houses and philosophical journals in Ljubljana, Beograd and Zagreb.

In the field of neo-Marxist theory, the Praxis group now faces fierce competition from a group of younger philosophers who often combine neo-Marxism with interests in phenomenology and hermeneutics. In their version of neo-Marxism, the concepts of human emancipation and self-understanding play the most prominent role; the concept of praxis has lost its centrality and is relegated to the role of one of the tools used in achieving philosophical understand-

---

7. Of all Praxis philosophers, Svetozar Stojanović seems to have moved away most from his earlier neo-Marxist views. In one of his latest papers, 'Marksizam, ideologija, demokratija', *Theoria*, No. 1–2(1985), he offers a systematic critique of Marx's analysis of class society and rejects not only the inevitability of the dictatorship of the proletariat but historical analysis in terms of the class struggle; further, he argues that in socialism one should retain the liberties gained in bourgeois society.

ing. In their view, the criterion by which a committed Marxist should assess his or her action – in the widest sense of the word – is the magnitude of the contribution which these actions make to general emancipation. The Praxis Marxists, therefore, have often failed this test by engaging in dissent which 'objectively' did not contribute much to emancipation; moreover, Praxis philosophers abandoned the Marxist historical and dialectical method as well as the Marxist (and Marx's) main goal – victory and the subsequent emancipation of the proletariat.[8]

The insistence of the new neo-Marxists on a return to Marx's fundamental ideas on dialectics and the role of the proletariat has earned them the name of 'fundamentalists'. But it was not so much their apparent theoretical orthodoxy as the means which they employed in their attempts to maintain control of the journal *Theoria* that brought them into direct conflict with both the Praxis neo-Marxists and the anti-Marxists. Their readiness to denounce their opponents to the authorities and to support Party attacks on analytic philosophers exhibited a lack of scruple characteristic of the Dia-Mat group. Fortunately, in spite of their readiness to serve the party, the party leadership seems not to have extended to these Marxists its official blessing, and, granted their small numbers and less than outstanding reputation, they have little chance of achieving dominance over philosophical life in Beograd, let alone other philosophical centres in Yugoslavia.[9]

Apart from non-Marxist philosophers who simply have no interest in any kind of Marxism, there is now in Yugoslavia a small group of anti-Marxists whose influence is growing. Unlike the other groups, these philosophers and social theorists share no more than a common rejection of Marxism. Some of them are interested in such Russian religious thinkers as Berdiaev; they usually accuse Lenin and the Bolsheviks of sheer immorality and consider them to be criminals. Others are interested in the classical liberal political theories of Mill and Constant and reject Marxism as incompatible

8. See the attacks by Slobodan Žunjić, Mladen Kozomara and Milorad Belančić published in *Theoria*, No. 1–2(1985), on Svetozar Stojanović's 'Marksizam, ideologija, demokratija' in the same issue of the journal. Stojanović in this paper goes beyond the previous Praxis interpretation of Marx. But his opponents accuse him of various failures in his earlier Praxis writings; one of the most serious charges is that he has abandoned the belief in the need for a revolutionary and violent overthrow of bourgeois society.
9. In addition to these two strands of Marxism, one might mention the Marxists of Sarajevo and various other apologists for the regime, who, recognized as apologists by most professional philosophers, play no significant role in the philosophical life of the country.

with the protection of individual human rights and liberties. A few philosophers also object to Marxism on purely intellectual grounds: they argue that Marxist theories are incoherent, unverifiable or simply false, both as philosophical theories and as theories about society and economics. The most prominent and consistent critic of Marxism of the latter kind is Neven Sesardić, an analytic philosopher from the University of Zagreb, who has recently extended his criticism to the concept of praxis and its use by Yugoslav philosophers.[10]

Given that Marxism is the official ideology of the Yugoslav Communist Party, one may well wonder why this proliferation of non-Marxist and anti-Marxist philosophical views was ever allowed. Perhaps an answer may be sought in the decrease of party leaders' interest in ideological questions and in the inability of anti-Marxist philosophers to present any real threat to the party's grip on power. The Yugoslav Party leadership has a long history of indifference to philosophical issues in the Marxist ideology. Tito himself never showed any interest in philosophy, and the party leadership which succeeded him has, until recently, felt so secure in its position of power that it has conceived of no need to call on philosophical theory to legitimize its rule. Confronted as they have been in recent years with a great variety of critics, dissidents and opponents, the party leaders probably find the philosophical dissent rather innocuous. Philosophers in their ever-growing disunity command no numbers. Nor do they have any significant influence, even among the intelligentsia. None of the present philosophical groups is able to achieve as dominant a position in the country as the Praxis group once held, nor can they, accordingly, match the Praxis group's erstwhile political influence.

Although non-Marxist philosophers present no threat to party rule, the Serbian Party leadership did make an attempt to stop the spread of one particular philosophical approach – the analytic. In the spring of 1985, the Ideological Commission of the Central Committee of the Serbian Communist Party issued a document which accused analytic philosophy of undermining the very foundations of Marxism. It called on all Communists to combat this approach to philosophy and to check its spread. Analytic philosophers, joined by some Praxis neo-Marxists, publicly protested; their protest led to a polemic in the Beograd literary weekly,

10. In his 'Razmišljanja o Praxis filozofiji', *Theoria*, No. 1–2(1987). A collection of anti-Marxist essays exemplifying the above three approaches was published in *Filozofske Studije*, Vol. 15, Beograd, 1983.

Književne novine (Literary News). Some older neo-Marxists, joined by younger fundamentalists (all of whom are present or former members of the Department of Philosophy at the University of Beograd), endorsed the party document and called for the containment and eventual eradication of analytic philosophy in Yugoslavia. Analytic philosophers replied by pointing out the ignorance and incoherence displayed by their opponents. The party issued no further instructions on this matter, nor has any attempt been made officially to ban analytic philosophers from publishing their work. This may indicate, as some analytic philosophers have argued, that the document was inspired by some of their Marxist colleagues who were fearful of being relegated to insignificance. But in the absence of further action by the party apparatus, some academic philosophers from Beograd seem to have taken on themselves the mission of checking the spread of this non-Marxist approach to philosophy.[11]

This may explain, at least to some extent, why the Serbian Party leaders have done nothing more to discourage analytic philosophy. Yet it is still unclear why, after the hard-won suspension and dismissal of members of the Praxis group in Beograd in 1975 – and the advance of non-Marxism dates from this event – no effort was made to replace them with reliable Marxists supporting the party line. Neither the party organization at the Faculty of Philosophy, nor higher party committees issued any guidelines concerning the selection and appointment of replacements for the Praxis Marxists. Nor did they put forward any candidates of their own. Moreover, no serious attempt was made to screen the ideological views of the applicants who were eventually appointed. No attempt was made to gain party control over the philosophical journals and professional philosophical organizations. The only explanation for this extraordinary ideological laxity is the sheer indolence of the party apparatus in the absence of any directives from the higher party organs. After years of campaigning to oust the Praxis philosophers from their posts, the Yugoslav and Serbian Party leadership, having achieved this goal, was content. Its main concern seems to have been to remove individually targeted philosophers. The University party apparatus, left without any instructions as to who should be appointed in their place, preferred not to act in any way.

Indifference of this kind was not perceived as extraordinary at the

---

11. For this often vitriolic polemic see the October and November 1985 issues of the weekly *Književne novine*. One should note that the weekly has had the reputation of being a dissident journal and that its editor at the time was a graduate in philosophy well versed in the philosophers' squabbles.

time. The party leadership since 1965 had refused to be drawn into any philosophical or literary dispute, and, in consequence, had no directives to offer on the ideological or philosophical stance of prospective candidates for university lectureships. The only political condition for appointment was, and seems still to be, that the candidate should not have a public record of opposition to the regime. This requirement is satisfied even by some of the present-day anti-Marxists.

In contrast to Yugoslav writers and poets, the philosophers in Yugoslavia seem to have acquired their (conditional) liberty without much effort of their own. For the pluralism of views, styles and approaches to literature characteristic of the present literary life in Yugoslavia, the so-called 'modernists' had to fight hard and long in the 1950s. The same pluralism in philosophy was achieved in the 1970s through inaction by the party machine.

–6–

Looking Back: The Past in the Soviet Russian Literary Journal of 1987

ZHANNA DOLGOPOLOVA

Unlike other spheres of contemporary social communication in the USSR, literature has not overused such words as *glasnost'*, *perestroika* or *uskorenie*, but it has, nevertheless, introduced its own cliché, 'liquidation of blank spaces' (*likvidatsiia belykh piaten*), for current changes in literary affairs. The expression 'blank space' was used primarily by geographers and cartographers to designate an unexplored territory; used figuratively, the expression signifies a problem which requires investigation. In the discussion of literature it has limited applicability: nobody would seriously claim that, say, Pushkin wrote *The Captain's Daughter* to liquidate the blank space of the Pugachev riots, or that Tolstoi liquidated the blank space of the Napoleonic wars by writing his novel *War and Peace*. Liquidation of blank spaces in literature is useful shorthand for liberal developments in publishing policy. In particular, it applies to the process of giving back to Russian readers those writers and works that were 'liquidated' some time ago, while granting living writers the opportunity to see their works published. In plain language, the 'liquidation of blank spaces' is tantamount to an amnesty for the (written) word.

This amnesty is supported by a number of leading literary magazines. 'Thick' and 'thin' journals, and paraliterary magazines like *Ogonek* and even *Krokodil*, publish several categories of previously proscribed works. In the first instance, they publish such Russian émigré writers as Vladimir Nabokov, Vladislav Khodasevich, Igor' Severianin and others of lesser status.[1] Second, they publish the

1. Vladimir Nabokov, 'Stikhi raznykh let', *Druzhba narodov*, 1987, No. 6, 170–5; 'O. Pushkine', *Iunost'*, 1987, No. 6, 90–3; Vladislav Khodasevich, 'iz liriki', *Druzhba narodov*, 1987, No. 2, 177–82; *Stikhi i memuarnaia proza*, *Znamia*, 1987, No. 5, 139–66; Igor Severianin, 'Stikhi', *Iunost'*, 1987, No. 4, 88–92; *Zvezda*, 1987, No. 5, 164–73; Poems by Georgii Ivanov in *Znamia*, 1987, No. 3, 140–57 and poems by Nikolai Otsup in *Literaturnaia Rossiia*, 1987, No. 34.

prose of living Soviet writers whose books, some ten years ago, appeared in the West.[2] Third, magazines have published the so-called 'confiscated prose' of Aleksandr Bek and Vasilii Grossman.[3] Fourth, magazines have made the first attempt to publish those so-called 'Soviet émigrés' who in the mid-1970s were stripped of Soviet citizenship.[4] Fifth, magazines have published rejected and banned works by Andrei Platonov, Mikhail Bulgakov, Anna Akhmatova, Aleksandr Tvardovskii, Boris Pil'niak, Osip Mandel'shtam, Marina Tsvetaeva and Daniil Kharms,[5] whom Soviet officials have feted as writers of Soviet classics in other contexts.

The 'liquidation of blank spaces' is proceeding rapidly and even in some haste. In the first half of 1987, five different journals published prose and plays by Mikhail Bulgakov,[6] while Aleksandr

2. Fazil Iskander's *Kroliki i udavy* (Rabbits and Boas) was first published in *Kontinent* in 1980, No. 22, 51–107 and No. 23, 79–136, now in *Iunost'*, 1987, No. 9, 21–62; Andrei Bitov's novel *Pushkinskii dom* (Pushkin's House) was published in 1978 by Ardis (Ann Arbor) and now in *Novyi mir*, 1987, Nos. 10–11, 3–92; 55–91.

3. Aleksandr Bek, *Novoe naznachenie* (New Appointment), *Znamia*, 1986, No. 10, 3–72, No. 11, 3–66; Vasilii Grossman's extract from the novel *Zhizn' i sud'ba* (Life and Fate), *Ogonek*, 1987, No. 40. The novel was published in 1988 (No. 1, 3–127, No. 2, 27–103, No. 3, 25–150, No. 4, 2–143). Towards the end of the 'thaw', when Grossman's novel *Zhizn' i sud'ba* was confiscated by the KGB, M. Suslov, the then chief ideologist of the Communist Party, warned the author that his novel could be published in perhaps one hundred years' time.

4. Iosif Brodskii's six poems, written since he left the Soviet Union, in *Novyi mir*, 1987, No. 12, 160–8; extract from Vasilii Aksenov's prose in *Krokodil*, 1988, No. 1, 14.

5. Andrei Platonov, *Kotlovan* (Foundation Pit), *Novyi mir*, 1987, No. 6, 50–123; Mikhail Bulgagov, *Bagrovyi ostrov* (The Scarlet Island), *Druzhba narodov*, 1987, No. 8, 140–4; *Adam i Eva* (Adam and Eve), *Oktiabr'*, 1987, No. 6, 137–91; *Sobach'e serdtse* (The Heart of a Dog), *Znamia*, 1987, No. 6, 73–141; 'Glava iz romana i pis'ma' (Chapter from a Novel and Letters), *Novyi mir*, 1987, No. 2, 138–80; 'Fel'etony i ocherki' (Féuilletons and Essays), *Iunost'*, 1987, No. 12, 18–22; Anna Akhmatova, *Rekviem*, *Oktiabr'*, 1987, No. 3, 130–5; *Neva*, 1987, No. 6, 74–9; Aleksandr Tvardovskii, *Po pravu pamiati* (By Right of Memory), *Znamia*, 1987, No. 2, 3–14; *Novyi mir*, 1987, No. 3, 162–205; Boris Pil'niak, *Zashtat*, *Znamia*, 1987, No. 2, 127–38; *Povest' nepogashennoi luny* (Tale of the Unextinguished Moon), *Znamia*, 1987, No. 12, 105–28; Osip Mandel'shtam, 'Stikhi i perevody' (Poems and Translations), *Druzhba narodov*, 1987, No. 8, 133–9; 'Iz neopublikovannoi knigi *Novye stikhi*' (From an Unpublished Book, *New Poems*), *Iunost'*, 1987, No. 9, 72–7; Marina Tsvetaeva, 'Poet i vremia' (Poet and Time), *Iunost'*, 1987, No. 8, 54–60; 'Iz literaturnogo naslediia' (From the Literary Heritage), *Oktiabr'*, 1987, No. 7, 185–201; Daniil Kharms, 'Iz neopublikovannogo' (From Unpublished Works), *Druzhba narodov*, 1987, No. 10, 176–7.

6. *Bagrovyi ostrov* (The Scarlet Island), *Druzhba narodov*, 1987, No. 8, 140–94; *Adam i Eva* (Adam and Eve), *Oktiabr'*, 1987, No. 6, 137–91; *Sobach'e serdtse* (The Heart of a Dog), *Znamia*, 1987, No. 6, 73–141; 'Glava iz romana i pis'ma' (Chapter from a Novel and Letters), *Novyi mir*, 1987, No. 2, 138–80; 'Fel'etony i ocherki' (Féuilletons and Essays) *Iunost'*, 1987, No. 12, 18–22.

Tvardovskii's poem *Po pravu pamiati* (By Right of Memory) was published at about the same time in two Moscow magazines.[7] Anna Akhmatova's *Rekviem* (Requiem) had been included in the publication plan of *Neva* and duly appeared in the sixth issue of that journal for 1987, but an impatient *Oktiabr'* upstaged the Leningrad journal by including this poem in its second issue, hinting that the editorial board had used a *samizdat* copy of 1963, the year in which Akhmatova personally released her poem to her many admirers.[8]

Publications from the so-called 'literary heritage' are generously advertised. The weekly *Ogonek*, for example, has become one of the leading promoters of the 'thick' literary journals, printing excerpts of works soon to appear in the literary monthlies. Published works in the 'thick' journals are accompanied by commentaries, introductions and prefaces, afterwords, memoirs, documentation[9] and critical articles, of which at least two, by Iurii Koriakin and Iurii Burtin,[10] became literary sensations.

In a very short time – no more than two years – literary magazines have brought to light various major and minor writers of different literary epochs who publicly disclosed what they knew and thought of their own times. Such fictionalized memoirs have appeared alongside works by contemporary, but hitherto unknown writers, about a past of which they have no first-hand experience. It would be interesting to compare two recently published interpretations of the Kronshtadt rebellion in 1921: that of Elizaveta Drabkina, who took part in a force that crushed the rebels, and that of the newly discovered contemporary writer M. Kuraev, who in his novel

7. *Po pravu pamiati* (By Right of Memory), *Znamia*, 1987, No. 2, 3–14; *Novyi mir*, 1987, No. 3, 162–205.
8. *Rekviem*, *Neva*, 1987, No. 6, 74–9; *Oktiabr'*, 1987, No. 3, 130–5. The *tamizdat* publication of *Rekviem* appeared in Poland and West Germany in the same year.
9. See, for instance, N. Tolstoy's vocabulary list and commentary for Nikolai Kliuev's poem *Pogorel'shchina* (The Burnt Land), *Novyi mir*, 1987, No. 7, 78–100, D. S. Likhachev's introductions to Bazunov's story *Moreplavatel* (Seafarer) in *Novyi mir*, 1987, No. 6, 7–44 and No. 7, 101–44, and Varlaam Shalamov's reminiscences about the early 1920s, *Dvadtsatye gody*, *Iunost'*, 1987, No. 11, 37–45, where, incidentally, for the first time in the Soviet press, Shalamov's *Kolymskie rasskazy* (Kolyma Stories) were not only mentioned, but also praised. Likhachev wrote 120 pages of introduction to Boris Pasternak's novel *Doctor Zhivago* in *Novyi mir*, 1988 No. 1, 5–10. See also M. Chudakova, 'Zhizneopisanie Mikhaila Bulgakova' (Life of Mikhail Bulgakov), *Moskva*, 1987, No. 6, 3–57, No. 7, 5–54, No. 8, 9–91.
10. Iurii Koriakin, 'Stoit li nastupat' na grabli?' (*Otkrytoe pis'mo odnomy Inkognito*), (Is There Any Use Stepping on the Rake? An Open Letter to Incognito), *Znamia*, 1987, No. 9, 200–24; Iurii Burtin, 'Vam iz drugogo pokolen'ia', *Oktiabr'*, 1987, No. 8, 191–202.

Kapitan Dikshtein (Captain Dikshtein)[11] gives a description of the same uprising as a demonstration of popular dissatisfaction with Communist policy.

Unlike publications in 1986, which placed considerable emphasis on contemporary matters, a distinctive feature of literary magazines in 1987 was the comparatively scant attention paid to contemporary topics.[12] The nation's past was presented and contemplated over and over again: the immediate past from the Brezhnev period onward, the past of the Khrushchev period, the distant past of the Stalin epoch and the remote past of Lenin's rule.[13]

The crimes of the Stalin era were an especially important theme in 1987, although the occasional piece about Stalin and Stalinism had already appeared in 1986. The Soviet critic Koriakin predicted that the next few years would continue to witness a flood of prose and poetry on this evidently inexhaustible theme.[14] In 1986 the few significant novels and stories in this category were set randomly throughout the Stalin period. Aleksandr Bek's novel *Novoe naznachenie* (New Appointment), for example, had the Second World War as a backdrop, and Iurii Trifonov's story *Nedolgoe prebyvanie v kamere pytok* (A Brief Stay in the Torture Chamber) dealt with the 'struggle against cosmopolitanism' in the early 1950s. Works printed in 1987, on the other hand, covered a narrower period beginning with the assasination in 1925, by Stalin's order, of his first comrade-in-arms, Frunze,[15] and ending with the suppression of Soviet genetics and the subsequent victimization of geneticists in 1948.[16] Prose writers and poets took as their themes several waves of Stalin's victims: the

11. Elizaveta Drabkina, *Kronshtadt, god 1921* (Kronshtadt, 1921), *Iunost'*, 1987, No. 10, 7–22; M. Kuraev, *Kapitan Dikshtein, Novyi mir*, 1987, No. 9, 5–80.
12. Although one should not miss Sergei Kaledin's story *Smirennoe kladbishche* (A Humble Cemetery), *Novyi mir*, 1987, No. 5, 39–81.
13. Read, for instance, Anatolii Genatulin's *Nepogod'* (Bad Weather), *Oktiabr'*, 1987, No. 4, 3–38; Boris Vasil'ev, *Zhila-byla Klavochka* (Once Upon a Time There Was Claudia), *Iunost'*, 1987, No. 1, 34–62, set in the late 1970s; Vladimir Soloukhin, *Pokhorony Stepanidy Ivanovny* (The Burial of Stepanida Ivanovna), *Novyi mir*, 1987, No. 9, 130–40; Vladimir Makanin, *Otstavshii* (Left Behind), *Znamia*, 1987, No. 9, 6–59, set in the Khrushchev period; or M. Kuraev's *Kapitan Dikshtein, Novyi mir*, 1987, No. 9, 5–80, set in the time of the New Economic Policy.
14. Iurii Koriakin, '. . . Stepping on the Rake?', p. 201.
15. Boris Pil'niak, *Povest' nepogashennoi luny* (Tale of the Unextinguished Moon), *Znamia*, 1987, No. 12, 105–28.
16. Vladimir Dudintsev, *Belye odezhdy* (White Robes), *Neva*, 1987, No. 1, 6–112, No. 2, 62–132, No. 3, 3–77, No. 4, 18–124; Daniil Granin, *Zubr* (The Aurochs), *Novyi mir*, No. 1, 19–95 and No. 2, 7–92.

former 'nepmen', beneficiaries of Lenin's New Economic Policy,[17] the so-called 'dekulakized' ('raskulachennye') peasants and, in particular, their children.[18] Other writers treated the kulaks' opponents, the poor peasants who were persuaded or forced to join the newly organized collective farms in 1928–32.[19] The intrigues surrounding Stalin's assassination of Kirov in 1934,[20] the beginning of the elimination of the Bolshevik Old Guard,[21] the Great Terror of 1937–8[22] and finally the deportation of nations accused of collaborating with Hitler's invading army[23] furnished further material.

Some of the above topics – collectivization, the deportation of 'traitor-peoples' and the crackdown on genetics – were treated by as many as two or three different works published in the course of 1987. Such thematic concentration was due, in part, to editorial policy. Journals now defrosted manuscripts (by authors both living and dead) which had previously been unpublishable because of their content, but which had survived in editors' safes and, even more fortuitously, in writers' desks. The publication of these 'liberated' manuscripts, mainly from the late 1950s and early 1960s, furthermore, bears witness to an undiminished public interest in the events which they relate.

Published simultaneously, works of the past and present are dramatically different in their moods and overtones. Prose and poetry written in the wake of events in the late 1950s or early 1960s (such as Akhmatova's *Requiem* or Tvardovskii's *By Right of Memory*) evince horror at the carnage in the wake of the chariot of history. Iurii Trifonov's unfinished novel *Ischeznovenie* (Disappearance), which was conceived in the 1970s, conveys a feeling of apathy: people accept the fate of their comrades-in-arms and wait for their

17. Iurii Nagibin, *Vstan' i idi* (Get Up and Be on Your Way), *Iunost'*, 1987, No. 10, 53–83.
18. Aleksandr Tvardovskii, *Po pravu pamiati* (By Right of Memory), *Znamia*, 1987, No. 2, 3–14; *Novyi mir*, 1987, No. 3, 160–205; Sergei Antonov, *Vas'ka*, *Iunost'*, 1987, No. 3, 5–45, No. 4, 68–87.
19. Nikolai Kliuev, *Pogorel'shchina*, *Novyi mir*, 1987, No. 7, 78–100; Boris Mozhaev, *Muzhiki i baby* (Peasants and Peasant Women), *Don*, 1987, Nos. 1–3; Vasilii Belov, *Kanuny* (Eves), *Novyi mir*, 1987, No. 8, 6–81.
20. Anatolii Rybakov, *Deti Arbata* (Children of the Arbat), *Druzhba narodov*, 1987, No. 4, 3–133, No. 5, 67–192, No. 6, 23–151.
21. Iurii Trifonov, *Ischeznovenie* (Disappearance), *Druzhba narodov*, 1987, No. 1, 6–95.
22. Anna Akhmatova, *Rekviem*, *Oktiabr'*, 1987, No. 3, 130–5, *Neva*, 1987, No. 6, 74–9.
23. Iosif Gerasimov, *Stuk v dver'* (Knock at the Door), *Oktiabr'*, 1987, No. 2, 120–51; Anatolii Pristavkin, *Nochevala tuchka zolotaia* (A Golden Cloud Passed the Night), *Znamia*, 1987, No. 3, 3–79, No. 4, 25–77; Fazil' Iskander, *Staryi dom pod kiparisom* (The Old House under the Cypress Tree), *Znamia*, 1987, No. 7, 3–85.

own 'disappearance'. Written in the 1980s, Iurii Nagibin's story *Vstan' i idi* (Get Up and Be On Your Way) is impregnated with the repentance a strong son feels for the failings of his weak father. Anatolii Rybakov's novel *Deti Arbata* (Children of the Arbat) attempts to investigate history freely and calmly, while in Sergei Antonov's *Vas'ka* a comic familiarization of images of history and humankind plays an essential role in understanding the past. Apparently, writers of the 1980s are less unified in their feelings for history than their predecessors and teachers had been.

In 1987 the Second World War seemed to have lost its attraction for writers. Vasil Bykov's short novel *V tumane* (In the Fog),[24] although set, characteristically for this author, in wartime, dealt rather with the manipulation of personal attitudes and actions by social opinion ('obshchestvennoe mnenie'). For many decades war had served as the only setting in which writers probed human nature under conditions of extreme stress. The ban on the discussion of vicissitudes in pre-war and post-war times has now been lifted, and literature has begun to make use of these changed circumstances. It is instructive to examine some examples of works dealing with themes that have become the property of *belles-lettres* for the first time.

Iosif Gerasimov's long short story *Stuk v dver'* (Knock at the Door)[25] is about the deportation of Moldavians. It was written in the early 1960s in the tradition of 'thaw' prose – a tradition which is best represented in Pavel Nilin's novel *Zhestokost'* (Cruelty) of 1956. Gerasimov's story is similar to Nilin's: a young and good man takes part in the nocturnal rounding-up of people to be deported. As a novice in such affairs, he occupies an insignificant place in the hierarchy of hunters and makes the mistakes of an innocent man. His more senior comrades correct him, and, although the round-up lasts only one night, throughout the subsequent years of his life he is tormented by a gnawing sensation of guilt. Gerasimov's story, which was not published during the Khrushchev 'thaw', does not speculate about reasons for the incident. Its aim is straightforward: to point to an indefinite 'them' who had trapped good and innocent people (like the main character) in their nets.

In another long short story, *Nochevala tuchka zolotaia* (A Golden Cloud Passed the Night),[26] Anatolii Pristavkin narrates the deportation of the Chechens in 1944. The work, written in 1981, features a

24. *Druzhba narodov*, 1987, No. 7, 3–61.
25. *Oktiabr'*, 1987, No. 2, 120–51.
26. *Znamia*, 1987, No. 3, 3–79, No. 4, 25–77.

new literary approach to the painful events of a traumatic past. The common practice of the 1960s and 1970s (from Boris Balter to Iurii Trifonov) had been to portray a character who had experienced the late 1930s or the Second World War as a raw youth, and who begins to reflect on these events many years later. Such characters usually regard themselves as innocent victims or inadvertent participants. Unlike them, Pristavkin's young heroes think about what is going on around them at present and endeavour there and then to resist the unfairness of the world.

The two main characters of the story are twelve-year-old orphaned twin brothers who have experienced homelessness, hunger and any number of other horrors of the war. Briefly, the story is as follows: in order to unburden overcrowded orphanages in Moscow and the Moscow region, five hundred orphans are chosen to be sent to the Caucasus. Since only volunteers may be selected, the authorities spare no bright colours painting the Caucasus as a land of plenty. But the promised land greets the newcomers with deserted houses, trampled fields and the sound of distant shooting. At night, strange riders (Chechens who have escaped deportation) make sudden plundering raids on the Russian settlers and their newly established kolkhoz and orphanage. After one of these night forays the orphanage is razed to the ground and everyone, except for one twin, is killed.

The Soviet army has been rushed to the area ('as if it were Stalingrad') to exterminate all remaining ethnic traces: vindictive mountaineers, houses, orchards and even burial-grounds. Extremely frightened, the little survivor hides, but eventually encounters a boy of his own age who turns out to be a Chechen escaping for the second time in his life from Russian troops. The two boys become inseparable friends and eventually call themselves twin brothers.

Pristavkin's story is composed or *sdelana* (to use Boris Eikhenbaum's notorious expression) in such a fashion as to create tension through the characters' adventures and pity in response to harrowing accounts of suffering – on the part of the newcomers in the 'land of plenty' no less than of the Chechen children who, for example, are crammed into cattle vans without food or water. The story eliminates the traditional opposition between 'them' and 'us', 'enemy' and 'friend', for in the situation depicted neither 'they' (the Chechens) nor 'we' (the Russians) are considered or treated as human beings.

Another feature of the story, which is of considerable importance in fuelling the reader's sense of outrage, is the narrator's free movement backward and forward in time. In the narrative present he often runs into people who, nearly half a century ago, had destroyed the life of a minority group in the name of Stalin. Getting older, they grow quiet and pass their time in steam baths, displaying their decorations ('as well-earned as for the Battle of Stalingrad'), repeating in harsh whispers: 'We should have put them all . . . all of them against the wall. We did not finish with them *then*, that's why we have all these troubles *now*.'[27]

Four years after the events depicted in the stories of Iosif Gerasimov and Anatolii Pristavkin, in August 1948, the party gave official sanction to Trofim Denisovich Lysenko, a biologist and agronomist who, since 1925, had filled a series of government posts in biology. His theory of 'acquired characteristics' was proclaimed as a uniquely genuine, patriotic and human contribution to science. Concomitantly, the research, scientific education and agricultural practice associated with orthodox genetics were suppressed as bourgeois, imperialistic, harmful, obscure and anti-national.

Vladimir Dudintsev wrote a voluminous novel, *Belye odezhdy* (White Robes),[28] about this period. The plot is straightforward: one of the characters, the 'right hand' of the academicians Lysenko and Riadno, is sent from Moscow to a remote research centre to implement an official resolution to remove the genetic researchers working there. He observes their experiments, becomes involved in their research, appreciates its significance and allies himself to the condemned group. He fails to protect either genetics or himself from the Lysenkoists and their supporters, who include the KGB, but finds a small number of friends from different quarters of life. Eventually, having gone through all manner of misfortune, he survives to witness the discreditation of Lysenkoism.

Dudintsev's novel contains the notion, not common among Soviet writers, that the human intellect and spirit become subject to demonic possession and destruction once they transcend their accus-

27. *Znamia*, 1987, No. 4, 68. Pristavkin's story was published in March–April 1987. At the beginning of October, the magazine *Ogonek* published an extract from V. Grossman's novel *Zhizn' i sud'ba*, which was due for publication in the journal *Oktiabr'* in 1988. *Ogonek* advised its readers that the extract was abridged. In fact the published fragment has only one omission, which reads: 'It was a time when the destiny of the Kalmyks, the Crimean tatars, Balkars and Chechens was being decided. At Stalin's behest they were deported to Siberia, lost their right to remember (*pomnit'*) their land, or teach their children their mother tongues.' This omission speaks for itself and for *Ogonek* as well. This magazine, which had acquired great popularity among readers because of its boldness, nevertheless restrained itself from adding fuel to the fire after the Crimean tatar demonstrations in June–July 1987. The example, however, does show that the haste (*uskorenie*) with which magazines publish literary works is fully justified; what is permissible today may prove to be impermissible tomorrow.
28. *Neva*, 1987, No. 1, 6–112, No. 2, 62–132, No. 3, 3–77, No. 4, 18–124.

tomed sphere and lay claim to universal dominion. In *White Robes*, formerly diligent, if not outstanding, agronomists become adversaries of truth and champions of destruction, slander and falsification.

On the other hand, the novel also demands to be read as an investigation of the ways in which good will, intelligence and moral action can prevail under the extreme conditions of a pogrom. As Georgii Gatchev puts it:

> It is as if a faithful devil, the right hand, supporter and advocate of Satan, had been subverted and, obsessed with Truth, had begun slowly and steadily to dissociate himself from the malevolent host. The disobedient devil is cast out and, as a fallen devil, becomes a human being. This metamorphosis is the essence of the development of the main character in Dudintsev's novel.[29]

Dudintsev's novel abounds in anachronism. His characters are jogging in 1948, and, what is more, they are jogging in the white running shoes that only become available in the USSR some two decades later; they drink bottled milk in an age of 'milk on tap' and grill meat in gas ovens at a time when gas stoves were scarcely seen in suburban Moscow, let alone the provinces. Not until the late 1950s or even the early 1960s did people begin to wear imported clothes, and ordinary scientists to conjecture whether they would be sent abroad to an international congress. Instead of seeking an 'authentic' restoration of the period, Dudintsev has created a world very much akin to contemporary reality. His characters think, speak and act as if they were offspring of the thaw of the 1950s (and later periods), enriched by the tragic experience of preceding generations and determined not to tolerate lies in whatever disguise. As a result the novel seems to be transposed from the past to an uninterrupted, continuous present. Resistance to evil is to be presented to the reader not as 'yesterday's' or 'today's' concern only, but as a universal human principle.

29. Georgii Gatchev, 'Arsenal dobroi voli' (An Arsenal of Good Will), *Oktiabr'*, 1987, No. 8, 183–90. The motif of the devil's descent from the host is also used in another contemporary story by Nikolai Evdokimov, in which Satan is angered by the fact that his devils have become too benevolent and sends one of them to earth to learn evil from man. The devil spends time on earth, meets decent people, himself becomes kind-hearted and on returning to the host, begins to disseminate human kindness. Nikolai Evdokimov, 'Trizhdy Velichaishii ili povestvovanie o byvshem iz nebyvshego', *Druzhba narodov*, 1987, No. 7, 113–60, No. 8, 86–131, No. 9, 146–77.

A completely opposite approach to the device of moving from one time-frame to another is introduced by Andrei Bitov in his fanciful novelette, *Fotografiia Pushkina (1979–2099)* (Pushkin's Photo, 1979–2099).[30] Its protagonist, Igor Odoevtsev, is sent on a business trip to the past to take Pushkin's photograph. He also takes some penicillin to save the great poet from an otherwise mortal wound. But he can do nothing to fulfil his plan, for the past was real and in full agreement with the established rules, customs and conduct of the period. Bitov's irony is directed against the presumption which is intrinsic in restructuring, remaking and correcting the past, or changing it to suit our present norms and standards. Bitov's novellete is a satirical attack on any remodelling of the past, whether it serves political or cultural imperatives. The hero's intention to return to the past to save Pushkin from death is as ridiculous and presumptuous, as, say, the 1987 intelligentsia's demand for the repeal of the 1946 decree condemning Akhmatova and Zoshchenko.

Interest in the past is not restricted to Stalin's time. A number of published works deal with the recent past, contemplating in particular the discontinuity between the periods of Khrushchev and Brezhnev. In 1987, at least three novels appeared on this topic, two of which, *Otstavshii* (Left Behind) and *Odin i odna* (A Lone Man and a Lone Woman), were written by the highly regarded writer Vladimir Makanin;[31] the third, *Pashkov dom* (The Pashkov Home), was written by Nikolai Shmelev, then an unknown.[32]

The theme of *Left Behind* is the reaction of young people of the early 1960s to the unmasking of the personality cult and to rehabilitations of the unlawfully accused. They feel the need to prostrate themselves before Stalin's victims and even to sacrifice themselves for them. Overwhelmed by the sudden freedom to talk openly about the country's past, they make impulsive and hasty decisions about their future. The novel also depicts a tiny layer of that generation which lives through this period, seemingly unaffected by it. It is they who eventually benefit from a maturity which allows them to see the nature of the times more clearly.

---

30. *Znamia*, 1987, No. 1, 98–120.
31. *Znamia*, 1987, No. 9, 6–59; *Oktiabr'*, 1987, No. 3, 3–116.
32. *Znamia*, 1987, No. 3, 80–139. Three months after Shmelev's novel was published in *Znamia*, *Novyi mir* (No. 6, 14–158) printed his article 'Avansy i dolgi' (Advances and Debts) on inadequacies in the Soviet economy and possible ways of overcoming its pervading backwardness. The article provoked vehement debate among Soviet intellectuals and earned the author some popularity. Nikolai Shmelev, an academician, works in the Institute of USA and Canada and is the author of more than twenty publications about international economics.

All three novels have the same leading theme: how the post-Khrushchevian period disillusioned people whose ideas and aspirations had been formed in the early 1960s. Makanin's and Shmelev's characters belong to the 'thaw' generation; they espouse hopes and listen to voices from the past which had seemed silenced once and for all. They are intoxicated with the notion of 'justice', and even more so with the heretofore undreamt-of privilege of social intercourse. In their youth the characters in all three novels had not simply lived; they had burned with enthusiasm to discuss life and to reflect on art and poetry, eternity and the recent past. What happens to them in the next thirty years? Times change, and a new selfish and acquisitive generation comes to life. Makanin's and Shmelev's characters refuse to stay in tune with this 'alien' generation and, as a result, are left in solitude. They find their cultural and intellectual refuge in books, culture and philosophy. Shmelev's hero, Aleksandr Ivanovich Gort, the last scion of an old Russian-German family dating from the eighteenth century, sees as the main purpose of his life the protection of cultural heritage. As he puts it: 'How many generations are needed to make up the deficiency which those massacres of recent decades have wrought on us, to regain the heritage of centuries, and not let it all vanish completely?'[33]

The title of Shmelev's novel, *The Pashkov Home*, refers to an eighteenth-century building which was once the private house of an aristocratic family. Now a section of the Moscow Public Library, it has become the 'home' where Gort has spent years working at his research project on 'kindness as a political instrument (a comparative study of certain Medieval doctrines)'. Submitted for publication in the mid-1970s, his manuscript is rejected on the grounds that his premises are wrong, and because, more importantly, 'Gort has not presented "our" point of view on kindness.' But the editor who deems Gort's manuscript unacceptable had been, in the 1950s, a senior lecturer at the university where Gort was working on his PhD dissertation. In 1956, at a meeting called to denounce Stalinist zealots, the editor had been unmasked as 'an informer, a slanderer, a murderer, who cast aspersions on hundreds of people innocent of any crime', expelled from the university, and threatened with a law suit. Gort alone had opposed the resolution, claiming that revenge is of no importance: 'what good comes of replacing the huge stream of people returning from Stalin's camps by a similarly large stream of people who had intially aided the imprisonment of those prisoners

33. Shmelev, *The Pashkov Home*, p. 138.

who have just acquired their liberty?'[34]

Nobody had agreed with Gort. The expelled lecturer, however, had found a post on the editorial board of a scientific publishing house, from which he continued his war against dissent from orthodoxy. It is this editor who returns Gort's manuscript, which thereafter remains in the bottom drawer of his desk.

Fortunately, by the time the journal *Znamia* printed Shmelev's novel, the question of kindness and mercy had acquired national importance.[35] For decades, people had been taught lessons of pitiless and harsh disregard for the life and well-being of others, and more or less unconsciously cultivated a disposition akin to that of the wild beast against which they had continually to be on their guard. In the early 1980s, they began to make provisions for a wider and more civilized and generous outlook towards life and human relationships. It is not impossible that Aleksandr Ivanovich Gort, who had been ahead of his time in the 1960s and had become a superfluous man in the 1970s, will finally be accepted as a righteous man in the late 1980s. In its moral attitude Shmelev's text is representative of the late 1980s, and differs markedly from the 'new prose' of the 1960s. The latter had also dealt with the past, but had treated its subject aloofly and from a distance. Hence its credo: 'In order to become an honest person, I have rid myself of the dishonest past.' The prose of the 1980s, created by those who began writing in the 1960s, considers the past to exist as part of the present. Its creed is quite different: 'We are all honest.'

---

34. Ibid., pp. 98–9.
35. Contemplation on the meaning of mercy, charity and kindness has taken place in the Soviet Union since the early 1980s and gained its peak in 1987, when Daniil Granin's article 'O miloserdii' (About Kindness) was published in *Literaturnaia gazeta*, 18 March 1987.

–7–

'Thaws' and the Visual Arts in the Soviet Union from the 1970s to 1987

PETER STUPPLES

A slow and gradual 'thaw' took place in many aspects of the visual arts after Khrushchev's de-Stalinization speech in 1956. It manifested itself in two particular developments: first, the rehabilitation of artists condemned to obscurity over the previous thirty years for a variety of reasons, and, second, the emergence of groups of artists creating, and sometimes exhibiting, work outside the three major controlling bodies of the visual arts – the Academy of Arts, the Ministry of Culture and the Union of Soviet Artists. Such work is generally known as 'unofficial art'.

Rehabilitation of an artist in the Soviet Union followed, and continued to follow until 1987, a pattern that was first established in 1956. The artist needed to be carefully selected by his sponsors. The chances of rehabilitation were less

(1) if the artist lived outside the Soviet Union after 1917. (For this reason, both Mikhail Larionov and Nataliia Goncharova were not formally rehabilitated, despite considerable interest in their work amongst art historians and museum curators, and despite parallels between contemporary Russian nationalist sentiment and Goncharova's advocacy of the rejuvenating vigour of 'Eastern' art in the future development of European painting.)

(2) if the artist produced canvases that were in any way be construed as non-representational. (Here again Goncharova and Larionov sinned with their production of 'rayist' works in 1913, and such painters as Kazimir Malevich, Il'ia Chashnik, Ivan Kliun and Vasilii Kandinsky were certainly confined to bottomless perdition, there to dwell in adamantine chains and penal fire.)

Pavel Kuznetsov and Kuz'ma Petrov-Vodkin were successfully

rehabilitated after 1956, at least in part, because they had some Socialist Realist works to their credit, never painted non-representational canvases and from the beginning threw in their lot with the Revolution.

Rehabilitation needed the support of prominent members of the hierarchies of art history, art criticism and the political establishment. Kuznetsov was supported by the liberal art historian Professor Mikhail Alpatov and later by the chief organizer of the rehabilitation programme, the professor of art history at Moscow University, Dmitrii Sarab'ianov, still an important figure in this process.[1]

In each 'rehabilitation' exhibition the organizers included works of incontrovertible Socialist Realist orthodoxy and others, such as still-lifes and landscapes, that may be stylistically unorthodox, to test the political water. If the exhibition was successful – that is, if it was not condemned in the political press – the organizers included at the next exhibition fewer Socialist Realist works, giving greater emphasis to early and stylistically innovative material, until eventually a substantially objective overview of the complete stylistic range of a particular painter was possible. The rehabilitation of Kuznetsov took the full twenty years of this period, from the first retrospective in 1956 to the appearance of Alla Rusakova's biography in 1977.[2]

For such artists as Malevich, Pavel Filonov and Kandinsky no similar campaign was attempted and, due to the foolishness of Western journalists, the limited access to their work and archives that had been granted to Western art historians was curtailed. For other painters rehabilitation began but never quite succeeded. When I visited Moscow in 1978 there were advertisements for a retrospective of the paintings of David Shterenberg, a leader of 'left' art after the Revolution, who had been charged with formalism in the late 1920s. The exhibition was difficult to find and get to. When I found the obscure building in the outer suburbs where the exhibition was supposed to be taking place, the doors were locked, venetian blinds were drawn and there was no notice of an exhibition. Advertisements in the centre of the city advertised this important event of rehabilitation, but no event was actually taking place. Shterenberg is still treated with polite caution.

The development of what Igor Golomshtok has called 'unofficial

1. For example: Dmitrii Sarab'ianov, 'Zhivopis' Vladimira Tatlina: vsled iubileiu', *Iskusstvo*, 1987, No. 8, 30–6.
2. *Zasluzhennyi deiatel' iskusstv professor zhivopisi Pavel Varfolomeevich Kuznetsov: 75 let so dnia rozhdeniia, 55 let tvorcheskoi deiatel'nosti. Katalog*, Moscow, 1956; Alla Rusakova, *Pavel Kuznetsov*, Leningrad Iskusstvo, 1977.

Russian art' in the years between 1956 and 1977 has been well documented in two books, both published in the United States following major exhibitions of this trend in New York and London in 1976–7: Golomshtok and Glezer's *Unofficial Art from the Soviet Union* and Dodge and Hilton's *New Art from the Soviet Union: The Known and the Unknown*.[3]

The 'unofficial artists' fell into two broad categories: (1) those, like the Leningrad Sterligov group, who had distinct links with the condemned tradition of formalism; and (2) the majority, like the Moscow Lianozovo group of kitchen-sink expressionists (*barachnaia shkola*), who had little knowledge of the history of Russian or Western art apart from Socialist Realism, and who were driven by an innate instinct for free expression.

'Official' artists are those who are members of the Union, whose work is exhibited in public collections and approved shows, and who receive commissions from the State authorities. 'Unofficial' artists are outside these sponsoring and sponsored institutions. Yet the dividing line was not and is not always clear-cut. Most unofficial artists have been taught their craft in official institutions, some continue to work as book illustrators, theatre set and costume designers or industrial and commercial artists, but a clear majority were excluded from all legitimate means of earning a living as artists either by choice or condemnation. Though unofficial artists were seldom overtly in political opposition, their work, by its very existence, was opposed to Socialist Realism and the privileged conformism of the art establishment.

Unofficial artists, whose work incorporated a multitude of themes, fell into four broad categories:

(1) the already mentioned *barachnaia shkola*, which depicted material symbols of the crude and graceless life that constituted the lot of a majority of city dwellers in Moscow in the 1960s and 1970s,

(2) the enigmatic symbolists, perhaps the majority of unofficial artists, whose works, such as the mixed media pieces of Il'ia Kabakov, are unashamedly formalist,

(3) the Kinetic artists, such as Galina Bitt and Francesco Infante, who move between official and unofficial positions, and

(4) such non-representational painters as Lidiia Masterkova,

3. Igor Golomshtok and Aleksandr Glezer, *Unofficial Art from the Soviet Union*, London: Secker and Warburg, 1977; and N. Dodge and A. Hilton (eds.), *New Art from the Soviet Union: The Known and the Unknown*, Washington: Acropolis, 1977.

whose style and subject matter placed them outside the acceptable parameters of Soviet art.

The so-called 'Group of Eight', though their number varied over time, attempted to work within the parameters of official art in order to extend them by incorporating themes and styles that had been previously condemned. Yet eventually they were forced by circumstances to choose between opposition and cooperation. Boris Birger, for example, was expelled from the Artists' Union twice, in 1962 and 1968, whilst Nikolai Andronov became head of the monumental art section of the Moscow Branch of the Union of Artists. Nevertheless, he continued to explore a mystical form of painterly primitivism that showed little affinity with the tenets of Socialist Realism. Over the twenty-year period following 1956, the achievements of the 'Group of Eight' and the rehabilitation programme re-established the legitimacy of the non-political subject, the landscape, the still-life and portrait, and reintroduced consideration of purely painterly issues. Art was no longer confined to the sphere of representational propaganda.

The significant events over this period were the Exhibition of Young Soviet Painters at the Sixth World Festival of Youth and Students held in Moscow in 1957 (at which the *barachnaia shkola* showed paintings); a number of foreign art shows held in the city, such as the exhibition to commemorate Picasso's birthday in the same year; and the appearance amongst students and artists of coffee-table books on Western art, particularly on American abstract expressionism, which played a significant role in the development of unofficial Russian painting.

The 'Group of Eight', and other painters within the Moscow Section of the Artists' Union who were known to be experimenting outside the parameters of Socialist Realism, were persuaded by Vladimir Serov, the President of the Academy of Arts, with malice most definitely aforethought, to take part in an exhibition to commemorate the thirtieth anniversary of the Section in the Manège at the end of 1962. Serov knew that by bringing the work of the innovators directly to the attention of the arch-philistine Khrushchev, who could be guaranteed to be outraged by any painting that was not strictly representational, the innovators would be condemned and a pernicious development would be nipped in the bud. The confrontation was wholly successful and this public shaming of the artists was followed by a concerted attack in the press, in a manner reminiscent of Stalin's time. However, the 'thaw' had affected the nature of political constraint, and no direct action was taken by the authorities against the painters at the time, despite Khrushchev's threat to send the offending artists to the West and notwithstanding his declaration that the party apparatus would declare war upon them. Representatives of the arts objected to this scurrilous attack by Khrushchev and the party felt obliged to call them together in December 1962, when they were addressed by Leonid Il'ichev, the Secretary of the Central Committee of the Communist Party responsible for ideological matters. He pointed out that because people were no longer arrested for political heterodoxy there were those who thought that there were no longer any restrictions and, indeed, that it was now 'Stalinist' to defend the party line on art. This was not the case, he went on; whilst the party approved of different styles and individual approaches to artistic expression, it rejected 'peaceful co-existence' between Socialist Realism and formalist art, which reflected 'opposite class positions'.[4]

The result of this confrontation was to draw more clearly the boundary lines between official and unofficial art. In order to find patrons and a public, unofficial artists were forced to contravene one of the principal tenets of conventional Soviet political morality – to sell their paintings to foreigners and show their works abroad. Unofficial art was unknown in the Soviet Union outside an almost hermetically sealed artistic intelligentsia in the main cities, but achieved a growing reputation in London, Paris, New York and West Germany. That reputation was often based on unrepresentative work and on paintings of small dimensions, which could be transported more easily to the West, particularly in the diplomatic bags of the smaller embassies. The only outlet for unofficial artists in the Soviet Union was created by staging exhibitions in private flats or in the scientific research institutes around Moscow, where powerful pressure groups permitted a greater discretion. However, in 1972 Brezhnev issued a decree, 'On Literary and Artistic Criticism', which began a new and vigorous initiative by State agencies to reimpose tighter control over the arts. Comparative toleration was replaced by a chilling arbitrary persecution. In February 1974 Solzhenitsyn was expelled from the Soviet Union. In Leningrad the windows in the studio of the painter Evgenii Rukhin were twice smashed. Another painter, Iurii Zharkikh, was picked up by the KGB. Oskar Rabin was interrogated in Moscow. Aleksandr Melamid and Vitalii Komar were subjected to abuse and interrogation for showing their paintings privately to friends in their apartments.

In their first collective action, the unofficial artists forced a show-

4. Leonid Il'ichev, 'Tvorit' dlia naroda, vo imia Kommunizma', *Literaturnaia gazeta*, 22 December 1962.

down with the authorities by attempting to hold an open-air exhibition of their work on a piece of waste ground in Moscow on 15 September 1974, known in the folklore of unofficial art as the First Autumn Open-Air Exhibition. Fourteen artists tried to show some thirty or forty works. The exhibition was dispersed by plain-clothes police, the works crushed by bulldozers and the artists drenched with water-cannon. The foreign press were present and created such a furore that, when the artists themselves made a formal protest to the Moscow authorities, permission was given for a Second Autumn Open-Air Exhibition at Izmailovo on 29 September. Seventy artists this time showed two hundred works to an estimated 10,000 to 15,000 spectators in the space of four hours.

This was not an unqualified victory. Though an exhibition of 'Fifty Leningrad Painters' was permitted at the Gaza House of Culture on 22 December 1974, and selected unofficial artists showed their work at the Beekeeping Pavilion of the Exhibition of Economic Achievements in Moscow in February 1975, the whole movement was subjected to intense criticism in the newspapers. Three unofficial artists were committed to mental hospitals.

The majority of these young artists showed works that were negative in sentiment, dealing with violence and death. The dominant mood of the paintings and painters, and the establishment they so recklessly confronted, was one of bitterness and anger.

There was, however, no unity between the unofficial artists. As one of their number, Nikolai Vechtomov, once remarked, 'all that unites us is a lack of freedom. Our philosophies and attitudes to art are so different that if we could all show our works we would become enemies.'[5]

Alongside the suppression of unofficial art, the authorities encouraged both Jewish and non-Jewish artists to apply for permission to go abroad. In 1976 Aleksandr Glezer was allowed to take his collection of unofficial art for exhibition abroad, but without the option of returning to the Soviet Union. Many senior members of the unofficial movement, such as Ernst Neizvestnyi, Oskar Rabin and Masterkova, followed. Those who remained were reportedly drafted into the Union of Soviet Artists. The expulsion of heterodox tendencies appeared to be a more efficient way of diffusing opposition than naked repression. The unofficial art movement that had grown successfully and powerfully out of de-Stalinization was effectively destroyed by the consistent expulsion of its more dynamic members.

5. Golomshtok and Glezer, *Unofficial Art*, p. 109.

At the same time, the Union of Soviet Artists did relax the parameters of officially recognized styles. Some former unofficial artists remained within the Union to facilitate precisely this development. Nikolai Andronov's newly acquired position of power within the establishment enabled him to encourage experimentation and high technical standards in the applied arts, which have achieved considerable public success since 1985. Il'ia Kabakov, Vladimir Nemukhin and Toomas Vint were able to establish their own official reputations and set standards for others to follow. The former unofficial artists who have chosen and been allowed to stay within the system, together with a growing number of younger artists, have so successfully altered the direction of Soviet painting that Socialist Realism, in its most restrictive sense, has almost been eclipsed in the past ten years and a new generation, which adheres to what might be called 'Lyrical Positivism', dominates the journals and exhibitions. The martyrs of that struggle are the many former Soviet artists who now live on the fringes of Western artistic communities, principally in Paris and New York.

The main issue which arose out of these events of the mid-1970s was whether artists should voluntarily exclude themselves from official artistic life in order to preserve their artistic integrity, or join public organizations in order to encourage and effect changes from within – a course which would inevitably lead to the compromising of their principles. The balance of this debate was upset by other issues. The preservation of artistic integrity, come what may, entailed loss of status, loss of income, loss of access to artist's materials and loss of any opportunity to exhibit. It exposed one's principles, one's friends and oneself to powerful criticism and official antagonism and resulted in powerlessness to improve the lot, not only of oneself, but of the cause of creative freedom. To work within the system implied the opposite of all these disadvantages.

The official organ of the Academy of Arts, the Union of Soviet Artists and the Ministry of Culture – that is to say, of the artistic establishment – is the monthly journal *Iskusstvo* (Art). Until 1989 it remained an unwavering supporter of Socialist Realism. The occasional appearance in its pages of articles dedicated to even the most slightly innovative painters of the early years of this century was due to Professor Mikhail Alpatov, one of the two deputy editors until his death in 1986. No articles had ever appeared on unofficial artists or the avant-garde of the early years of the century until Sarab'ianov's article on Tatlin in 1987.[6] After 1977, however, official

6. Dmitrii Sarab'ianov, 'Zhivopis' Vladimira Tatlina', *Iskusstvo*, 1987, No. 8, 30–6.

circles began to encourage younger painters who were less firmly attached to Socialist Realism and whom I have described above as 'Lyrical Positivists'. Though their canvases are not strictly political, they nevertheless adhere to a politically approved set of narrative subjects – motherhood, collective farm life and domestic themes. Their painterly treatment is often quite free-ranging, from the urban photorealism of Nasipova to the haunting naturalism of the Armenian Akop Akopian and the remarkable lyrical washes of the Estonian painter Olav Subbi.

The Lyrical Positivists are distinguished from the Socialist Realists by their modesty and lack of narrative ostentation, but above all by their remarkable originality and freshness of painterly innovation. They also differ in manner and subject matter from the unofficial painters in their display of meticulous craftsmanship and their adherence to the representational subject. It is of some significance that many of these painters belong to vigorous non-Russian national schools in Estonia, Latvia and, in particular, Armenia. Since 1977 the Lyrical Positivists have also gathered to themselves a growing number of Russian painters. Though their work has been reported at the exhibitions of young painters in *Iskusstvo*, they have received greater coverage in the journal *Tvorchestvo* (Creativity), the 'theoretical and critical' monthly of the Union of Soviet Artists. This journal includes on its editorial board a senior founder of the Lyrical Positivist movement, Dmitrii Zhilinskii, whose work may be represented by *Voskresnyi den'* (The Day of Rest and Recreation) (1973), a remarkable recollection of Florentine prototypes. Somewhat predating the development of Lyrical Positivism is the vigorous school of Vladimir landscape painters, with their love of brilliant colour and their dominating interest in texture and the overall design of a composition, which, in the hands of Valerii Kokurin, for example, almost threatens to destroy the representational subject. The Vladimir school came together in the early 1960s and their tradition has been developed in recent years by such superb painters as Andrei Tutunov and the mystical Igor Orlov, whose work is strangely reminiscent of the 'Blue Rose' of the beginning of the century. The Vladimir painters and Tutunov are both innovative and traditional. They find support in the establishment because of their affinity to the wave of Russian nationalism and nostalgia in the contemporary Russian consciousness. Such popular sentiments have been responsible, in the sphere of more populist painting, for the overinflated reputation of Il'ia Glazunov.

Tangential to such lusty nationalism is the work of Vladimir Stozharov, Nikolai Troshin and Gelii Korzhev, whose still-lifes, in what has become known as the 'severe style', combine a nostalgia for the objects of old Russia with a remarkable compositional gift which throws those very objects into the immediate attention of the spectator. Their works evoke an aesthetic appreciation of the quality of craftsmanship and of the texture, the shape and dignity of a way of life which appreciates objects not only for their usefulness but for the pleasure in their touch and visible rightness.

In this way, during the late 1970s and early 1980s, after the defeat of unofficial art, and when the party under Brezhnev, Andropov and Chernenko attempted to reimpose the domination of Socialist Realism and the narrative subjects of war, industrial construction and the glorification of the political leadership, gifted painters, sculptors and applied artists were able to extend the parameters of the permissible by using Lyrical Positivism to celebrate the everyday and the here and now, and painters of landscape and still life were able to utilize an unassailable nationalism to justify their own explorations of colour, texture and composition. In this way a 'thaw' in style was possible during a period when restrictions on subject matter were being reimposed.

During this same period of severe reaction, 1976–85, which became most repressive in 1981–4, the spirit of the unofficial artists was maintained by a second generation of radicals, adhering to such Western fashions as Pop Art, Minimalism and Conceptualism. Their achievements were less substantial than those of the generation now largely in exile. They were able to show their work only in their apartments in the outer suburbs of Moscow or outside the city in forest clearings. The intelligentsia would be invited to their exhibitions by phone only a day or two beforehand. One group, which called itself Apt Art or Apartment Art, was characterized by a bitter sense of irony that often undermined any overt serious intention, treating life as a nonsense which deserves only mockery. A multiplicity of these anarchic groups – Collective Action, Moscow Archive of the New Art, Mukhomor and others – flourished in Moscow until 1983, when Andropov passed the law which stated that any persons using their living space 'against the interests of society' would be exiled from the capital.[7]

On 11 March 1985 Mikhail Gorbachev succeeded Chernenko as First Secretary of the Central Committee of the Communist Party. The art journals showed no change in tone, but profound changes

---

7. Margarita Tupitsyn, 'The Decade "B.C." (Before Chernenko) in Contemporary Russian Art', in the catalogue *Apt Art: Moscow Vanguard in the '80s*, ed. Norton Dodge, Mechanicsville, Maryland, 1985, p. 13.

took place in the art world almost immediately. In October 1985 an unprecedented number of artists took part in a Moscow Regional Exhibition. A wide range of media was represented – painting, sculpture, graphics and three-dimensional constructions, such as the remarkable *Vremia, prostranstvo, tsvet* (Time, Space, Colour) installation by A. Zimonenko, A. Konov, A. Mitin and V. Rafailov. Though some works were in the broad tradition of Socialist Realism, others were extensions of the 'severe style'. In discussing this exhibition, Miuda Iablonskaia emphasized two attitudes to tradition:

> Traditionalism, by confessing to a tradition, develops it. Tradition outside a context of development is imitation. Any such non-creative treatment of tradition draws attention to itself, because it gives rise to an impression of inertia, monotony and featurelessness. In these circumstances an artist presents himself, as it were, 'anonymously.' An impersonal attitude towards the object of representation draws many works close together and destroys the specific quality of individual creativity.[8]

The development of the traditions of art and the unashamed manifestation of artistic individuality, Iablonskaia went on, have led young artists to reject the ostentation, pseudoromanticism and pseudoheroism of much Socialist Realism. Socialist Realism, unrelated to the specifics of the spectator's life, and merely repeating the subjects and painterly mannerisms of the 1930s and 1940s, is already 'art history', art of the past in the present. In putting forward this criticism, Iablonskaia was not articulating a heresy but explaining the function of the current 'thaw' in bringing the Soviet Union face to face with its own reality: by channelling the tradition of Socialist Realism into subjects and manners of presentation that will return to the visual arts the quality of relevance to the present, it will be possible to maintain cultural continuity and to avoid encouraging confrontation between opposing points of view.

The unambiguous intention of publicistic art gave way at this exhibition to a richer ambiguity and variety of means of expression, particularly in the work of Lyrical Positivists such as Igor' Orlov, the 'severe' canvases of Zhilinskii and Korzhev, and the playful sculpture of Marianna Romanovskaia. This exhibition also included works which incorporated sentiments of the second generation of unofficial artists (though they did not specifically take part in the exhibition): irony, self-irony and the grotesque. It was a modest but firm declaration of a new intent, not to destroy Socialist Realism, but to undermine and reject some of its most absurd manifestations,

8. Miusa Iablonskaia, 'Problemy, razmyshleniia', *Tvorchestvo*, 1986, No. 1, 7.

such as *paradnost'* (ostentation), *melkoe bytopisatel'stvo* (the petty treatment of social themes), and above all *tipichnost'* (typicality), and to promote individual creative approaches, the specificity of the image and the richness of metaphor and ambiguity.

These tendencies were given full realization at the end of 1986 in the remarkable Seventeenth Young Artists' Exhibition held in various venues in Moscow. The selection committee included young people, art historians and sociologists. The censorship was no longer obliged to approve each piece. A professional group of exhibition designers was employed to mount the show, and separate committees, largely made up of young painters, organized relations with the media, as well as evening discussions and musical events. The exhibition had what many commentators described as a 'carnival atmosphere', using this phrase as a mark of approval or disparagement, depending on their point of view. To the disgust of the establishment, works by unofficial Conceptualist groups were also included. Unlike the Lyrical Positivists, the conceptual artists reject Socialist Realism *tout à fait*. They link their self-appointed mission to the notion of the avant-garde, ever ahead of cultural development and derisively undermining established conventions.

There were many aspects of the show that were naïve. It was reminiscent of an undergraduate review. There was a deliberate mocking of the Soviet establishment, an almost incredulous joy that, to present themselves and their work, artists were given a degree of responsibility unknown since the early years of the Revolution and a level of material support unknown since before the Revolution. The exhibits were displayed in a remarkable fashion on and among constructions reminiscent of enlarged picture frames linked together. The walls were self-consciously draped with black and white paper. Loudspeakers endlessly droned songs by Ella Fitzgerald and the Beatles. Queues stretched down Kuznetsky Most as 70,000 visited the exhibition in twenty days. The practice of 'open discussion' became established and has remained a hallmark of such exhibitions ever since, reminiscent of the 'ultra-democracy' of the period of War Communism. Artists explain their work to those interested. The public are asked to voice their opinion or fill in questionnaires. The press publishes the views of a broad cross-section of people, so that it is less possible to establish the 'official' response to any exhibition.

Tvorchestvo carried a series of such assessments of the Seventeenth Young Artists' Exhibition.[9] Many commentators reiterated the

9. 'XVII molodezhnaia', *Tvorchestvo*, 1987, No. 3, 7–13.

opinions of Iablonskaia, rejecting any 'idealization' of Soviet reality. They re-emphasized the rejection of 'typicality' and reasserted the value of a variety of personal approaches to subject and medium of expression in deepening our apprehension of the contemporary world. In a notable statement Genrikh Igitian wrote:

> [In the Soviet Union], you do not have either to be cast out and rejected, or to have a dogmatic, surface literacy that kills the living idea and the creative source. 'It is not the artistic system that gives rise to genius but opposition to the system'. The whole of world culture emphasizes these words of Gauguin [. . .]. Often, concerned with slogans about realism, gigantic, meaningless paintings force themselves onto our attention, absolutely devoid of any artistic quality.[10]

The greatest interest was shown in the work of Aleksei Sundukov. *Kogda v ocheredi* (When in a Queue) is painted in such a way that the spectator is invited to join the patient proletariat regardless of what might be for sale, and in *Beskonechnyi poezd* (The Endless Train) the spectator is assumed to be leaning against a door, looking and feeling as bored and depressed as the other passengers, locked into their own grim thoughts. Maksim Kantor's *Zal ozhidaniia* (Waiting Room), with the implication of interminable tedium, created much interest. Evgenii Dybskii's *Trevoga* (Anxiety), from a cycle of *Trevozhnoe prostranstvo* (Anxious Landscapes), gave infinite possibilities for interpretation: figures in a wasteland, fences and freedom, the black cloud of oppression, the mist of contamination issuing from a disintegrating building, creating, as one critic put it, 'a suspicious estrangement'.[11]

Those opposed to the exhibition pointed out its weaknesses. Valerii Turchin called it 'a carnival of all styles and 'isms' . . . kitsch, with all its ambiguities, pseudosignificance, qualities of the grotesque and banal (*groteskovost', poshlovatost'*).'[12]

What is at stake here is the role of a work of art. Conservatives in the Soviet Union point to the constants of Socialist Realism, as if works of art, like icons of the Orthodox Church, may relate unassailable visions of an unwavering truth. Lyrical Positivists and adherents of the 'severe style' are anxious to create convincing visions of a particular truth relevant to a contemporary moment. Whereas Socialist Realism, narrowly conceived, relates to the supreme need for political conformity, the Lyrical Positivists revive an older notion

10. Ibid., 9.
11. Ibid., Ol'ga Sviblova, 9.
12. Ibid., 11.

of art as answering the supreme need of the spirit.

The journals, however, even *Tvorchestvo* and the liberal *Dekorativnoe iskusstvo*, give no indication of the speed with which the present 'thaw' is progressing. In February 1987 an exhibition took place near the Kashirskaia Metro station in the south-east sector of the city. Half the organizers came from the Moscow Section of the Union of Soviet Artists and the other half from one of the newly formed art groups, the First Creative Society. In May the exhibition hall on Malaia Gruzinskaia, given over since 1974 to tamed members of former unofficial groups, held an exhibition entitled 'Object', with sensational works of explicit sexuality. Throughout the northern summer of 1987 new art groups and former unofficial groups came out into the open with shows by Apt Art, the Hermitage Society and the Moscow Club of Avant-Gardists. In March 1987 Zhilinskii showed a painting entitled *1937* depicting a man about to be arrested.

Whilst some old institutions continue unchanged, others are being modified by the new liberality. New groups are being created with an almost unbelievable freedom to exhibit and publicize their work and ideas. Some institutions appear to be established with the approval of the Central Committee to goad the more conservative into change. The Soviet Culture Fund, for example, supported by Gorbachev, with his wife Raisa on the board, seems to be gathering funds to rival some of the functions of the Ministry of Culture.

What are the parameters of this new 'thaw'? Will the popular involvement of a wide spectrum of the public ensure that the art produced under its umbrella does not become esoteric? The problem for experimental artists in the past was that they had no opportunity to meet and exchange views with an engaged and literate public. That seems no longer to be the case. The economic conditions under which artists exist in the Soviet Union appear to be under review. The monopoly of patronage by the Union of Soviet Artists seems under threat.

All previous 'thaws' have depended upon the political climate. The Hungarian uprising in 1956 brought an end to the gains that followed Khrushchev's de-Stalinization speech the same year. The Prague Spring of 1968 heralded the gloom of Brezhnev's autumn. The Second Open Air Show of 1974 was followed by the consistent exile of unofficial artists. Is this 'thaw' different, directed as it is from above, joined with enthusiasm by the young, openly debated between those for and against, with many taking a more mature position and finding words to articulate both the gains and the failures? Perhaps, *un grand peut-être*, the visual arts in the Soviet

Union are coming of age and a glittering renaissance is at hand.

A word of caution. In the West we are apt to interpret Soviet 'thaws' as good or bad, strong or weak, to the extent that they bring Soviet writers or painters towards current stylistic or content pre-occupations in the West, or to the extent that they undermine the hegemony of the Soviet establishment. Though there are those in the Soviet Union, of all generations and persuasions, who are attracted towards Western, particularly American, trends in painting, Soviet art has become a robust and vigorous movement since the late 1950s, developing its own expressive styles and significations. The 'mythical speech' or secondary sign-system of Soviet art must be seen as a commentary upon the cultural antecedents of Soviet artists. Socialist Realism remains the officially approved style, conveying polemical, political messages. Modern Soviet art, despite the vicissitudes of the 'thaws', has consistently side-stepped Socialist Realism and has begun to dismantle at least one of its tenets, *tipichnost'*. The new freedom will only attract a few to American 'Post-modernism', dominated by a sense of hopelessness, despair and violent anarchy. Western signifiers have often been used for Soviet significations. Yet Soviet art, despite persecution, is more likely to be characterized by lyricism and a positive celebration of the here and now. Whereas many Soviet artists are climbing aboard the magical ship of modernism, many others are sailing alongside in the well-trimmed barque of lyricism. It makes for a brave and colourful flotilla.

–8–

The Thaw in the Soviet Theatre in 1953–4

ROSH IRELAND

The Soviet theatre is a particularly fruitful topic to discuss in the context of the series of 'thaws' which have been observable in cultural and intellectual life in the Soviet Union since the death of Stalin. The theatre is one signal area in which impasse had been reached by the time of Stalin's death; it was a field in which there were generally acknowledged outstanding events in 1953 (connected by commentators with the influence of Georgii Malenkov),[1] and in which a distinct revival had occurred by the end of the decade, even though the dramatists of the 'thaw' period were slow in claiming their place in the new literature. As in 1953, in 1986–7 some extraordinary measures were taken and extraordinary suggestions made in respect of the theatre. Some of the myriad unofficial theatres which had come into precarious existence in the 1970s gained recognition; the 'experiment' of permitting some theatres limited autonomy indicated a relaxation of central control over the repertoire and made possible the dismissal of actors who had hitherto enjoyed security of employment; and the All-Russian Theatrical Society was transformed into the new Union of Theatrical Workers, apparently with the objective of establishing an organization which would be a counterweight to the Ministry of Culture at a national level. As a consequence, expectations in the years 1986–7 included a theatrical boom and even the possibility of the return of private theatres.

As in many of the areas subject to change in the Soviet Union at present, it makes sense to go back to the first 'thaw' of 1953–4 and to look at the sequence of events in those remote years in order to discover whether the agenda of 1986–7 was connected with earlier discussions. One is particularly encouraged to do so when one notes

1. E. R. Frankel, *'Novy mir': A Case Study in the Politics of Literature 1952–1958*, Cambridge: Cambridge University Press, 1981, pp. 29 and 67.

certain parallelisms: whereas in 1954 a theatre had been named after Maiakovskii, in 1987 a public suggestion was made to name a theatre after his most notable collaborator, Meierkhol'd.[2]

In October 1953 the Fourteenth Plenum of the Board of the Union of Soviet Writers took place. It was devoted to problems of drama and canvassed three central problems: the damage caused by adherence to the (by then notorious) *teoriia bezkonfliktnosti* (no-conflict theory), notably in creating too egregious a gap between the version of life displayed on the stage and its real counterpart; the concomitant problem of developing in drama a better presentation of conflict and character; and the need to create conditions favouring drama in the writers' organizations, the Ministry of Culture, and the theatres.[3]

The two theatre productions which were to have particular resonance followed in December and February. Maiakovskii's *Bania* (The Bath-house) at the Satire Theatre had its first performance on 5 December. The revival of Maiakovskii's drama was one of the outstanding events of 1953–4: *The Bath-house* had thirty full houses in its first four months and seems to have occasioned the first complaints from visitors to the capital that tickets were unobtainable – long before the Moscow theatre 'boom' of the 1960s and 1970s. Leonid Zorin's *Gosti* (Guests) opened at the Leningrad Bol'shoi Dramatic Theatre on 24 February. It was published in the February issue of the journal *Teatr* (Theatre), which came out after a delay of two months, twice the average delay for the journal in those years.

In June 1954, Vladimir Ermilov published an article in *Pravda* in which he attacked four plays, comparing them with Vladimir Pomerantsev's article on sincerity in literature, which had appeared in the December 1953 issue of *Novyi mir*. The four plays were Anatolii Mariengof's *Naslednyi prints* (The Crown Prince), I. Gorodetskii's *Deiatel'* (Public Figure), Anatolii Surov's *Poriadochnye liudi* (Decent People) and *Guests*.[4]

Relatively few plays in those years achieved publication. Most were distributed in steklograph form. The critic Tamara Trifonova complained at the time about the limited distribution of plays in this manner, since it conferred on them only the status of manuscripts and, by restricting the number of people with access to them,

2. The suggestion was made by Valentin Pluchek, *Teatr*, 1987, No. 4, 45.
3. *Literaturnaia gazeta* 22, 24, 27 and 29 October 1953. Also 'Za vysokoe masterstvo dramaturgii', *Teatr*, 1954, No. 1, 118–34.
4. V. Ermilov, 'Za sotsrealizm', *Pravda*, 3 June 1954.

ensured that few were aware of cuts, changes and other distortions of the text in production; she commented especially on the new policy of 1953 which saw the publication of no more than twenty plays in central journals in that year.[5] (As a result of such restrictions on distribution, of the notorious plays of 1953–4 only *Guests* has been available to this commentator. Nor is it a straightforward task to determine from later sources where and when the controversial plays were staged. *Guests* was produced at the Bol'shoi Dramatic Theatre in Leningrad and was rehearsed by Andrei Lobanov at the Ermolova Theatre in Moscow, but the play is absent from the repertoire of the former and does not appear in the *Theatrical Encyclopaedia's* summary of the contemporary plays staged by the Ermolova.)[6]

Then as now, there were two sides to the problems of the theatre: the repertoire and the theatre itself. In 1953–4 it was the problem of the repertoire which achieved publicity. The application of the 'no-conflict' theory and a concentration on modern plays had emptied the theatres, creating a crisis. A strong comment by the dramatist Mikhail Roshchin on the situation in theatre in 1986 seems curiously apposite for the earlier period:

> Unfortunately, [. . .] the situation in the 'Kingdom of Denmark' of our theatre is such that the *specifics* of the work of the dramatist are of interest to very few. They all clamour, 'Give us a quality play!' Yet they all stage any old thing which has some topical connection. Hence our theatres are full of pot-boilers and ephemeral pieces. The lowering of artistic standards; a primitive interpretation and a profanation of the notion of the positive, together with an overwhelming terror of adding a little of the negative; a substitution of ersatz-art and ersatz-creativity for real theatre art and real creativity; contempt for the dramatist as an individual, which stems from a desire 'not to rock the boat' and to have a middle-of-the-road play or stage version in preference to risky artistic experiments – all this and many other things destroy the desire to be oneself, and teach or direct people (above all young dramatists) to go no further than the accepted, mass-produced plays that our masters require.[7]

What achieved publicity in 1986 was the problem of the theatre and its organization; hence the 'experiment' referred to above. However, the problems caused by the establishment in the early 1930s of permanent theatre troupes (*statsionarnye teatry*) were being

5. T. Trifonova, 'Zametki o p'esakh 1953 goda', *Teatr*, 1954, No. 4, 49–50.
6. *Teatral'naia entsiklopediia*, Moscow: Sovetskaia entsiklopediia, Vol. 1, 1961, p. 639, and vol. 3, 1964, p. 947.
7. *Teatr*, 1986, No. 2, 124.

discussed in the earlier period. The inbuilt rigidity of the system made it impossible for theatres to change or increase their troupes of actors: the Kemerovo Theatre was reported to have on its strength eight aging actresses of similar professional profile. This stability meant that actors were in a position virtually to dictate to directors, while directors, moving from one provincial theatre to another and isolated from new developments (they were discouraged from contact with one another and from making visits to Moscow), slipped inexorably down the hierarchy.[8] There existed, nevertheless, the notorious *akterskaia birzha* (actors' employment exchange), which in 1953 was described in these terms: 'Each year there gather in Moscow those actors and directors who, through whatever conflicts and breakdowns in the system, find themselves unemployed. There they fill the corridors of some institution or club. This year, the oil industry workers' club was chosen as the meeting place.'[9] During discussion of the 'experiment' in 1986, concern was expressed that this unofficial employment exchange for the profession might be revived. It reappeared, with official approval, in 1988.

The theatre troupes, despite their strength in dealing with virtually itinerant directors, were dependent in respect of the repertoire on the central organs through which plays were distributed. This dependence was aggravated by the absence of literary departments in theatres at regional (*oblast'*) and territorial (*krai*) levels. The arbitrary control of local party and government organs over the repertoire of theatres was also complained of in the 1950s: 'In our republics it still happens that, when one of the VIPs says that he did not like something in a play, the Directorate of the Affairs of the Arts (*Upravleni po delam iskusstv*) and the theatre capitulate. They say it could lead to trouble. Each one of them hangs on to his desk and chair so hard that one might think they were afraid of being sacked.'[10]

The solutions suggested at that time are identical with two of the principal proposals that were given effect in the 1986–7 period: the proposal that the studio approach in all of its aspects be revived, and that theatres be given the freedom to manage their companies as they think best.[11]

The reforms introduced by the Ministry of Culture in the 1950s addressed problems of presentation. Theatres were required to publish, and observe, starting and finishing times for performances;

8. P. Vasil'ev, 'Glavnyi rezhisser pokidaet teatr', *Teatr*, 1953, No. 9, 59–67.
9. A. Volgin, 'Ne sluzhba, a priviazannost'', *Teatr*, 1953, No. 12, 141–6.
10. Ibid., 88.
11. V. Danilov, 'Staraia sistema', *Teatr*, 1954, No. 8, 88.

to present their best productions with their strongest casts on Sundays and holidays; and to cut interval times, speed up cloak-room service and improve buffet service. Current productions were to remain under surveillance by the directors responsible for them.[12]

The door to the interesting productions of the period was opened by Malenkov with his call for a revival of satire – for modern Gogols and Shchedrins – at the Nineteenth Party Congress in 1952. Nikolai Akimov used that speech to justify his production of Mikhail Saltykov-Shchedrin's *Teni* (Shadows) at the Novyi Theatre in Leningrad in December 1952. Akimov was at liberty to reconstruct a play which had been attempted on the stage only once or twice before and therefore enjoyed, as director, greater freedom in casting than usual. Contemporary comment emphasized that it was difficult to perceive where vaudeville ended and tragedy began.[13] There followed a series of such productions of nineteenth-century satirical comedies, often with Moscow following Leningrad. All of them were noted at the time as being outstanding, and were praised for displaying dramatic qualities that were absent from productions of contemporary plays: the interweaving of genres, character development, inventive staging and success in conveying a generalized meaning.

Shadows was then staged by Aleksei Dikii at the Pushkin Theatre (the former Kamernyi Theatre) in Moscow. In 1954, Akimov produced Aleksandr Sukhovo-Kobylin's *Delo* (The Lawsuit) at the Leningrad Novyi Theatre, while, also in Leningrad, Georgii Tovstonogov adapted Saltykov-Shchedrin's *Pompadury i Pompadurshi* (Pompadours) for the Comedy Theatre, following that with *Smert' Pazukhina* (The Death of Pazukhin) at the Bol'shoi Dramatic Theatre in 1955.

It is notable that, although all these plays have a civil service milieu, military elements were prominent in the sets and effects used in production. Emphasis was often placed on the uniform as a motif. A vast civil service uniform might form a backdrop, or the curtain might open on an empty uniform sitting in a chair; green walls and mahogany furniture might repeat uniform colours or drum and fife music outside impose its rhythm on the characters. Given this emphasis, it is not hard to imagine that actors and audiences alike tacitly imputed to the spectacle a high degree of contemporary relevance.

12. 'V glavnom upravlenii po delam iskusstv Ministerstva kul'tury SSSR', *Teatr*, 1954, No. 3, 146.
13. N. P. Akimov, *Teatral'noe nasledie*, Vol. 2, Moscow: Iskusstvo, 1978, pp. 190–202. V. Metal'nikov, 'Rozhdenia shchedrinskogo spektaklia', *Teatr*, 1953, No. 5, 90–7.

Once the acceptability of political and social satire written seventy-five years ago had been established, the theatre was able to move on to satire no more than twenty-five years old. The reappearance of Maiakovskii's *Bath-house* at the Satire Theatre in Moscow had also been prepared for by official encouragement of experiment and novelty in staging,[14] by work at the Satire on plays outside the official tradition,[15] by the Maiakovskii jubilee, which was to bring the dramatist's name back into prominence and to lead to the renaming of the Moscow Drama Theatre in 1954, and by the appearance of excerpts from his plays on the variety stage.[16] Once Maiakovskii had been re-established on the stage, the way was open for Evgenii Shvarts, Mikhail Bulgakov and Nikolai Erdman.

The challenge which was presented to the theatre in the mid-1950s was formulated by one contemporary as follows: 'We long for the return of lyricism, tenderness and sadness in our plays and of sincerity (*zadushevnost'*) in human relationships.'[17] For this order to be fulfilled, of course, the theatre was to wait until Aleksandr Vampilov's plays reached the stage a quarter of a century later. However, dramatists did turn away from ideologically sound, 'big' questions and positive characters to plays on the family and on the frictions of everyday life.[18] Plays on contemporary themes were described as differing from those of previous years in that they did attempt such topics as slander, officials who turn a blind eye to facts (*ochkovtiratel'stvo*), demagogy, time-serving and unscrupulous factory managers.[19] These themes were, of course, well within the bounds set for social criticism in a period of 'thaw'. On the positive side, the critic Dmitrii Shcheglov perceived that a move had been made away from descriptive pieces towards character, and especially towards the study of character in unusual circumstances.[20]

Critics attempting to use the milder political climate to encourage a more radical approach by dramatists to their subject matter saw them as holding off or failing to push their chosen topics to a logical end. They pointed out that often it was impossible to discern the views of a character, since no adequate biography was given. To provide a career record for characters has not ceased to be a problem

14. 'Pravda i dolg teatra', *Pravda*, 27 November 1953.
15. N. Petrov, *Vstrechi s dramaturgami*, Moscow: Iskusstvo, 1957, p. 178.
16. 'Dramaturgiia Maiakovskogo na estrade', *Teatr*, 1954, No. 3, 154–5.
17. Dm. Shcheglov, 'Novatorstvo i inertsiia formy', *Teatr*, 1954, No. 8, 72.
18. 'O kritike', *Teatr*, 1954, No. 4, 45.
19. Vl. Sappak, 'Zamysel obiazyvaet', *Teatr*, 1954, No. 3, 93–102.
20. Dm. Shcheglov, 'Priroda konflikta i masterstvo dramaturga', *Teatr*, 1954, No. 3, 118.

for dramatists, who continue to be vague in that area. Progressive critics also complained that social conflict was frequently touched on, but rarely dealt with: 'we often use as a substitute for conflict of ideas an external difference between bad and good characters, where we should, through character, uncover and reflect *social contradictions.*' They saw dramatists as afraid of making use of details lest they be accused of naturalism, and subject to their 'internal censor' who deprived them of 'the courage to think their own ideas through'.[21]

Perhaps the fault for which the 'vicious' plays of 1953–4 were attacked lay precisely in the ability of their authors to think their subjects through in the manner sought by the critics. It may also be, however, that the plays themselves were not of a high standard as plays. Mariengof's *Crown Prince* was described as a 'panopticon of misfits', a play which a group of spoilt youngsters fill with their trivial clashes and bickering. Virta's *Gibel' Pompeeva* (The Destruction of Pompeii), which occurred in some lists of plays under official disapproval, clearly contained the conflict required, since Pogodin described it as a play in which conflict was taken to an extreme.[22] It and Gorodetskii's *Public Figure* upset the approved balance between positive and negative characters: 'The scheme of relationships among the characters in them is arranged so that good Soviet people in conflict with bureaucrats and careerists appear helpless, are presented as stupid and fail to recognize blatant villainy.' In effect, the plays seem to have followed the model of *Guests*, which was notorious because it had been published and because the journal had been made to admit its mistake.[23]

In terms of what was possible in 1953, Zorin achieved a great deal. He took as his central figure a bureaucrat evidently from the central *nomenklatura*, hinted at his having been a procurator in the mid-1930s, and then involved him in the sacking of a lawyer who looked like mounting too good a defence in a case in which the position of a high flier in the regional bureaucracy was threatened. The arrogance of the central figure's treatment of the lawyer, premised on the requirement that the 'honour of the uniform' be preserved, is reinforced by his arrogance toward his family. As a consequence, he suffers isolation and expulsion from his father's house, the symbolic home of the Revolution. Zorin concedes to orthodoxy the final line (*'Pravda* has a big article about the case in

21. Sappak, 'Zamysel obiazyvaet', 102.
22. 'Za vysokoe masterstvo dramaturgii', *Teatr*, 1954, No. 1, 121.
23. 'Glavnaia zabota dramaturga', *Teatr*, 1954, No. 6, 51–2.

today's edition'), leaving society on the side of the oppressed. *Guests* succeeds because it concentrates on the political clash in the confined space of the family, so intensifying it, and because the elementary symbolism of the title carries the implication that the bureaucracy trained by Stalin is a transient and unwelcome phenomenon in the history of the state.

While the outstanding pieces published during the greater 'thaw' of 1956 are reappearing in the 1980s, one looks in vain for any reference to the plays of 1953–4. One is led to the surmise that the key factor here is technical quality. If one looks at the plays of recent years which might be regarded as comparable with them – Rozov's *Gnezdo Glukharia* (The Nest of the Woodgrouse) and Radzinskii's *Sportivnye igry 1980 goda* (The Games of 1980), for example – one finds the themes to be very similar. The dramatist is still constrained in reporting the biography of his characters. Sometimes such forced constraint is exploited as the basis for subversive hints. There has been, however, an enormous step forward in the degree of sophistication of play construction – in the interweaving of public and private plots, the balancing and doubling of characters, the operation of the play at several levels and the use of symbolic elements. The relative crudity of the earlier plays is too great a handicap when the expectations of a modern audience are taken into consideration.

–9–

1940: Not So Much a Thaw – More a Change in the Air

AMANDA METCALF AND JANET NEVILLE

If one were to plot on a graph a 'profile of Soviet literature' for the 1930s and up until the beginning of the Second World War – an admittedly subjective and impressionistic profile, based on a general idea of which were the 'good years' and which the 'bad' from the point of view of good works published or staged – there would probably be a gap in the line. Beginning fairly low in 1930, the heyday of the Russian Association of Proletarian Writers (RAPP), the line would take a sudden swing upwards following the dissolution of RAPP in 1932, run along a plateau until about eighteen months after the Writers' Union congress in 1934, and then take a sudden nose-dive at the beginning of 1936, when the literary world, like the rest of Soviet society, began to feel the pinch of the purge days. The lowest point would be reached in 1937, when the joy with which the journals and publishing houses hailed the 100th anniversary of Pushkin's death was only partly due to their love of the 'great Russian poet'. They were also, no doubt, delighted to have an undisputed, uncontroversial and already safely long-deceased subject with which to fill their norm of pages for the year. The theatre, meanwhile, was being levelled out to a set of clones of the two major theatres, and writers in general were staying as safe as possible, turning to translation for survival if they feared the consequences of original creation. In 1938 the graph would continue at the same low level – but thereafter the imaginary line peters out.

As a rule, the Soviet general histories of literature, journals or the theatre contain a chapter on the 'thirties' (with very few concrete examples later than 1938), followed by a chapter on the war years (beginning, of course, in 1941). It is a well-established fact that the beginning of the war marked a time of some relaxation in Soviet literature. A much wider variety of works became acceptable, as long as the criterion of supporting the war effort was adhered to.

One might, therefore, expect the graph line to continue at a uniformly low elevation from the years 1937–8 to the outbreak of war in mid-1941. The purpose of this paper is to show that such an assumption would be a mistake; that there should, in fact, be a small peak in the middle of this low-lying plain, covering a period from some time in late 1939 to September 1940. We have at the moment no explanation of the downhill slide which followed, but hope at least to prove that there is a question here which is worth asking.

The progress of Soviet literature during the late 1930s is demonstrated with particular clarity in the theatre, if only because it is often easier to chart the 'life' of a play on the stage than of a book once it is published. If the three years following January 1936 constituted a very low period for the theatre, with plays being removed at the last minute and various theatres being closed or merged, then, by early 1939, a reaction was beginning to set in.

Complaints are usually the first signs of a thaw, and at a drama conference in January 1939 complaints were expressed about the low standards of the theatre.[1] Later, in April of that year, Aleksandr Fadeev, addressing a meeting of the Writers' Union on the tasks of Soviet literature, said that although the Moscow Arts Theatre was undoubtedly the best of the Soviet theatres, its style should not be the only possible one in a Soviet context, and that there existed in the theatre a need for such things as satire, the grotesque and fantasy.[2]

During 1939 the 'Komitet po delam iskusstv' (Committee on Artistic Affairs), which had been running the theatre world since 1936, and which was always a convenient scapegoat if only because of its manifest inefficiency, also came in for much criticism. On this occasion it was being asked to provide better, stronger guidance.[3] The original 1936 head, Platon Kerzhentsev, had been replaced during 1938 by Mikhail Khrapchenko. The new head presumably took the hint, because in September 1939 the Committee acquired an 'Artistic Council' with sections covering music, art and theatre/drama – the latter including directors such as Vladimir Nemirovich-Danchenko and Solomon Mikhoels, playwrights such as Konstantin Trenev, Nikolai Pogodin and Aleksei Tolstoi, and even

1. See B. A. Nazarov and O. V. Gridneva, 'K voprosu ob otstavanii dramaturgii i teatra', *Voprosy filosofii*, 1956, No. 5, 89. This article cites a reference (unattributed) to 'the theory, harmful to art, which justifies the low quality of a play by the importance of the theme it addresses'. (From *Sovetskoe iskusstvo*, 1939, No. 12.)
2. 'Doklad tov. A. Fadeeva', *Literaturnaia gazeta*, 20 April 1939, 2.
3. Nazarov and Gridneva, 'K voprosu ob otstavanii . . .' *Voprosy filosofii*, 1956, No. 5, pp. 89–90.

an actor, Boris Shchukin.[4] Presumably the idea was to defuse criticism of the Committee as a nest of administrators, divorced from the realities of the theatre. At any rate, it seems to have been a step in the right direction, and may have been the cause of the subsequent opening of one or two new theatres in 1940 – a change from the history of closures and amalgamations which had prevailed for the preceding few years.[5]

Starting from the second half of 1939, various unexpected and interesting items rose to the surface of Soviet literature. They give some idea of why this would prove a difficult and embarrassing time for the Soviet writers of general literary histories to summarize in a few paragraphs. The examples given below are in no particular order of chronology or importance, but one may as well start at the beginning of the alphabet – with Anna Akhmatova.

In 1940, after a long drought, a few of Akhmatova's poems began to appear in journals. In the early summer a collection of various old and new works under the title *Iz shesti knig* (From Six Books) was published. This was reviewed quite favourably in the summer by the critic Viktor Pertsov, who acknowledged the poet's mastery, while noting (rather than attacking) her irrelevance to the contemporary world.[6] The book was, however, withdrawn from sale a few months later (certainly before November 1940).[7] In the meantime, though, there had apparently been a move to recommend Akhmatova for the poetry award in the first round of the newly established Stalin prizes.[8]

From A to Z is closer in Russian than in English, and from Akhmatova to Zoshchenko is hardly any distance at all, at least as far as the level of official approval is concerned. Zoshchenko, however, was apparently not as lucky as Akhmatova on this occasion. Collections of stories promised by publishing houses in Moscow and

4. *Teatral'naia entsiklopediia*, Vol. 3, Moscow: Sovetskaia entsiklopediia, 1964, p. 166.
5. For example, the variety theatre 'Os'minog' (Octopus), the opening of which is mentioned in *Literary Gazette* in June ('Novyi estradnyi teatr"Os'minog"', *Literaturnaia gazeta*, 26 June 1940, 6) and the Molodoi Teatr (Young Theatre) which opened in the autumn ('Molodoi Teatr', *Literaturnaia Gazeta*, 8 Sept. 1940, 5).
6. 'Chitaia Akhmatovu', *Literaturnaia gazeta*, 10 July 1940, 3.
7. See Amanda Haight, *Anna Akhmatova: A Poetic Pilgrimage*, New York and London: Oxford University Press, 1976, p. 112.
8. See the comment by A. Surkov in his speech at the discussion on Maiakovskii (published in *Literary Gazette* during November and December 1940): '. . . the discussion ought to have begun with a clarification of the political significance of such phenomena as the attempt to put forward Anna Akhmatova as a candidate for the Stalin Prize for poetry, or the assertion by the Leningrad critic Grinberg that this . . . poetess is the only one after Maiakovskii who expresses the feeling of the time' (*Literaturnaia gazeta*, 1 December 1940, 5.)

Leningrad for both 1940 and 1941 did not appear.[9] None of these collections is mentioned in the Zoshchenko bibliography in the *Kratkaia literaturnaia entsiklopediia* (The Short Literary Encyclopedia), which usually does mention any edition which appears in the middle of a long silence, although it may not mention every edition in the better years.

Moreover, Zoshchenko's play *Opasnye sviazi* (Dangerous Liaisons/ Les liaisons dangereuses), dealing with a particularly unpleasant petty party functionary who oppresses his employees, does not seem to have reached the stage, although it was published in the Leningrad journal *Zvezda* (The Star).[10] Even the ultimate exposure of the 'hero' as a former member of the Tsarist security police did not save the play from becoming a target for attack later in the year, when targets were being sought, but the fact that it was at least published is noteworthy.[11]

The theatre offers some of the best examples of unlikely appearances and near-appearances at this time. In the realm of the classics, the return of Chekhov's *Tri sestry* (Three Sisters) is worthy of at least a passing mention. It had only appeared in two or three theatres since the Revolution, and hitherto had not been restaged in the Moscow Arts Theatre, since the passivity of Chekhov's heroes, particularly in that play, had been difficult to fit into the new times. However, since 1940 was Chekhov's eightieth anniversary year, it is probably not due solely to any change in climate that the Moscow Arts Theatre and a few others should have brought back *Three Sisters* for the occasion – albeit with an appropriate shift of emphasis towards the active and the positive, particularly in the final scene.[12]

More surprising is the brief return of Aleksandr Sukhovo-Kobylin. His satirical trilogy of plays was published as early as 1938, for the first time between the nineteenth century and 1959. In 1940 at least one book appeared about his works (the next appeared only in 1957).[13] In April, a production of the second part of the

9. See, for example, 'Knigi 1940 goda', *Literaturnaia gazeta*, 11 November 1939, 8 (a list for the Lengoslit publishing house), and 'Knigi budushchego goda', *Literaturnaia gazeta*, 8 December 1940, 1 (the plans of Moscow's Goslitizdat). In each year Zoshchenko was promised for both cities.
10. *Zvezda*, 1940, No. 2.
11. Attacks included references in the leader 'Ideinoe vospitanie sovetskogo pisatelia', *Literaturnaia gazeta*, 22 September 1940, 1.
12. See V. I. Nemirovich-Danchenko, 'Vstupitel'noe slovo pered nachalom repetitsii spektaklia "Tri sestry"', in *MKhAT v sovetskuiu epokhu*, Moscow: Iskusstvo, 1974, pp. 233–9; A. Roskin, *Tri sestry na stsene MKhAT*, Leningrad: VTO, 1946, p. 122.
13. See *Teatral'naia entsiklopediia*, Vol. 4, Moscow: Sovetskaia entsiklopediia, 1965, p. 1138.

trilogy, the anti-bureaucratic satire *Delo* (The Lawsuit) was staged at the Central Theatre of the Red Army. The length of the run is, however, unknown.

On the contemporary side, February 1940 saw the appearance of a fairy tale for adults – Evgenii Shvarts's *Ten'* (The Shadow) – the only one of the three plays which he wrote under Stalin to be produced during that period. The satire in the play ranges from specifically anti-Western to universal, but there is enough of the latter, potentially applicable within a Soviet context, for the play to be an unexpected arrival in the post-1936 climate. The idea had certainly been in Shvarts's mind since 1938, and it is therefore possible that a slight change in climate was necessary for its realization.[14] Staged by the Leningrad Comedy Theatre under Nikolai Akimov, the play was generally approved of, but this production does not appear to have continued beyond the 1940 season.

Another slightly dubious Comedy Theatre production was Vasilii Shkvarkin's *Strashnyi sud* (The Last Judgement), which displayed a rogues' gallery of bribetakers and sycophants, including the director of an unspecified Soviet institution. This play reached the stage in 1939, although it is not clear how long it lasted, and the theatre's historian says that it 'called forth a variety of opinions'.[15]

One work which nearly managed a come-back at this time was Bulgakov's play *Pushkin. Poslednie dni* (Pushkin. The Last Days), which had been originally written in 1935, with the 1937 Pushkin anniversary in mind. The project was, however, postponed after the 1936 crackdown, in which another Bulgakov play, *Mol'er* (Molière), had been among those removed in disgrace from the stage. However, June 1939 saw *Pushkin. The Last Days* finally passed by the Repertoire Committee and June 1940 produced a new contract for its production by the Moscow Arts Theatre during the 1940–1 season. In the event, the actual production date was 1943, which suggests that this play, too, was caught in whatever caused the late-1940 slide.[16]

Perhaps one of the most striking examples of the change in the air is the shift in the status of Vladimir Maiakovskii's works. Of course, since 1936 he had been compulsorily recognized as a Great Poet, and one could expect this to be reiterated *ad nauseam* in 1940, the

14. A portrait of Shvarts, by the director and artist Nikolai Akimov in 1938, includes in the background a shadowy figure in a top hat – the prototype of the Shadow.
15. M. Iankovskii, *Leningradskii teatr komedii*, Leningrad: Iskusstvo, 1968, p. 47.
16. See Ellendea Proffer, 'Alexander Pushkin (Last Days)', in *Bulgakov. Life and Work*, Ann Arbor: Ardis, 1984, pp. 445–58.

tenth anniversary of his death.[17] However, hitherto he had been regarded solely as a Great *Poet*. His plays – such as *Klop* (The Bedbug), his satire on the New Economic Policy, and the anti-bureaucratic *Bania* (The Bath-house) – had been languishing in the oblivion appropriate to such embarrassingly non-Socialist-Realist phenomena. Nonetheless, in 1940 a combination of the changed climate and the anniversary saw even the plays beginning to stir. *The Bath-house*, always the more dangerous of the pair, does not seem to have been published in 1940, but it did rate a chapter in a collection of articles about Maiakovskii which appeared in that year. The less contentious *Bedbug* did rather better – it was published in 1941.[18] What is more, it was even staged – by Aleksandr Tairov's Chamber Theatre, in Khabarovsk, in the course of an extended eastern tour in early 1940.[19] Tairov's plans (or, rather, dreams) of putting on *The Bedbug* in Moscow in 1941 came to nothing, but Leningrad did hear a radio production of the play, produced in May 1940 by one of Vsevolod Meierkhol'd's disciples, Erast Garin, with actors from the Comedy Theatre. Apparently the same group intended to follow *The Bedbug* with a similar production of *The Bath-house*, but it is unlikely that it was ever realized.[20]

Of the works listed above, some appeared on stage or in print unexpectedly, but with comparatively little trouble, while others never quite made it. Of those which did appear, most disappeared again before the end of 1940. Having considered some which sank quietly without trace, we should also look at a couple which ended with a loud explosion. In these cases, the manner of their going is probably less remarkable than the fact of their original appearance.

The first is Anatolii Glebov's play *Nachistotu* (Come Clean!). The hero of this work is a backward peasant from a rural community who returns home after many years of exile for the murder of a kolkhoz chairman. The point around which the plot revolves is whether he will decide to reassimilate into society or take revenge by sabotaging the life of the community. The play was on during 1939

17. For example, the exhaustive publication of all the speeches in the discussion on Maiakovskii and various recent books about him in *Literary Gazette* between mid-November and mid-December 1940.
18. *Teatral'naia entsiklopediia*, Vol. III, Moscow: Sovetskaia entsiklopediia, 1964, p. 80.
19. 'Kamerny i Teatr na Dal'nem Vostoke', *Literaturnaia gazeta*, 5 February 1940, 7. *The Bedbug* is later mentioned as being in preparation by the theatre for a Moscow premiere ('Nakanune novogo teatral'nogo sezona', *Literaturnaia gazeta*, 25 August 1940, 5).
20. For this production, see A. Fevral'skii, '"Klop" . . .' radiospektakl'', *Literaturnaia gazeta*, 20 May 1940, 5.

and early 1940 in the Mossovet Theatre and, according to the theatre's historian, the director had edited the stage version to make the hero somewhat more respectable than the rabidly anti-party figure of the author's original.[21] By March 1940, however, the play was under violent attack in *Literaturnaia gazeta* (Literary Gazette) as a 'harmful production', and was presumably removed thereafter. Gone but not forgotten, it was referred to in discussions later in the year, of which more below.[22]

Another work with a very similar history, but played out a few months later than Glebov's, was Leonid Leonov's *Metel'* (Snowstorm). This concerns two peasant brothers, one of whom emigrated 20 years previously, at the time of the Civil War, but now returns to his village. Meanwhile, the 'good' brother who stayed 'loyal' to the Revolution married the other's wife and has gradually become a local tyrant who oppresses his family and all those around him. He is finally rejected and leaves, in his turn, for Paris. Having been approved by the Repertoire Committee early in 1940, the play went on stage in various Moscow and provincial theatres. It had good reviews in journals such as *Teatr* (Theatre) and *Sovetskoe iskusstvo* (Soviet Art), and various other theatres planned to add it to their repertoires during the 1940–1 season.[23] However, they changed their plans when the journals changed their minds: in September 1940 *Theatre* and *Soviet Art* turned against the play and attacked it, and *Literary Gazette* joined the hunt with an article called 'A Slanderous Play', which maintained that the characters were all archaic types and that the play was lacking in really good Soviet people.[24]

In enumerating all these unlikely appearances, or near-appearances, it is not intended to suggest that every slightly unexpected publication or production of 1940 would necessarily have been rejected out of hand in the pre-1939 climate. The contention is that before mid-1939 such publications and productions would not have been attempted – the works would have remained 'in the drawer'. For some as yet unknown reason, the climate of 1940 produced a readiness to make the attempt.

One possible explanation takes into account the non-aggression

21. A. Obraztsova, *Teatr imeni Mossoveta*, Moscow: Gosudarstvennoe izdatel'stvo 'Iskusstvo', 1959, pp. 120–1. She is citing the review 'Vrednyi spektakl'', *Vechernaia Moskva*, 28 March 1940.

22. For example, O. Khvalebnova, 'Ideinoe rukovodstvo literaturoi', *Literaturnaia gazeta*, 22 September 1940, 2, and the leader 'Dramaturgiia, teatr i kritika', 27 October 1940, 1.

23. See V. A. Kobalev, *Leonid Leonov: Semenarii*, Moscow and Leningrad: Prosveshchenie, 1964, p. 32.

24. B. Fomenko, 'Klevetnicheskaia p'esa', *Literaturnaia gazeta*, 22 September 1940, 3.

pact signed by the USSR and Germany in August 1939. Suddenly, one of the mainstays of Soviet literature of the late 1930s had gone – it was no longer possible to write the works on 'defence themes' which had been becoming increasingly popular. The potential 'enemy' was now officially a good friend, and to suggest otherwise was unacceptable. It may be that all kinds of unexpected works slipped into the vacuum thus created. They may well have been greeted with relief, rather than suspicion, by publishing houses and theatres with a norm to fill and part of their material suddenly rendered obsolete.

Another factor could have been the apparent change in official policy towards the intelligentsia. The party now set out deliberately to recruit 'the best people' from the 'new Soviet intelligentsia', reversing the trend of the mid-1930s towards proletarianization of the party.[25] Moreover, as it had been the elite of the party who had fared worst in the recent purges of the late 1930s, it would not be surprising if a need were felt for some noticeable degree of relaxation to woo the white-collar sector of society back to the fold.

The end of this small and short-lived thaw is even less easy to explain, but that it did end, around September 1940, there is little doubt. Many of the case histories dealt with above have an explicit or implicit ending some time in the second half of the year, quite compatible with a crackdown during the autumn. Such an autumn frost would account very well for the various plays cited above which appeared in the 1939–40 theatrical season but never reappeared in the 1940–1 season (which, of course, began in September). Further confirmation can be found in the literary discussions of the time. While Shvarts's *Shadow*, Maiakovskii's *Bedbug* and Akhmatova's book of poems disappeared from sight with little publicity, such works as Leonov's *Snowstorm* were openly condemned and, suddenly, in September 1940, the presidium of the Writers' Union itself was in trouble.

This is a somewhat odd phenomenon: the criticism voiced during the autumn must be considered largely as 'self-criticism', since much of it went on in leaders in the *Literary Gazette* – the Writers' Union's own newspaper.[26] The charges against the Union's leadership included excessive concentration on administrative matters at

25. See T. H. Rigby, *Communist Party Membership in the U.S.S.R. 1917–1967*, Princeton: Princeton University Press, 1968, pp. 214–7.
26. The chief example is the article 'Ideinoe vospitanie sovetskogo pisatelia', *Literaturnaia gazeta*, 29 September 1940, 1, but see also footnote 27. Note that this 'self-criticism' does not seem to have been marked by any editorial change in the newspaper.

the expense of providing responsible guidance on ideological and artistic questions (presumably a general reproach for permitting the 'thaw' to occur), allowing the wrong sort of plays on the stage, permitting harmful theories to gain currency, and not listening to the party organization when it pointed out the presidium's faults. Obviously, for whatever reason, the party had decided that enough was enough.

One of the theoretical exchanges which the presidium was criticized for having allowed was, interestingly, the debate on the relative merits of form and content. Apparently, the issue had once again reared its head, despite the attacks on 'Formalism' which had been at their height in 1936. At the end of September a whole *Literary Gazette* leader was devoted to this question, which had apparently been occasionally canvassed 'in recent years'.[27] The supporters of 'form' were, of course, held to be the 'not yet unmasked representatives of the remains of the bourgeois tendency to formalism which we have already smashed', but this does not indicate the presidium's support of the other side of the argument. According to the leaders, the protagonists of pure 'content' were merely 'bad writers'. The chief fault of the presidium lay not in letting the 'wrong' side win, since both sides were wrong, but in allowing the discussion to start up again and, having started, to continue.

Another aspect of the literary scene touched on in discussions at the time bears out the suggestion of a vacuum left by the demise of the 'defence theme'. Writers were criticized for complaining of the lack of vital themes ('ostrye temy'), and for producing such plays as *The Snowstorm* in a mistaken attempt to find such themes.[28] There were, said *Literary Gazette*, plenty of suitable themes available, but it is noteworthy that all its suggestions (including the Revolution, the Civil War and the period of the first Five-Year Plan) were historical. *Literary Gazette*, too, could find no vital themes in 1940, since the most vital of all was unmentionable.

In one phase of the discussion the paper attempted to deal specifically with the problem of the treatment of The Enemy in a literary work. The Enemy was not defined, of course, being just the obligatory enemy necessary for the production of dramatic conflict in literature (this being well before the days of the 'no-conflict' theory). A distinction was drawn between those who took The Enemy so seriously that he/she/it became the focus and the aim of the whole work, and those who did not take The Enemy seriously

27. 'Soderzhanie i forma', *Literaturnaia gazeta*, 29 September 1940, 1.
28. 'Ideinoe vospitanie sovetskogo pisatelia'.

enough, creating an undesirable mood of euphoria. According to *Literary Gazette* the important thing was to be true to the Soviet cause; the correct approach to The Enemy would follow: 'the enemies are not imaginary, but are such as they have been and still are at every historical stage of the struggle for communism.' Thus, the solution to the problem of presenting The Enemy was seen as an emphasis either on historical enemies, or on the process by which Soviet life and communism *had been* established. Once again, the contemporary world of 1940 was too difficult to handle.[29]

More wide-ranging complaints followed in October 1940. There were complaints about misconceptions about the direction of the Soviet theatre; about the heroes of various plays – that they did not set a good example, but were disaffected citizens (as in Glebov's play) or prodigal sons (as in Leonov's); about the failure of literature to modify the old characters and concepts of comedy and tragedy to match the new society.[30]

In December 1940, even the literary journals, which had been more or less constantly under fire throughout the 1930s for not conducting literary criticism of appropriate quality, but had enjoyed something of a respite from such attacks during the magic year, now came suddenly under fire again and were told to refurbish their criticism sections.[31] This development coincided with the abolition of the Critics' Section of the Writers' Union, and supplies further proof of a need, perceived by the authorities, to correct some kind of adverse trend in various sectors of Soviet literary life.

Although a full explanation of this phenomenon is still to be sought, it should by now be beyond doubt that the period from mid-1939 to late 1940 had a somewhat milder micro-climate than its precursors, and also that it was separated from the wartime 'thaw' by a fairly sharp frost.

29. Ibid.
30. 'Dramaturgiia, teatr i kritika', *Literaturnaia gazeta*, 27 October 1940, 1.
31. 'O literaturnoi kritike i bibliografii', Central Committee decree, 2 December 1940, in *KPSS v rezoliutsiiakh i resheniakh s"ezdov, konferentsii i plenumov TsK*, Vol. 5, Moscow: Izdatel'stvo politicheskoi literatury, 1971, pp. 448–51.

–10–

April Thaws in the Poetry of Osip Mandel'shtam and Irina Ratushinskaia

JUDITH ARMSTRONG

Irina Ratushinskaia is one of the many Russian and Soviet writers who excite interest as much by their fate (usually suffering or exile) as by their literary output. It becomes important, therefore, to separate the art from the cause, however poignant the latter might be, and however vivid the biographical events that were the original raw material of the poetry. Thus, judged simply by artistic criteria, Marina Tsvetaeva's short, elegiac fragment on the death of her little daughter, which ends,

> Svetlaia – na sheike tonen'koi –
> Oduvanchik na steble!
> Mnoi eshche sovsem ne poniato,
> Chto ditia moe v zemle . . .[1]

(Bright and with a slender neck / A dandelion on a stalk – / I still cannot believe at all / That my own child is in the earth . . .)

and Anna Akhmatova's enormously different, long, complex and explicitly crafted *Rekviem* (Requiem) – suggested by the woman with lips blue from the cold who waited in line with Akhmatova to get food-parcels into a Leningrad prison – are both poems which, despite their profound difference of style, superbly transcend, through their art, even the numbing pain of knowing that one's children have starved. Can one say that Ratushinskaia's poetry similarly transforms the admittedly shocking experience of baseless accusations, separation from her husband, and incarceration in a labour camp? The purpose of this essay is to consider the influence on her poetry of a poet of the 1920s and 1930s, Osip Mandel'shtam, to argue that her reading of Mandel'shtam not only inspires, but

---

1. Marina Tsvetaeva, Khudozheshvennaia literatura *Sochineniia*, Vol. 1, Moscow: 1980, p. 132.

also matures her work, and to consider this effect in the light of Iurii Lotman's theory of internal communication in regard to both poetry and politics.

Ratushinskaia's story is becoming well known, thanks mainly to the efforts of such bodies as Amnesty International and International PEN to draw attention to her plight and her poetry, and to the dedication of many individuals who have worked to collect, publish and translate the poems which filtered through to the West during the time when their author was in prison.

In 1988 a volume of Ratushinskaia's verses in the original Russian became available.[2] Her work had previously appeared in three English translations: a trilingual edition published in 1985;[3] a combination of biographical information, diary excerpts and translated poems under the title *No, I'm Not Afraid* (1986)[4]; and *Beyond the Limit*, a bilingual American collection which appeared a year later.[5]

The latter two provide the details of the poet's upbringing, studies, arrest and imprisonment. Born in Kiev in 1954, she early adopted the Catholic religion of her Polish ancestors. From school she went on to study natural science and became a teacher at the Odessa Pedagogical Institute. It was at this time that, after categorizing herself as being of a scientific turn of mind, she suddenly discovered the poets of Russia's Silver Age, and also the famous, more recent quartet – the two men and the two women, the two Muscovites and the two from Leningrad – consisting of Mandel'shtam, Tsvetaeva, Pasternak and Akhmatova, and thus became aware of her love for literature and of her own embryonic talents. In 1979 she married Igor' Gerashchenko, a human rights activist; both were arrested in 1981 for demonstrating in Red Square in support of Andrei Sakharov. Irina was imprisoned for ten days, as was her husband, and her poetry was cited in the evidence against her. She was finally sentenced to seven years of hard labour in a strict regime concentration camp, to be followed by five years' exile. It was from the Bareshevo Camp that her poems were smuggled to the West. As well as being anthologized, they have appeared in many newspapers and magazines, including *The New York Review of Books* and *Cosmopolitan*. Public pressure succeeded in getting Ratushinskaia released from the so-called 'Small Zone' of Bareshevo Camp – the special

2. Irina Ratushinskaia, *Stikhi*, Chicago: Literaturnyi kur'er, 1988.
3. *Stikhi. Poems. Poèmes*, Ann Arbor: Hermitage Press, 1985.
4. Irina Ratushinskaia, *No, I'm Not Afraid*, trans. David McDuff, introduced by Joseph Brodsky, Newcastle upon Tyne: Bloodaxe Books, 1986.
5. Irina Ratushinskaia, *Beyond the Limit. Poems*, Evanston, Illinois: Northwestern University Press, 1987.

unit for female political prisoners – and at the time of this writing she and her husband were living in England.

With the growing awareness of this trickle of poetry from a woman in exile, it was inevitable that comparisons should be made between Ratushinskaia and Marina Tsvetaeva. But the evidence is that it was rather Osip Mandel'shtam whose influence over Ratushinskaia was the most significant. He is certainly the one to be singled out in relation to the theme of literary thaws.

Let us take by way of example two early poems by Mandel'shtam, both from the *Tristia* collection, written between 1916 and 1920. They begin, 'Kogda Psykheia-zhizn' spuskaetsia k teniam' (When Psyche, who is life, steps down into the shadows), and 'Ia slovo pozabyl, chto ia khotel skazat'' (I have forgotten the word that I wanted to say).[6] They are often referred to as twin poems, since both treat the same theme by means of similar classical images. Both allude to the myth of Persephone, whose mother, Demeter, goddess of corn and agriculture, was worshipped as a principle of life. The second Homeric Hymn tells how Persephone was abducted by Hades, to which Demeter responded angrily by making the earth barren. Zeus saved the world from famine by ordering Hermes to lead Persephone back to her mother, but Hades had tricked Persephone into eating pomegranate seeds, which meant that she had to return to him for one third of every year. Each year, therefore, Persephone was kept in the underworld for four months, during which the earth mourned, the sun hid, and seeds would not grow. For the remaining eight months Persephone was permitted to return above ground, and Demeter joyfully allowed the earth to be warm and fertile. It is no great intellectual feat to recognize the myth as an attempt to reconcile human beings to the rigours of winter, and comfortingly to remind them of the cyclical nature of seasonal time.

But Mandel'shtam's two poems take that notion much further. The first one certainly shows us Persephone in the Underworld, but it also introduces another female figure, who has been set the task of following Persephone down into the world of shadows to bring back from her a box containing beauty. This figure is Psyche, whose name is the Greek symbol, and word, for Thought. To atone for her transgression of daring to look on the face of her sleeping lover Cupid, when this had been specifically forbidden, Psyche had to wander around the world seeking her lost lover and performing various tasks set for her by Zeus.

6. Osip Mandel'stham, *Sobranie sochinenii* in two volumes, ed. G. P. Struve and B. A. Filipoff, Washington: Interlanguage Library Associates, 1964, Vol. 1, pp. 80–1.

In the first line of the poem, quoted above, Mandel'shtam states that she is not only thought, but life, and, later, 'soul'. As this second girl of more complex connotations follows Persephone into the netherworld, a blind swallow casts itself at her feet 'with Stygian tenderness and a green branch'. The bird presumably has come from the world above, but has lost its sight in the dark, leafless and silent forest of the underworld. It offers Psyche the only living thing there is in this 'leafless forest', while the shades 'wring their frail arms before her in awe and trouble and shy hope'.

So, amongst other things, the first of the twin poems by Mandel'-shtam speaks of spring and fertility, of life and thought, and of the human soul all being lost in a world of sadness, silence and confusing unfamiliarity.

It becomes clearer in the next poem why these thoughts preoccupied their author. The poet was working round – one critic, Peter France, has aptly likened Mandel'shtam's poetry to a web which stretches further and further, encompassing more and more in its expanding circles[7] – a delicate and poignant image, perhaps only half-comprehended at first, of the moment when he, or perhaps any poet, finds it impossible to be fertile or productive. The second poem's claim that the poet has 'forgotten what he wanted to say' links the poetic 'word' directly to the image of the swallow, for although Mandel'shtam claims to have forgotten his lines, he nevertheless creates a clearer picture of his swallow, still blind in that 'hall of shadows', but now mutilated as well, since it flies on 'clipped wings'. The swallow occurs three times in this second poem. Having returned, still with 'Stygian tenderness and a green branch', it now falls at Persephone's feet (previously it had cast itself there). It seems, in fact, that it is now dead, and, dead, becomes a bitterly appropriate image for the creative inspiration which the poet felt to be failing in him. Having 'forgotten' what he wanted to say, he sees the thought which he failed to embody return, like both Psyche and the swallow, to the palace of the shades.

Now it can also be seen that the whole poem is a subtle allusion to an upper world which has more in common with the desolate and empty underworld than we had realized. Instead of a contrast being drawn between the two, as in the original myth of Demeter and Persephone, the two worlds above and below ground now seem each to echo the other. It is true of both poems, though only stated in the second, that the Muses are grieving, Antigone has gone mad, and

---

7. Peter France, *Poets of Modern Russia*, Cambridge: Cambridge University Press, 1982, p. 100.

the poet is fearful.

Fearful of what? The second poem was written in 1920, not long before Mandel'shtam's essay 'Slovo i kul'tura' (The Word and Culture), which, as Peter France points out, provides a connecting link between the two poems[8] and also expresses more overtly Mandel'shtam's disquiet over the cultural consequences of the Revolution. In this essay Mandel'shtam states quite baldly that 'the separation of Church and State is the most significant event of our revolution,'[9] and goes on to make a more complex point which has considerable significance for today's *glasnost'* -born optimism. Referring to what he describes as a secularization more profound than that which had occurred at the time of the French Revolution, Mandel'shtam remarks that this is based, paradoxically, on a relation of 'tolerance' between Church and State. 'The isolation of the State insofar as cultural values are concerned makes it fully dependent on culture. Cultural values insure the State against the ravages of time.' 'Time,' he asserts, 'wants to devour the State.' Culture, by implication, is not so perishable. In other words, Mandel'shtam seems here (for the passage is almost as enigmatic as his poetry) to be accusing the State of attempting to appropriate the word in order to insure itself against its own ephemeral and culturally empty existence. But of this act of cultural terrorism Mandel'shtam is naturally scornful; when the State borrows or claims the word, it does so by compelling poets to celebrate and glorify its power, and this compulsion becomes a yoke of intolerable weight.

Mandel'shtam the poet is afraid, therefore, because he feels alone in his grim understanding of the fact that, far from being subordinated to political power, the word cannot be equated with, or mastered by, any 'thing' at all, not even by the object it designates. For the word is a Psyche, which does not 'designate an object but freely chooses it for its dwelling-place.'[10] The poet's duty is to preserve the life of the word, which can only be guaranteed if it has a free choice of dwelling-place. Such a choice has been provided by poets of all ages, by Pushkin, of course, but also by Catullus and Ovid in much more remote times – in the classical period that Mandel'shtam so loved. So any 'forgetting' of the word is not just the personal frustration of what we might call writer's block, but the betrayal of a sacred trust. The underworld without sound or live swallows symbolizes the life-in-death endured by poets who fear

8. Ibid., p. 103.
9. Mandel'shtam, *Sobranie sochinenii*, Vol. 2, pp. 265 ff.
10. Ibid., Vol. 2, p. 286.

that their voices will be stilled not simply by lack of inspiration, but by an all-powerful state that may intimidate them into silence.

These poems are obviously products of a fear that dared not speak its name, the symbol of the dead swallow a haunting link between the myths of antiquity and the realities of the 1920s. But at that period Mandel'shtam had not yet reached the despair that he was to endure during his last years. In 'The Word and Culture' he speaks of poetry as the 'plough that turns up time in such a way that the abyssal strata of time, its black earth, appear on the surface'. So now there is a new thematic image, that of Russia's famous black earth, whose utterance gives forth a metonymic cluster of allusions: black earth, Mother earth, fecundity both natural and spiritual. When dissatisfied or horrified by the present, mankind must seek the black virgin soil of time, still untrammelled, unsullied, and must look to the poet-ploughman to turn it up.

A resurgence of hope in the revivifying effect of the word churned up from the past (which to Mandel'shtam at least conjured up the classical era) was aroused for him both symbolically and in actuality when, in 1935, fifteen years later, he was exiled with his wife to the town of Voronezh. After nearly a year of the silence which he had prophetically dreaded in the poem 'I have forgotten the word . . . ,' the cycle of poems begun in the spring of 1935 is suddenly vigorous and full of the celebration of life. It is explicitly triggered off by the sight of the newly ploughed steppe all around the outskirts of the town. 'Chernozem' (Black Earth), a poem in the first Voronezh notebook, launches a group of poems generated by the idea of the richness of the 'abyssal stratum' of earth, turned up in practice by the ploughman and in allegory by the poet.[11] The poet's task is again insisted on; he must 'labour without tools', while the black earth itself is exhorted to keep up its courage and be 'the dark speech of silence labouring'.

Other poems in the same cycle then take up this theme, some extending to more general celebrations of spring and the month of April, others returning to the stirrings of rebirth in the earth and to Mandel'shtam's concept of the turning over of thawed earth so that the 'abyssal strata' can be brought to the light of day. Never does the poetry lose sight of this great theme – the connection, in his mind at least, between the thawed earth and the creativity of the poet. The stanzas written in May make the point quite clearly:

11. See Jennifer Baines, *Mandelstam: The Later Poetry*, New York: Cambridge University Press , 1976, pp. 112–20.

I v golose moem posle udush'ia
Zvuchit zemlia – poslednee oruzh'e –
Sukhaia vlazhnost' chernozemnykh ha.[12]

(And in my voice, when I can breathe again / The earth rings out – my last weapon – / The dry dampness of the acres of black earth.)

As Jennifer Baines comments, 'in the heavy clods of earth saturated with rain and melt-water, he sees his freedom: "Komochki vlazhnye moei zemli i voli!" (The damp lumps of my earth and liberty).'[13] The silence of the earth is like the silence that precedes creation, as the poet strains to catch the word before it slips back into Lethe. Below the surface the earth is in fermentation, belying its apparent frozen passivity; in a cheery fancy the poet suggests that the melt-water is so strong that it will even intoxicate the townspeople. With this upsurge of vitality, warmth and fecundity Mandel'shtam was able to believe that the thaw of 1935 was more than just a seasonal change.

That there are direct connections between the themes and convictions of Mandel'shtam's poetry and that of Ratushinskaia can be guessed at from the evidence of dedication and mention-by-name. The collection entitled *Beyond the Limit*, begun in June 1983 and completed in the August of the following year,[14] contains one poem to 'O. M.' and several others with unmistakable references, such as one, reminiscent of the *Tristia* poems, which begins,

Mandel'shtamovskoi lastochkoi
Padaet k serdtsu razluka . . .[15]

(Like Mandel'shtam's swallow / Parting falls to the heart).

Another poem (No. 9, p. 24) begins with these two lines:

Vot i stikhli kriki. Penelopa
Pokryvalo v storonu!

(Now the cries have died down, Penelope, / Lay aside your cloth.)

If it is true, however – and it is certainly at least arguable – that

---

12. 'Khochu sred' Stansy (ia ne khochu sred' iunoshei teplichnykh . . .), as quoted by Baines, *Mandelstam: The Later Poetry*, p. 114.
13. Ibid., p. 114.
14. Later poems have been added by the translators.
15. Ratushinskaia, *Beyond the Limit*, Poem No. 29, p. 68.

many of the earlier poems of Ratushinskaia can only be called jejune, it can just as strongly be suggested that the Mandel'shtamian themes which I have been addressing lend the gravity of literary tradition to an otherwise slight collection. There is a whole matrix of images which sets up reverberations between the one set of poems and the other, both through association – swallow, spring, April, black earth, creativity, poetry, the living world – and also through the negatives of these concepts: underworld, the stifling of freedom and of the freedom of expression, imprisonment (which Mandel'-shtam also knew) and camp life (which he did not). Thus the activation of a doubled response on the part of Ratushinskaia's readers, who are reminded of another poet standing just behind the one whom they are reading, seems to strengthen and reinforce what might otherwise appear facile.

It should be noted that Irina had discovered Mandel'shtam in 1978, when she was twenty-four. It could be said that there are already echoes of Mandel'shtam – his 'black earth' theme and the prominence of the notion of thaw – in her very earliest poems, such as 'I vot ia lechu po stupeniam' (Here I Go Flying Down the Steps), written in Kiev in 1980. This lyrical piece celebrates a day in which she, in a response which parallels the renascence of spring, 'pants with April':

> A den' do bezumiia beshenyi
> I dvor s prostyniami – vesennyi![16]

(And the day is springlike to the point of madness / And the yard with its streets is – springlike!)

However, although the general idea might be similar, no one could claim that the resemblance goes beyond that. The poem conveys great happiness, but is essentially naïve, as is a good deal of Ratushinskaia's poetry. Indeed, a first view of her *oeuvre*, judged by the Bloodaxe collection, conveys exactly that. It also has the freshness and charming spontaneity of a young, sincere, and later brave girl – but it misses the power even of the most self-indulgent poems of Marina Tsvetaeva.

However, the later poems, those written in the 'Small Zone', are the work of a poet for whom April's thaws have an entirely new meaning, amplified by both the terrible rigours of her life in prison and her sober, serious, and at the same time desperate awareness of the values she shared with other martyr-poets.

16. Ratushinskaia, *Stikhi*, p. 9.

In the poem which begins 'Est' u nashei sovesti dva ottenka' (Our conscience has two inflections), which is a delightful play on the two silent signs in Russian orthography, one 'banned', one retained, Ratushinskaia has the same understanding as Mandel'shtam of what she calls the 'double-voicedness' of silence. Silence can outwardly represent stifling and extinction; but it can also veil, as does the silence of the black earth, the turmoil of creativity:

> Pomolchi – skazhi
> Slovo – i spasi
> Sam sebia![17]

(Be silent – say / The word – and save / Yourself!)

Ratushinskaia thus sees her poetry as carrying on the 'word' cherished by Mandel'shtam; and, like him, she must compose in silence – often in the silence of solitary confinement, without even the comforting sound of the scratch of pen on paper, since her method was to write with a match on soap and then memorize the lines before washing them away.

Ratushinskaia arrived in Bareshevo on the 12 April 1983. The poems which she wrote that summer and in the following autumn and winter are stalwart, but not hopeful. Naturally, she is often terribly cold; frequently she thinks and writes nostalgically of her past. But as early as the 4th February a 'spring wind blew',

> I na vspenennoi loshadi vestovoi
> V nelepom mundyre starinnykh voin
> Promchal po merzlym poliam. [. . .]
> I po grud' v vesne proveli konei,
> I namokli vesnoi plashchi. [. . .]
> I eto byl nikakoi ne son:
> Bylo uzhe svetlo.[18]

(And on a foaming horse a courier / In the absurd uniform of ancient wars / Dashed across the frozen fields. [. . .] / And they led their steeds up to their chests in spring, / And drenched with spring their cloaks. [. . .] / And this was no dream: / It was already light.)

This perception of the passing of winter and the melting of the ice makes her shout that 'we' (a 'we' that includes her fellow inmates and friends) will 'go mad in a sorrowful spring [. . .] when the snows

17. Ratushinskaia, *Beyond the Limit*, No. 1, p. 2.
18. Ibid., No. 17, p. 44.

sigh for April.' And again she insists that it will not be just a dream: 'I vse ispolnitsia' (It will all come about).[19]

Later in the same month the urgency of hanging on to hope by remembering spring generates another poem. Ratushinskaia's inspiration leaps ahead of chronological time, and she proclaims, 'It's April and already light . . .'[20]

On the 25th April she writes the poem which begins, 'Like Mandel'shtam's swallow parting falls to the heart,' and, invoking also Pasternak and Tsvetaeva, repeats Mandel'shtam's insistence on the world's need for the word – the living, not the false, word, the word which only poets can be asked for. Yet she registers with some bitterness that so far the word has been impotent; no one's voice has yet rendered freedom, even though '*svoboda* [liberty] *is* a Russian word.'[21]

This mental affinity between Ratushinskaia and her dead mentor, and its ability to engender and, as it were, sponsor her poetry, operates even when the differences rather than the similarities of their situations are paramount. Ratushinskaia was separated from her husband during her period of greatest tribulation, whereas Mandel'shtam was able to derive enormous consolation from a wife who almost never left his side. Ratushinskaia was forced to create her own comfort from any company that she could find – mostly from her beloved co-detainees, but sometimes from almost nothing. She cannot have a dog in prison, but she can have a tame mouse, who will remind her of her husband's presence 'when the letters suddenly stop'. This mouse, she tells him, she will keep till after her term is up, and when she is released he will go too, in her secret pocket. She will share her sugar with him ('10 grams per nose'). They will make a home anywhere, 'beyond any February, in springtime.'[22]

Even with the mouse, the longing for the warmth of April remains a persistent metaphor for all the blessings that lie outside the prison walls. But a more elevating consolation can always be relied on in her spiritual friendship with Mandel'shtam. He was not afraid, she says, when he was arrested, 'lifted mid-verse into blizzard', and she was 'blessed by him' on the same frozen road, greeted by him when she arrived, and given a hand by him so that when they came to walk on 'unearth' the water of oblivion would not lap any higher

19. Ibid., No. 23, p. 56.
20. Ibid., No. 25, p. 60.
21. Ibid., No. 29, p. 68.
22. Ibid., No. 42, pp. 100–2.

than her knees.[23]

Nevertheless, the mere expression of comfort received does not necessarily make good poetry. The threads that Mandel'shtam wove, like Penelope, into a tapestry whose symbolism far outweighed its everyday value, were produced by a craft whose secrets were not really transmissible. Ratushinskaia is not steeped in the richness of classicism, as was her mentor; the resonances that are her link to him and, through him, to Greek mythology add depth without conferring greatness. Even Mandel'shtam's very earliest lyrics are crafted in such a way as to impose stern respect, bordering on reverence, in the reader. Such comparisons notwithstanding, it has to be said that the last poem of *Beyond the Limit* is complex, obscure, and superb. It talks of an evening flight, but implied is the notion of death, as the subjects of the poem ('we') spread their arms like children and are carried through dreams, recognizing those whom they have tried to remember. The poem reminds one of Mandel'shtam's insistence that Revolution breeds a return to the past, to the order and stability of classicism, to some Golden Age when harmony reigned; for the 'we' of Ratushinskaia's poems have also turned in the direction of the 'translucent memory of centuries', although, like Mandel'shtam, who turned to ancient Greece and found himself in the underworld, they have arrived elsewhere:

> My v nee svoiu zhizn' navodili, kak vstrechnoe zerkalo,
> No glaza osleplial svet nevedomykh nam beregov.
>
> V ozaren'i poleta my budem besstrashny i mudry,
> I pridut k nam krilatye zveri s nebesnykh vorot . . .
> A v kogo prevratimsia, udarivshis' ozem', nautro –
> Nam eshche ne izvestno, i stoit li znat' napered?[24]

(We have led our lives in its direction, as if to an oncoming mirror, / But the light of unknown shores has blinded our eyes./
  In the illumination of flight we shall be fearless and wise. / And winged beasts will come towards us from the heavenly gates. / But what we'll be turned into in the morning, when we hit the ground / Is still unknown to us. But must we know what's ahead?)

In this poem, the death motif is clear enough in the allusion to heaven's gates, but the 'we' of the poem are now, above all, wise and fearless, since they do not require to know what is ahead.

The calm courage of the verse is no less remarkable for the fact

23. Ibid., No. 46, p. 110.
24. Ibid., No. 47, p. 112.

that what lay ahead of its author was not death, but release – a salvation engineered by international pressure. Between that poem and the day on which Ratushinskaia was let out (the eve of the Reykjavik Summit), she was kept in a prison within the labour camp, deprived of all outside contact, had her head shaved, and was forced, later, to sign a self-incriminating statement. From coping with such experiences must have come some of the extraordinary strength that enabled her to write poems like the one on evening flight, in which she achieved a maturity and stature lacking from the bulk of her poetry. Yet the theme itself has not changed since those earlier, youthful poems. Throughout her work she persists in the assertion, 'Ia dozhivu, i vyzhivu' (I will live and survive),[25] and proclaims in the imagery of her mentor, which is for her both an end and a means, 'Ia doidu, ia doidu do aprelia!' (I will reach, I will reach April!)[26]

No one would wish to underestimate or devalue the sacrifices that, because Ratushinskaia was forced to endure them, were able to work in her poetry a maturing and deepening of expression that might otherwise have eluded her all her life. Yet it is not only these bitter experiences that have lent her the seriousness of the later poems. It was through becoming not only a reader of poetry, but also, more importantly, a rememberer of it, in the same way that, for example, Siniavskii remembered Pushkin, that Irina Ratushinskaia also became a poet.

A growth phenomenon such as this probably does not surprise us. We take for granted that one of the effects of deeply lived experience is a refinement of sensibility – so long, that is, as an opposite, brutalizing result does not occur. Guided by common-sense psychology, we assume that something will be added to the raw, undeveloped or immature psyche of the suffering subject. The Mandel'shtamian input into Ratushinskaia's creativity, however, may better be understood through a more general theory of psychic accretion put forward by one of Ratushinskaia's compatriots. An attempt to probe the reasons why there should be an effect of increase in creative force can be found in a short article by Iurii Lotman, 'O dvukh modeliakh kommunikatsii v sisteme kul'tury' (On Two Models of Communication in the System of Culture).[27]

Here Lotman suggests that the generally accepted and predomi-

25. Ibid., No. 11, p. 28.
26. Ratushinskaia, *Stikhi*, p. 151.
27. Published in *Trudy po znakovym sistemam*, Vol. 6, 1973, the essay is quoted here from an earlier version in *Soviet Semiotics: An Anthology*, ed., trans. and intro. by Daniel P. Lucid, Baltimore: Johns Hopkins University Press, 1977, pp. 99–101.

nating model of communication, originally advanced by Roman Jakobson and based on the schema 'transmitter–message–receiver' – which Lotman labels the 'I–he' model or the model of external communication – can describe only messages sent from the self into the world. External communication is constructed on the basis that a message or text is encoded by the sender, transmitted, and decoded by the receiver. Ideally, the text coincides at entrance and exit, although in practice a loss of information usually occurs. Another model, however, is required to account for the phenomenon of internal communication, which Lotman calls the 'I–I' model. In internal communication a message or text is encoded in a certain system, another code is introduced, and in this process the text is transformed, while the addresser and the receiver remain one and the same. The message or text varies at entrance and exit because an increase in information has occurred through interaction with the new code.

Internal communication operates in two cumulative stages, and thus may serve more than one purpose. In the first step the text is simply encoded in a particular system and later read off by the encoder. In this case its purpose is simply mnemonic: it serves to retain information, reminding the self of things that risk being forgotten. But if the further step of re-encoding is taken, so that the text or message is transformed, and yet retained for the transmitting self, internal communication of the inventive type takes place; its purpose is an increase in information. Thus, 'words and images are transformed into indices in the system of internal language.'[28] Lotman provides the example of Pushkin's manuscripts, where his notes are mere hieroglyphs, meaningful only to himself; but once they had reminded him of what he wanted to say, they would be transformed into new text whose information yield is far higher than that of the notes. This new text is intelligible to readers, and constitutes a message of the I–he variety. The prior process of turning jottings into poetry, on the other hand, constitutes an operation of the I–I model of communication. The combination of the two processes is, of course, a general function of all culture: 'Art is engendered in the sphere of internal speech as the antithesis to the practical speech of external messages, but oscillates historically between these poles, approaching now one, now the other.'[29]

In the Mandel'shtam–Ratushinskaia case, however, we have an illustration of internal communication that is clear, sophisticated,

28. Ibid., p. 100.
29. Ibid., p. 100.

and peculiarly Russian. Ratushinskaia's encoded memories of Mandel'shtam's poems, re-encoded so as to be constitutive of her own poetry, repeat the practices of many prison writers, including Siniavskii and Solzhenitsyn, in a way which allows the prison experience to offer a paradigm case of normal human action. Moreover, the combination of external and internal communication models, with more than usual reliance on the latter, is, in a sense, responsible for the maturing of Ratushinskaia's prison poetry. While many of the poems admittedly swing more towards the first model (that is, they convey *to us* a message *about* what it was like in Bareshevo), others, particularly those discussed in this essay, are a reworking of already held knowledge transformed into a new text. Ratushinskaia's Psyche and Penelope poems re-encode 'message 1' – not Mandel'shtam's poems themselves, but the imprint of their reception on Ratushinskaia's mind – and are then contextually displaced and re-rendered as 'message 2'.

However, this is not the only use that can be made of Lotman's communication models. The present volume of essays contains Katerina Clark's analysis of the nature of political thaws, which, she argues, are essentially recurrent phenomena. In the Soviet context, in particular, they are occasions of revaluation, when it is felt, usually most strongly by the intelligentsia, that a subjective discontent can allowably be expressed and a new direction taken. They appear, that is, to be optimistic, looking forward to a brighter future which almost seems already to be taking shape. Clark's analysis, however, shows this perspective to be an illusion. Innately retrospective and repetitive, thaws are instances of a search for points of orientation in the past; some 'canonical' aspect of an earlier period is presumed to be able to throw light on the present. Clark uses Bakhtin's argument and terminology to suggest that the present is in fact but a reworking, a 'reaccentuation' of the 'canonical' past. If D. S. Likhachev's present status as a 'guru' rests partly on the fact that he explicitly approves Dostoevskii's idealization of Pushkin, this is only one of several indications that the Petersburg myth is being revived in the present rehabilitation of writers associated with the Leningrad of the 1920s. These writers include Gumilev and, of course, Mandel'shtam.

In other words, not only is the release of Ratushinskaia one of the many thankful results of Gorbachev's thaw, but her reminiscences of Mandel'shtam are not accidental events at this particular time. Her *case* is the political aspect, her *poetry* the artistic example, of the phenomenon of internal communication, which, as Lotman explicitly says, includes 'examination of patterns'. The picture of an isolated prisoner sustaining herself by her memories of a poet of the 1920s is yoked to the image of the Soviet leadership revitalizing itself through reference to that same point in the past. Both are, or have been, engaged in a search for a model of authority – or author-ity. Both are attempting to use what Lotman calls a 'poetics of identity' in order to find a new voice ('golos') in their own variant of *glasnost'*.

–11–

In Expectation of a Thaw:
Literary Tradition as Code in
Akhmatova's *Poem Without a Hero*

DAVID WELLS

Wherever literature is subject to rigorous political control, writers make use of whatever means are at their disposal to undermine the ruling authority and to let their opinions be heard. Some writers, inevitably, prove unequal to the struggle and either conform to the dominant ideology or fade into the obscurity of non-publication. For others, however, the necessity to submit their works to censorship leads to a particular inventiveness in discovering ways to subvert it. There arises a literature of hints and allusions, an Aesopian style where what is not stated directly is as important as the overt message of the text. This phenomenon has been discussed at length in the context of Russian literature in recent works on Soviet censorship.[1] Political control, of course, rarely remains at a constant level, and writers under such a system come to expect a continual alternation between freeze and thaw. In response to a severe period of 'freeze', therefore, instead of writing solely for the desk drawer, an author might consciously choose to write in a manner calculated to guarantee publication during the next period of relative thaw, even though this was not expected to grant full freedom of expression. Through Aesopian language texts could appear in print containing matter potentially disapproved of by the state, and these would ideally be decoded by the alert future reader.

One such work, begun during a period of repression but aimed at the 'sensitive' reader of the future, is Anna Akhmatova's *Poema bez geroia* (Poem Without a Hero). This paper will consider one aspect of the subtextual message of this highly complex poem and investi-

---

1. See, for example, Lev Loseff, *On the Beneficence of Censorship: Aesopian Language in Modern Russian Literature*, Arbeiten und Texte zur Slavistik, 31, Munich: Otto Sagner, 1984; M. Dewhirst and R. Farrell (eds), *The Soviet Censorship*, Metuchen, N.J.: Scarecrow Press, 1973.

gate an Aesopian technique through which it is simultaneously revealed and concealed, namely Akhmatova's use of reference to other literary works. Before looking in detail at this characteristic of the poem, however, it will be helpful briefly to survey Akhmatova's writing career in the light of changes in political control of the arts.[2]

At the time of the Revolution Akhmatova was at the peak of her early fame. Her first books had gone through several editions, her poetry had begun to receive serious critical attention, and she was already something of a celebrity in literary and artistic circles. This success continued with the appearance of *Belaia staia* (White Flock) in the first half of 1917 and with a string of editions and re-editions of her works over the next six years. After the publication of *Anno Domini* in Petrograd in 1921 and in Berlin the following year, Akhmatova found it increasingly difficult to publish new work. Her poems nevertheless remained extremely popular, and in 1925 a large selection was published in an anthology of twentieth-century poetry. However, after this date, notwithstanding the Communist Party's relatively liberal approach to the arts during the 1920s and Bukharin's doctrine of 'anarchic competition', Akhmatova appears to have become subject to an unofficial party ban. Like several other writers who did not fulfil the new requirements of Soviet literature but who were respected and well-established, Akhmatova received a small pension from the state. She was to publish virtually no more poetry until 1940.[3]

With the consolidation of Stalinist control over literature in the late 1920s and early 1930s, there could be no question of publishing Akhmatova's relatively low-key lyrics. It was at this time that she began the serious scholarly investigation of Pushkin and the study of the history and architecture of St Petersburg. Although she never stopped writing poetry altogether, she was isolated from the audience which she had built up, and her output during this period was quite small. Some of the poems written at this time are among the best she ever wrote, although these, including the famous cycle *Rekviem* (Requiem), were mostly composed towards the end of the period, between 1936 and 1940. When in 1940 the ban against her was lifted, the volume that appeared as a result, *Iz shesti knig* (From

2. For a more detailed account of the vicissitudes of Akhmatova's literary career, see Amanda Haight, *Anna Akhmatova: A Poetic Pilgrimage*, New York and London: Oxford University Press, 1976, on which I have drawn freely in the following paragraphs. For Akhmatova's publications, see the bibliography in Anna Akhmatova, *Sochineniia*, ed. Gleb Struve and Boris Filippov, Vol. II, Washington: Inter-Language Literary Associates, 1968, pp. 437–76.
3. One poem was published in a Pushkin almanac in 1926: see Akhmatova, *Sochineniia*, Vol. 2, p. 447.

Six Books), devoted only 37 out of 327 pages to poems written after *Anno Domini*. The decision to publish *From Six Books*, however, appears not to have satisfied all levels of the party hierarchy and the volume was withdrawn after a few months.

In 1941 Akhmatova, along with many other writers, was evacuated from Leningrad to Tashkent. Here, in the relatively open atmosphere of the war years, she contributed to the national effort by writing and giving recitals of her poetry to the wounded. A volume of her poems, *Izbrannye stikhi* (Selected Poems), was published in 1943. When she returned to Leningrad in 1944, Akhmatova was appearing regularly in journals and her status seemed secure. However, Zhdanov's reimposition of strict party control over literature in 1946 rendered her once more unpublishable, and two volumes of her poetry which had been printed but not distributed were pulped.

In the years following the Zhdanov resolution Akhmatova was able to preserve a degree of official recognition as a translator, if not as a writer, though naturally the time spent on translating other people's work meant that her own original output was reduced. Shortly after the death of Stalin in 1953, Akhmatova received substantial financial support in the form of payment for her translations of Hugo, and she was permitted to attend the Second Congress of the Union of Writers in 1954. Her full rehabilitation as a poet took place after Khrushchev's secret speech in 1956. By the time of her death in 1966, three new collections of her poetry had appeared and Akhmatova had been allowed to travel twice to Western Europe, to receive an Italian literary award and an Oxford honorary doctorate.

Akhmatova took her responsibilities as a poet very seriously, and acted in the long tradition of Russian poetry, dating back to Pushkin and earlier, according to which the writer has an important part to play in social, moral and political issues. Although her early verse concentrates on the emotions caused by love, there are poems in Akhmatova's first books which address a wider range of themes, particularly in relation to the First World War. A good example of this type of poem is the prophetic 'Iiul' 1914' (July 1914).[4] By the late 1930s Akhmatova felt increasingly that she was one of the few people still able and willing to chronicle the era through which she was living and to keep alive the literary and social traditions of the past. In the introduction to the cycle *Requiem*, which describes in penetrating detail the experiences of a generation of women in the

4. Akhmatova, *Sochineniia*, Vol. 1, 2nd ed., 1967, pp. 133–4.

queues outside Stalin's prisons, Akhmatova notes with pride the duty which has fallen on her shoulders:

'Can you describe this?'
And I said,
'I can.'
Then something like a smile lit up what had once been her face.[5]

When Akhmatova wrote the poems of *Requiem*, she can have had no expectation that the cycle would be published. In order to ensure its survival, a small group of people learnt it by heart. It was obviously preferable, nevertheless, for the poems to appear in print in however mitigated a form, and an opportunity presented itself when *From Six Books* was allowed to appear in 1940. In this collection Akhmatova managed to include one poem, 'I upalo kamennoe slovo' (And the Word Fell Like a Stone),[6] which, taken out of the context of the *Requiem* cycle, appeared to refer not to an unjust sentence of imprisonment, but to a broken love affair. In several other poems published in this volume Akhmatova broaches the theme of political persecution under Stalin in a similarly veiled manner. Thus, when she describes Dante, exiled from his native city, or Cleopatra, attempting to maintain her dignity after defeat at the battle of Actium,[7] Akhmatova is at the same time drawing attention to her own insecure position.

In *Poem Without a Hero* Akhmatova continues this practice of encoding statements about past and present persecution in her work. When she began the poem in the dark days of late 1940 she must have thought that if her ideas were presented in sufficiently cryptic form it might subsequently prove possible to publish them during a period of relaxation such as that which had so recently seen the appearance of *From Six Books*. Sections of the poem were indeed published during the war years and later during the post-Stalin thaw, although conditions were not sufficiently favourable for the work to appear in the Soviet Union in its entirety during Akhmatova's lifetime.[8]

In the event, Akhmatova's project in writing *Poem Without a Hero*

5. Ibid., p. 361.
6. Ibid., p. 365–66.
7. Ibid., pp. 236, 238.
8. For the publication history of *Poem Without a Hero*, see Akhmatova, *Sochineniia*, Vol. 2, pp. 359–65; Akhmatova, *Stikhotvoreniia i poemy*, Biblioteka poeta, bol'shaia seriia, ed. Viktor Zhirmunskii, 2nd ed., Leningrad: Sovetskii pisatel', 1977, pp. 512–13. Akhmatova's introduction of increasingly sensitive material into the text of *Poem Without a Hero* after the death of Stalin deserves further study.

was to prove far more difficult than she had initially imagined. Many of her first readers found it difficult to understand, and Akhmatova continued to work on the poem for many years, partly to make it more accessible, only declaring it finished in 1962. However, although perhaps at first only readers from within Akhmatova's immediate circle were able to decipher the code, the work itself declares its cryptographic nature quite openly. Even the earliest complete version (1942) contains, for example, the following lines:

> No soznaius', chto primenila
> Simpaticheskie chernila,
> Chto zerkal'nym pis'mom pishu.[9]

(But I confess that I have used / Invisible ink, / That I am writing in mirror writing.)

Akhmatova's main subtextual purpose in *Poem Without a Hero* is not so much to continue the 'Requiem theme', though this is certainly present,[10] as to preserve the literary traditions of the early years of the century and the memory of her contemporaries in St Petersburg. The upheavals of war and revolution in the years following 1914 led inevitably to a certain discontinuity in Russian literature in which many significant achievements of the past were forgotten. This natural process was strengthened by the new Soviet policy on the arts, which tended to reject the more 'aesthetic' elements of pre-revolutionary literature and to brand them as 'decadent'. As a poet whose work was already established before the hiatus, Akhmatova felt responsible for ensuring that ideas and images from the earlier period were not altogether lost to the contemporary reader. One of the ways in which she achieves this aim is through constant reference to other literary works.

Even on the surface the extent of such allusion is striking. The numerous epigraphs to the different chapters and sections of *Poem Without a Hero* show a wide range of quotation from the writers of several centuries and cultures. The authors represented include, for example, Pushkin, Zhukovskii, Mandel'shtam, Mozart's librettist Da Ponte and T. S. Eliot. The text of '1913', the first part of the poem, contains numerous allusions to the verse of the Symbolists and on one level enters into a dialogue with them. On a structural

9. Akhmatova, *Stikhotvoreniia i poemy*, p. 439.
10. Akhmatova indirectly refers to its presence in some versions of the prose introduction to 'Reverse': see *Stikhotvoreniia i poemy*, p. 370. A passage in some versions of 'Epilogue' refers directly to the camps and to a prisoner who is the double of the narrator: see Akhmatova, *Sochineniia*, Vol. 2, pp. 130–1, lines 31–50.

plane, too, the poem is deeply dependent on other literary models. In writing it Akhmatova was highly aware of the pervasive example of Pushkin's *Evgenii Onegin* (Eugene Onegin), which she saw as the culminating point of the narrative poem genre, and struggled not to fall into imitation of it. In discussing the composition of '1913' in the second part of her poem, 'Reshka' (Reverse), Akhmatova makes several comparisons with representatives of the English Romantic tradition, referring notably to Byron, Shelley and Keats.[11] Akhmatova's contemporaries are especially well represented. Most obviously, the characters of the love-triangle which is central to '1913' are modelled on the poet Vsevolod Kniazev, the actress Ol'ga Glebova-Sudeikina and Aleksandr Blok (although their relations in real life were quite different). There are many correspondences in biography. Kniazev, for example, like the young dragoon cornet-poet in '1913', served in the army and took his own life at an early age. Akhmatova's heroine acted in the same plays as Sudeikina. There are also many direct and indirect quotations in Akhmatova's text from the works of writers of the 1910s. Compare, for example, the following:

Akhmatova	*Source*
Na ch'em serdtse 'palevyi lokon'. . .	Skol'ko raz videl palevyi lokon . . . !
(On whose heart lies a 'straw-coloured curl'. . . ?)	(How many times have I seen a straw-coloured curl . . !)
	(Kniazev)
No mne strashno: voidu sama ia Kryzhevnuiu shal' ne snimaia Ulybnus' vsem i zamolchu.	'Krasota strashna' – vam skazhut – Vy nakinete lenivo Shal' ispanskuiu na plechi.
(But I am frightened: I myself will come in / Without taking off my lace shawl. / I will smile to everyone and fall silent.)	('Beauty is terrible,' they will tell you. / You will throw your Spanish shawl lazily. / Onto your shoulders.) (Blok, 'Anne Akhmatovoi' [To Anna Akhmatova])

11. Many critics have discussed Akhmatova's dependence on other writers. Among the most important studies are: Roman Timenchik, Vladimir Toporov and T. V. Tsiv'ian, 'Akhmatova i Kuzmin', *Russian Literature*, 6(1978), No. 3, 213–305; Toporov, *Akhmatova i Blok (k probleme postroeniia poeticheskogo dialoga: 'blokovskii tekst' Akhmatovoi)*, Modern Russian Literature and Culture, Studies and Texts, No. 5, Berkeley: Berkeley Slavic Specialties, 1981; Rory Childers and Anna Lisa Crone, 'The Mandel'štam Presence in the Dedications of Poèma bez geroja', *Russian Literature*, – 51–82; L. L. Saulenko, 'Pushkinskaia traditsiia v "Poème bez geroia" Anny Akhmatovoi', *Voprosy russkoi literatury* (L'viv), 1980, No. 2, 42–50.

Kruzhevoi roniaet platochek . . .
I briullovskim manit plechom.

(She drops her lace handker-
chief. . . / And beckons with a
Briullovesque shoulder.)

Krasavitsa, kak polotno Briullova . . .
Ne popravliala alogo platochka,
Chto spolz u nei s zhemchuzhnogo
plecha.

(A beauty, like a canvas by Briullov . . .
Not adjusting her scarlet shawl / Which
has fallen from her pearl shoulders.)
(Kuzmin)[12]

An expression in Akhmatova may well have more than one origin. This is true, for example, of the words spoken by the dragoon cornet in '1913': 'Ia k smerti gotov' (I am ready for death). This phrase has several sources, including an oral statement by Mandel'shtam and Gumilev's play *Gondla* (Gondla).[13]

The allusions, frequently covert, to Kniazev, Kuzmin, Mandel'shtam and others which abound in *Poem Without a Hero* were for a long time the only way in which these poets, in many respects typical of Akhmatova's generation, and of the poetry of the 1910s and 1920s, could be represented in print, even in periods of relative thaw. Many of the people she refers to in this way were not in sympathy with the Soviet government, and had been destroyed or exiled by it. Akhmatova's work thus becomes a tribute to her colleagues, who would otherwise be forced into permanent silence.

This layer of textual reference is not, however, the only way in which these figures are restored to the reader, or at least to the reader initiated into the often labyrinthine complexities of Akhmatova's late style. *Poem Without a Hero* contains what might be called 'hidden portraits' of Akhmatova's contemporaries, independent of allusion to their work. In order to announce the existence of these encoded tributes to the attentive reader, Akhmatova uses literary reference as a signalling device. In this technique it is generally the nineteenth-century literary tradition which is evoked.

The operation of this feature of *Poem Without a Hero* will become clear from a detailed investigation of the epigraph 'Inykh uzh net, a te daleche' (Some are already dead, and the others are far away). This phrase is one of the first things to strike the reader's eye in the later redactions of the poem. It precedes an introductory prose

12. Akhmatova, *Sochineniia*, Vol. II, pp. 106, 119, 127; see Timenchik et al., 'Akhmatova i Kuzmin', pp. 224, 240; Toporov, *Akhmatova i Blok*, p. 46.
13. See Akhmatova's memoir of Mandel'shtam: *Sochineniia*, Vol. 2, p. 179; Nikolai Gumilev, *Sobranie sochinenii*, ed. Gleb Struve and Boris Filippov, Vol. 3, Washington: Victor Kamkin, 1966, p. 91: 'ia vinom blagodati / Op'ianilsia i k smerti gotov . . .' (I am drunk on the wine of grace / And am ready for death).

section, in which the author describes the poem's composition and original inspiration. By its position, this phrase can be considered a sub-title for the work, and consequently a key for its understanding. The line is taken from the last stanza of chapter eight of *Eugene Onegin*. Pushkin, concluding his novel, takes leave of his readers, and notes that those to whom he read the first chapters are by now either dead or far away. The immediate context reads:

> No te kotorym v druzhnoi vstreche
> Ia strofy pervye chital . . .
> Inykh uzh net, a te daleche,
> Kak Sadi nekogda skazal.[14]

(But [of] those to whom, as friends, / I read the first stanzas . . . / Some are already dead and the others are far away, / As Sadi once said.)

Nabokov has traced the complex literary history of the phrase 'Some are already dead, and the others are far away' in other authors as well as in Pushkin.[15] Its origins in the Persian poet Sadi are obscure. Nabokov concludes that the expression derives from a mistranslation in an unknown French version of Sadi's *Rustan* (Orchard). The first Russian rendering he mentions occurs in an 1814 poem by the little-known poet Vladimir Filimonov (1787–1858), where it takes the form: 'Druzei inykh uzh net; drugie v otdalen'e' (Some friends are already dead; others are distant).[16] In 1824 Pushkin used a similar expression as an epigraph to *Bakhchisaraiskii fontan* (The Fountain of Bakhchisarai): "Many, like myself, have visited this fountain; but some are already dead, others are wandering afar' – Sadi."[17] Here the phrase is designed to intensify the Romantic atmosphere of the poem and to add to the pathos and mysteriousness of the story of Mariia. Nabokov calls Pushkin's words an 'innocent bit of nostalgic literature in the pseudo-Oriental style of the day'. By 1827, however, they had acquired a political overlay. In a review of Russian literature of 1825 and 1826 published

14. Aleksandr Pushkin, *Polnoe sobranie sochinenii v desiati tomakh*, 3rd ed., Moscow: AN SSSR, 1962–6, Vol. 5, p. 191.
15. See Pushkin, *Eugene Onegin*, a novel in verse by Alexander Pushkin, translated from the Russian, with a commentary by Vladimir Nabokov, Vol. III, London: Routledge and Kegan Paul, 1964, pp. 245–7, on which much of my discussion of the phrase in Pushkin is based.
16. Iurii Ivask examines other possible borrowings of Pushkin from Filimonov: 'Filosof v duratskom kolpake (Vladimir Filimonov)', *Opyty*, VIII, 1957, p. 78.
17. Pushkin, *Polnoe sobranie sochinenii*, Vol. IV, p. 175. This epigraph was retained for the 1827 and 1830 editions of *The Fountain of Bakhchisarai*, although it was dropped in 1835.

in early 1827, Nikolai Polevoi included the following passage: 'I look at the circle of our friends, once lively and cheerful, and often . . . repeat with sadness the words of Sadi (or of Pushkin who gave us the words of Sadi): *Some are already dead, the others are wandering afar!*[18] (Emphasis in original.) This was taken by government agents as a clear allusion to the Decembrists. The result of this series of events was that the epigraph to *The Fountain of Bakhchisarai* acquired a retrospective meaning and was read as a dedication to the Decembrists, Pushkin's sympathy for whom had been well known ever since his famous declaration to Nicholas I in 1825.

In the wake of Polevoi's article, Baratynskii made use of the idea of Pushkin's epigraph in his poem 'Mara (Stansy)' (Mara [Stanzas]), written in 1827, though not published in full until 1835. When Baratynskii writes, in the context of a lost past:

> Daleche bedstvuiut inye
> I v mire net uzhe drugikh.[19]

(Some are wandering afar in poverty, / The others are no longer in this world),

he is again making a political point and referring to the Decembrists.

Yet another rephrasing of the same idea occurs in a draft version of Pushkin's elegy 'Na kholmakh Gruzii lezhit nochnaia mgla' (The Shadows of the Night Lie Over the Hills of Georgia), written in 1829. In a cancelled stanza Pushkin wrote:

> bestsennye sozdaniia
> Inye daleko, inykh uzh v mire net.[20]

(priceless creatures, / Some are far away, some are no longer in this world.)

The connection between the Decembrists and the phrase, 'some are already dead, and the others are far away', then, was already well established by the time Pushkin came to publish chapter eight of *Eugene Onegin*, and, as Nabokov notes, his contemporary readers would have had no trouble 'deciphering the enriched allusion'.[21]

18. Nikolai Polevoi, 'Vzgliad na russkuiu literaturu 1825 i 1826 gg. (Pis'mo v N'iu-Iork k S.D.P.)', *Moskovskii telegraf*, 13(1827), No. 1, 9.
19. Evgenii Baratynskii, *Polnoe sobranie stikhotvorenii*, Biblioteka poeta, bol'shaia seriia, ed. E. N. Kupreianova, 2nd ed., Leningrad: Sovetskii pisatel', 1957, p. 133.
20. Pushkin, *Polnoe sobranie sochinenii*, Vol. III, p. 114.
21. Nabokov, in the commentary on *Eugene Onegin*, p. 247.

Pushkin's action in publishing these lines was a political act of some significance, as Iurii Lotman remarks: 'The story of persecution for the epigraph from Sadi, of course, was known to Pushkin from Viazemskii, and by using it in the conclusion to *Eugene Onegin* he not only accomplished a bold act, hinting at the Decembrists, but also deliberately provoked Benkendorf, demonstrating that he could not be stopped . . .'[22]

When the expression 'Some are already dead, and the others are far away' came to be attached to *Poem Without a Hero* it was thus clearly associated with both a literary and a political tradition. It can be seen to continue the literary tradition by reinterpreting the works of earlier writers, and also to preserve the political awareness demonstrated by Pushkin.

The implicit comparison between Akhmatova's contemporaries and the Decembrists is revealed on several different levels. In the prose introduction, which is the immediate context of the epigraph, Akhmatova dedicates her poem to the memory of its first audience: 'I dedicate this poem to the memory of its first listeners – my friends and fellow citizens who perished in Leningrad during the siege'.[23] A note at the end of the passage indicates that at the time of writing the author was in Tashkent. Thus a contrast between the dead and the distant, those in exile, is immediately established.

This contrast in fact dominates the whole poem. Of the three dedications, the first two are clearly written to dead addressees. They bear the dates of the deaths of Mandel'shtam and of Ol'ga Glebova-Sudeikina respectively, and both terminate with funereal images: the first with Chopin's funeral march, the second with the words 'il' podsnezhnik v mogil'nom rvu' (or a snowdrop in an open grave). The third dedication is associated with the 'guest from the future' who appears later and who is not dead, only distant from the speaker in time and place. The dichotomy continues into '1913'. In the 'Pis'mo k N' (Letter to N), which forms an introduction to some early versions of *Poem Without a Hero*, Akhmatova, echoing the epigraph, notes some early reactions to her poem in Tashkent: '. . . he [a critic] said that I was settling some old accounts with the epoch (1910s) and with people either who were dead, or who were unable to answer me'.[24]

Akhmatova's critic here, although he has misunderstood her poem, has none the less noted correctly the categories of people to

22. Iu. M. Lotman, *Roman A. S. Pushkina 'Evgenii Onegin': kommentarii*, Leningrad: Prosveshchenie, 1980, p. 373.
23. Akhmatova, *Sochineniia*, Vol. II, p. 99.
24. Ibid., p. 97.

whom it is devoted. Nearly all of Akhmatova's contemporaries who are referred to in *Poem Without a Hero* were either dead or in exile. Some of those alluded to, like Blok, died through natural causes; others, like Kliuev, whose work provides an epigraph to later redactions of 'Reverse', as a result of political circumstances. Others still were distant either because, like the composer Arthur Lourié, whose libretto Akhmatova imagines she is writing in 'Reverse',[25] they had emigrated to the West, or because they had been sent to prison camps. The epilogue to the poem transfers the temporal viewpoint from the past to the present. Again death and distance are stressed. The inhabitants of Leningrad, to which this section is addressed, are either dead in the siege, or scattered 'kto v Tashkente, kto v N'iu-Iorke' (some in Tashkent, some in New York). Reference is also made to the camps in the east, another cause of death and distance.

Reference to the literary tradition is also an important component of specific hidden portraits which are contained in *Poem Without a Hero*. Allusion to Pushkin especially is often a sign that such a portrait is to be found. One example – that of Akhmatova's hidden reference to Nikolai Vladimirovich Nedobrovo – will indicate the high degree of complexity attending these situations.

Chapter three of '1913', which is on one level a self-contained unit and bears the title 'liricheskoe otstuplenie' (lyrical digression), is particularly rich in Pushkinian allusions. The prose introduction to the chapter describes the section as 'poslednee Vospominanie v Tsarskoe Selo' (last recollections in Tsarskoe Selo), deliberately evoking Pushkin's two poems entitled 'Vospominaniia v Tsarskom Sele' (Recollections in Tsarskoe Selo).[26] Both of these poems present an idyllic view of the past, which is contrasted sharply with the present. The earlier of the two, although it goes on to celebrate the military triumphs of the past, paints an idealized picture of Tsarskoe Selo in the first few stanzas, and laments the passing of time. The later poem similarly idealizes Tsarskoe Selo and develops the analogy of the prodigal son returning home. The accompanying mixture of joy and shame is similar to the contrast found in *Poem Without a Hero*.

The beginning of chapter three of '1913' describes a series of ominous events: carriages sliding from the bridges across the Neva, drums beating for an execution, the city succumbing to the curse of

25. Ibid., p. 123: 'A vo sne vse kazalos', chto eto / Ia pishu dlia kogo-to libretto . . .' (And I dreamed that / I was writing this as a libretto for someone). Zhirmunskii relates this passage to Lourié: see Akhmatova, *Stikhotvoreniia i poemy*, p. 518.
26. Pushkin, *Polnoe sobranie sochinenii*, Vol. 1, pp. 83–8; Vol. 3, pp. 155–6.

the Empress Evdokiia. These lead up to the onset of the terrible
True Twentieth Century (Nastoiashchii dvadtsatyi vek) and the
realization of a degree of guilt for its coming. The sense of foreboding
is increased by a series of indirect references to scenes of ill omen
in Pushkin's *Mednyi vsadnik* (The Bronze Horseman) and *Skazka o
zolotom petushke* (The Tale of the Golden Cockerel), which serve to
highlight the contrast between the present situation and the idealized
past. For example, the account of the flood in *The Bronze
Horseman* can be compared with Akhmatova's description of the river
Neva. In both cases the Neva is uncontrollable. Akhmatova's lines
'Po Neve i protiv techen'ia / Tol'ko proch' ot svoikh mogil' (along
the Neva and against the current only away from its graves) echo a
similar mention of graves in Pushkin: 'Groba s razmytogo klad-
bishcha / Plyvut po ulitsam' (coffins from a flooded cemetery float
along the streets). Similarly, Akhmatova's line 'V Letnem tonko
pela fliugarka' (the weather-vane sang thinly in the Summer Garden)
recalls the fateful calling of Pushkin's golden cockerel.[27]

The scene of destruction and guilt is contrasted with the italicized
passage which concludes the chapter. This evokes several expressions
from Pushkin's Tsarskoe Selo elegies, referring to waterfalls,
gardens and the Muses. It ends by confirming the importance
of the garden for Akhmatova and stressing the association between it
and a specific but unnamed person who is a proponent of the lost
ideal:

> Razve ty mne ne skazhesh' snova
> Pobedivshee smert' slovo
> I razgadku zhizni moei?[28]

(Won't you say to me again the word which overcomes death and
explain to me the puzzle of my life?)

In a passage not included in the final version of this section there
is a further reference to Pushkin. The passage begins:

> Chto nad iunost' vstal miatezhnoi
> Nezabvennyi moi drug i nezhnyi . . .[29]

27. Akhmatova, *Sochineniia*, Vol. II, p. 117; Pushkin, *Polnoe sobranie sochinenii*, Vol. IV,
pp. 387, 486; see T. V. Tsiv'ian, 'Zametki k deshifrovke "Poemy bez geroia"',
Trudy po znakovym sistemam, 5, 1971, p. 272.
28. Akhmatova, *Sochineniia*, Vol. II, p. 118; Tsiv'ian, 'Zametki k deshifrovke "Poemy
bez geroia"', p. 272.
29. Akhmatova, *Sochineniia*, Vol. III, ed. Gleb Struve, Nikita Struve and Boris
Filippov, Paris: YMCA-Press, 1983, p. 117.

(You rose above my tempestuous youth, my unforgettable and affection-
ate friend[. . .].)

The idea of 'tempestuous youth' is a commonplace going back at
least to Horace. However, one variant of the expression in Pushkin is
relevant here. In a poem to Chaadaev written in 1821, in which
Akhmatova elsewhere showed considerable interest, Pushkin writes
of his opportunity in exile to reflect and study, and contrasts this
with the behaviour of his tempestuous youth.[30] He goes on to discuss
the important role played by Tsarskoe Selo in his creativity, and to
lament the absence of his friend Chaadaev. Comparison with the
Pushkin context emphasizes several features of the passage in Akhmatova. Like Pushkin, she feels a degree of guilt for missed oppor-
tunities in her youth (she had not heard the approach of the True
Twentieth Century); she draws attention to the absence of a friend;
and she confirms her idealistic view of Tsarskoe Selo, with which
this friend was strongly associated.

The Pushkinian references in general thus highlight and expand
the themes of Akhmatova's elegy to Tsarskoe Selo. The question of
the identity of the friend to whom Akhmatova refers can be resolved
from sources outside *Poem Without a Hero*. It is known from Akhmatova's prose notes on the poem that the third chapter of '1913' is
dedicated to the memory of Nikolai Vladimirovich Nedobrovo. Poet
and arbiter of taste, Nedobrovo was a prominent figure in literary
circles in Tsarskoe Selo and Petersburg in the early years of the
century and was particularly close to Akhmatova in 1913–14.
Although the period of their intimacy in Tsarskoe Selo was short
and Nedobrovo was to die of tuberculosis in 1919, his memory
remained important to Akhmatova for the rest of her life. It seems
that in 1940, at about the time when Akhmatova began to write *Poem
Without a Hero*, she was thinking of Nedobrovo particularly. Lidiia
Chukovskaia in her detailed diary of her meetings with Akhmatova
recalls that at this time the latter was very anxious to re-read the
article which Nedobrovo had written about her work in 1914.
Akhmatova considered this to be the best early piece written about
her, and was especially impressed by Nedobrovo's prediction of the
future path of her poetry.[31]

30. Pushkin, *Polnoe sobranie sochinenii*, Vol. II, pp. 51–3. Parts of this poem are
    marked in an annotated copy of Pushkin's works from Akhmatova's library.
31. See Lidiia Chukovskaia, *Zapiski ob Anne Akhmatovoi*, Vol. I, Paris: YMCA-Press,
    1976, p. 108. Nedobrovo's article has been reprinted in Akhmatova, *Sochineniia*,
    Vol. III, pp. 473–95. For further information on Nedobrovo see the article by
    Gleb Struve, 'Akhmatova i N. V. Nedobrovo', in this same volume, pp. 371–427.

By combining the portrayal of Nedobrovo with the extensive use of reference to Pushkin, Akhmatova is alluding to one specific aspect of his literary activity. Nedobrovo was widely recognized as an authority on the early nineteenth-century poets and was even compared to Pushkin by one or two contemporary witnesses.[32] At the same time, by confirming this comparison, and herself perpetuating the identification of Nedobrovo with Pushkin, Akhmatova attempts to rescue Nedobrovo from the oblivion into which he had fallen, and to accord him a type of rehabilitation.

On the association between Nedobrovo and Pushkin in Akhmatova's verse see especially Roman Timenchik, 'Akhmatova i Pushkin. Zametki k teme', *Pushkinskii sbornik*, 2, Riga, 1974, pp. 32–55.

32. See I. Ia. Aizenshtok, 'Iz rannikh let nauchno-literaturnoi deiatel'nosti A. I. Beletskogo', in *Iskusstvo slova: sbornik statei k 80-letiiu chlena-korrespondenta AN SSSR Dmitriia Dmitrievicha Blagogo*, Moscow: AN SSSR, 1973, p. 399.

–12–

Borys Antonenko-Davydovych's
Behind the Curtain: Limits of the Thaw

DAVID FARRER

Though his published works comprise only a small *oeuvre*, Borys Antonenko-Davydovych (1899–1984) is considered, especially by critics in the West, to be one of the more notable Ukrainian prose writers of the twentieth century.[1] An active participant in the Ukrainian literary renascence of the 1920s, Antonenko-Davydovych was arrested and imprisoned amidst accusations of nationalism in 1935. His return to Kiev in 1956 after more than twenty years in prison and exile was due to, and part of, the Khrushchevian thaw. From the 1960s until his death he was a symbolic figure for the Ukrainian dissident movement. Though not an organizer, or even an active participant, in campaigns to defend human rights or Ukrainian cultural values, he was respected by the 'shistdesiatnyky' ('people of the sixties') and their successors as an exemplar of dignified, stoical opposition.

Antonenko-Davydovych wrote his novel *Za shyrmoiu* (Behind the Curtain) in the 1950s, the first draft while still in prison.[2] Its publication in Kiev in 1963 was one of the high-water marks of the thaw in Ukraine. The novel was subject to considerable criticism for its political standpoint, and has not been republished in the Soviet Union since.[3] The reason for its uncongenial official reception lies,

The final version of this paper was written in consultation with Marko Pavlyshyn.

1. For the consensus of Ukrainian critics in the West, see, e.g., the articles and bibliographies in *Ukraine: A Concise Encyclopaedia*, Vol. 1, Toronto: University of Toronto Press, 1963, p. 1054, and *Encyclopedia of Ukraine*, Vol. 1, Toronto: University of Toronto Press, 1984, p. 83.
2. See Oleksander Khakhulia, *B. Antonenko-Davydovych u pazuriakh chekistiv*, Melbourne: Lastivka, 1987, p. 14.
3. For an official Soviet treatment of the novel, rather ambiguous in its judgement, see *Istoriia ukrains'koi literatury*, Vol. 8, Kiev: Naukova dumka, 1971, pp. 367–8. A sympathetic account of *Za shyrmoiu* was given by Leonid Boiko in a longish review of Antonenko-Davydovych's life and work, 'Borys Antonenko-Davydovych', in *Ukrains'ki radians'ki pys'mennyky*, No. 6, Kiev: Radians'kyi pys'mennyk, 1968, pp. 125–74.

doubtless, in the fact that it attributes profound psychological significance to issues of nationality and national roots, and that its symbolism can be interpreted as expressing disapprobation of contemporary Soviet reality and of the prevailing position of Ukraine within the USSR.

The disloyal point of view which the novel's critics detected in *Behind the Curtain* is not programmatically formulated, nor does it emerge through an indirect critical strategy such as satire. It takes shape more subtly at the level of character through the novel's representation of psychological repression. 'Repression', of course, is the category employed by most psychoanalytic discourses to describe the forcing of certain mental contents – memories, impulses, feelings – into the unconscious, either because they are too painful to deal with, or because they are socially unacceptable.[4]

We shall argue in the following that what brings the novel into conflict with the prevailing official ideology is its depiction of the psychological development of the central character – Alexander Postolovsky, a doctor – as a development toward conscious awareness of what he has repressed: the roots, traditions and values of his native Ukrainian village. Impressed by science and progress and inspired by the ideal of the improvement of mankind, he had as a youth left his village to study medicine in Moscow. Yet his native values, abandoned because not reconcilable with the values of the modern world, ultimately prove to him their incalculable worth.

This juxtaposition of modern and primeval is on the one hand a reiteration of romantic nostalgia for an allegedly simple and organic past; on the other, within a Soviet context it also has the aspect of an ideological statement. For in *Behind the Curtain* values highly prized by the Enlightenment tradition, sanctioned by the authority of Marx and enshrined in scientific socialism, are discovered to be less applicable to the human condition than such a 'reactionary', even 'nationalist', attitude as dedication to the place of one's birth and to the people with whom one shares it.

Postolovsky is presented to the reader initially as a man who, having with some success repressed his attachment to his roots, has integrated his ideologically inspired idealism into the routine of his

4. This analysis uses the term in its Jungian, rather than its Freudian, sense, in so far as it does not see the repressed psychic contents as limited to instinctive, and primarily sexual, behavioural patterns, and follows the lines of the definition in Arthur S. Reber, *The Penguin Dictionary of Psychology*, Harmondsworth: Viking, 1980, p. 640. For a more narrowly Freudian and clinical definition, see, e.g., *Encyclopedia of Psychology*, ed. H. J. Eysenck, et al., Vol. 3, New York: Herder and Herder, 1972, p. 148.

life. He has volunteered to live and work in a backwoods area of Soviet Uzbekistan, where he runs a hospital and clinic. Personal virtues which identify him with the tradition of the Enlightenment include honesty, an intolerance of fools and self-servers, and a conscientious concern for people's needs. He has expended great efforts to improve the hospital to meet the needs of the local population. Yet, lacking roots in Uzbekistan, he fails to win the full confidence of the indigenous population and remains unable to implement his well-meaning plans except through local figures of authority.

It is Postolovsky's development beyond his rationalist's optimism that is the controversial content of the novel. Antonenko-Davydovych traces Postolovsky's progress through three psychological points of crisis, which are the main focus of this discussion. The points of orientation between which this linear unfolding is framed are two women characters: Postolovsky's aged mother, Odarka Pylypivna, and his wife, Nina. As characters, each is somewhat static and schematic – the consequence of their being products of a symbolic intention.

Nina's portrait in the novel is very negative. She is portrayed as being insensitive to the point of callousness, as exemplified in her treatment both of her young son and of her mother-in-law. Amorally opportunistic and manipulative, she lies in order to get her own way or to maintain her public image. Her vice of perceiving people mainly in terms of stereotypes manifests itself especially in her racist categorization of Uzbeks: 'I can perhaps envisage an Uzbek as a teacher, an actor, even a poet . . . but a doctor, an engineer, or an artist – never! . . . It just doesn't suit them' (127, 187).[5] For herself she selects a stereotypically 'feminine' role as a sensitive, artistically inclined doctor's wife.

While eliciting from the reader a negative judgement of Nina's pretensions to high culture and sophistication, the novel draws Nina as unselfconsciously superstitious: she accepts wholeheartedly, for example, her mother-in-law's claim that a dog's howling prophesies misfortune (128, 189). Within the psychological terms of reference of the novel, such readiness to revert to forms of belief and behaviour learnt in childhood explains Nina's apparently inconsistent behaviour at Odarka Pylypivna's deathbed: she looks after Alexander's

5. Quotations from the novel are from the English translation by Yuri Tkach: *Behind the Curtain*, Melbourne: Bayda Books, 1980. The second bracketed page reference is to the text of the Ukrainian edition, Borys Antonenko-Davydovych, *Za shyrmoiu*, Kiev: Radians'kyi pys'mennyk, 1963, rpt. Melbourne: Slovo, 1972. Transcriptions of proper names adopted in Tkach's translation are retained in this article.

mother capably and even sensitively. Faced with a human situation – death and a dying person's need for care – for which her Moscow life has not prepared her, she draws on the experience and instincts of her small-town country background. (As the novel is careful to note, she was born in Kobeliaky, a town in the Poltava oblast' of Ukraine [79, 113].)[6]

Nina's construction as a character, then, brings to the fore a dissociation between the conscious and unconscious levels of her mental life. She possesses little insight into the relation between her own socially conditioned persona and her inner self, and therefore lives at what Jungian analysis would regard as a relatively low level of consciousness.[7] Consciousness implies an ability to draw together disparate parts of one's life experience into a coherent whole, or, where this is not possible, to be aware of the lack of cohesion in one's life or outlook. The latter variant involves suffering or at least a degree of psychic discomfort. In the Jungian tradition, overcoming neurosis involves becoming aware of one's contradictions and learning to face them squarely. If, as T. S. Eliot suggests, it is the chief task of culture to assist the individual in developing and maintaining a coherent world-view, which is to say a relatively contradiction-free approach to life,[8] then Nina's problems arise from being bereft of culture, or being 'deracinated'. In the case of the Soviet Union – thus we might read the critical subtext of Antonenko-Davydovych's characterization of Nina – the problem of deracination is exacerbated by the authoritarian and dogmatic implementation of Marxism-Leninism, with its rigid adherence to a nineteenth-century version of philosophical materialism and concomitant downgrading of the role and importance of culture in human affairs.

Alexander's mother, Odarka Pylypivna, is in essential respects Nina's polar opposite. A product of a traditional, rural-based society, she is loving, gentle, patient and self-effacing.[9] She is affection-

---

6. In the first, unpublished version of the story, however, Nina was a Russian. See Dmytro Chub, *Borys Antonenko-Davydovych: zhyttia i tvorchist'*, Melbourne: Lastivka, 1979, p. 26.

7. The subject of dissociation between the conscious and unconscious contents of the psyche in modern man – a result of the demise of traditional culture, most notably of its religious or spiritual component – is a major theme of many of Jung's writings. For a major treatment of the theme, see 'The Undiscovered Self', in C. G. Jung, *Collected Works*, transl. F. C. Hull, London: Routledge and Kegan Paul, 1953–73 (henceforth *CW*), Vol. 8, pp. 247–305.

8. T. S. Eliot, *Notes Towards the Definition of Culture*, New York: Harcourt Brace, 1949, especially Chapter 1.

9. According to Khakhulia (p. 14), in the first draft of the novel Odarka Pylypivna was also portrayed as devoutly religious.

ately portrayed as a prototypical, yet still quite individual, Ukrainian (or generally Slavic) babushka. If Nina's is a personality rendered disharmonious by estrangement from cultural roots, Odarka Pylypivna retains her harmony and inner happiness because she remains culturally intact, though transplanted physically to Central Asia. Her folkloric knowledge, her system of beliefs and superstitions, as well as her sense of correct familial and domestic relationships, guarantee her a personal harmony, authority and self-confidence. It is this which, the novel suggests, is the source of the respect which Alexander's son Sashko feels for Odarka; the values which Nina represents, by contrast, lack authenticity and persuasiveness. Furthermore, the confidence born of cultural harmony enables Odarka to relate to people in a simple and direct way, without defensively categorizing or judging; thus she communicates easily with those Uzbeks who befriend her, and, while puzzled by some of their Islamic customs,[10] has no difficulty in recognizing and treasuring their humanity. Her immediate rapport with the Uzbek doctor Khodzhaev, and his with her, are in marked contrast to Nina's hypocritical fawning.[11]

Nina and Odarka, then, are at opposite extremes of the range of possible responses to culture and roots; in the course of his psychological development in the novel, Postolovsky shifts his position relative to the two women as he passes through his three psychological crisis points. The first such point occurs when Alexander comes to realize that he neither loves his wife nor knows why he married her. He speculates that he must have been intoxicated at the time of his marriage – a conclusion which coincides closely with his mother's thoughts on the subject: 'She must have bewitched him, enveloped him in delusion (prycharuvala, manu napustyla na ii Sashka), as the old people would have said back in Pereyaslav' (79, 113). The expression is not coincidental: as a representative voice of the folkloric genius of her people, Odarka equates Postolovsky's marriage, the event which symbolizes his estrangement from his roots, with a bewitchment – an event which estranges the victim, in Ukrainian folklore and literary tradition, from his or her right mind.[12]

10. She notes with disapproval the veils worn by some Muslim women (96, 138). These constitute one of the novel's numerous references to the symbolic 'curtain' of the title, which here can be seen to conceal the feminine aspect of existence (cf. below).
11. See especially Chapter 22.
12. The best-known literary realization of this motif is Taras Shevchenko's 'Prychynna' (The Bewitched Woman, 1837).

David Farrer

Postolovsky's realization that he does not love Nina begins to confront him while she is away shopping in Tashkent. Distanced from her immediate influence, Postolovsky has a dream which is set in his native Pereyaslav. In the dream he experiences once more his youthful idealism and desire to break out of the narrowness of traditional small-town existence: 'To live, not selfishly, but for people, for good, for life!' (89, 127). Beside him in the dream is a 'fiery stallion' ('bas'kyi kin''), which he mounts, and which then carries him into the world of modernity. The appearance of the horse in Alexander's dream accords well with the findings of archetypal theory regarding the horse, which signifies an essentially masculine form of animal vitality.[13]

Then follows the passage: 'But why was there sorrow creeping into his heart and covering the bright horizon with clouds? Sashko already knew why. Before him lay not only a bright path to the future, but escape as well. Escape from the past . . . And back there, behind him, stood Pereyaslav, containing his childhood, his youth, and Marusia – his first love.' This is the reader's first encounter with the name of Marusia, who never enters the novel as a character, but remains a disembodied presence. She clearly functions as a positive feminine figure; her very name, Marusia, one of the Ukrainian diminutives of 'Maria', links her with the most positive, powerful, and yet human archetypal figure in Christian culture.[14] We learn that Alexander dreams of Marusia about twice a year, and always feels refreshed and cleansed afterwards.

The dream is the first point at which Alexander becomes conscious of the pain he had felt at leaving his village and Marusia. He had repressed those feelings, and had therefore made the decision to depart not in full consciousness, but by blocking out a vital part of his being. What he had blocked out is identified at various points with the feminine – mother, Marusia, Ukraine. Even his home town, Pereyaslav, where the treaty uniting Ukraine with Russia was signed in 1654, has been interpreted by one tradition of Ukrainian historical mythology as the scene of a rape or at least a forced marriage.[15]

13. Cf. Jung, CW, Vol. 5, p. 287: 'On account of their speed, horses signify the wind . . . German legend knows the wind as the wild huntsman in lustful pursuit of the maiden. Wotan gallops along after the wind-bride (Frigg).'
14. Treatment of the Virgin Mary from an archetypal perspective occurs frequently in the writings of Jung and of those influenced by him. See, e.g., Jung, CW, Vol. 11, pp. 397–9; Joseph Campbell, The Masks of God: Oriental Mythology, New York: Viking, 1964, pp. 42–5.
15. See John Basarab, Pereiaslav: A Historiographical Study, Edmonton: Canadian Institute of Ukrainian Studies, 1982, and especially the Introduction by Ivan L.

The first crisis point, then, can be interpreted as beginning for Postolovsky the painful process of re-integrating the repressed, feminine part of himself into his conscious life.

The second crisis point of the novel advances the process begun by the first, and occurs when Postolovsky unexpectedly receives a letter from this same Marusia.[16] The letter informs the reader that, like Postolovsky, Marusia has entered the modern world and has lost much of her innocence, but – and in this respect, too, she is like the friend of her youth – without succumbing to cynicism, despair, or the temptation to live unconsciously like Nina. Clearly, she represents a feminine counterpart to what is positive and life-affirming in Alexander. His youthful view of her as a soul-mate is confirmed. Yet he tears the letter up and throws it away, deliberately not noting the return address.

There may be two reasons for this motif of self-denial. First, Antonenko-Davydovych may be denying in advance the possibility of any crudely sexual interpretation of Postolovsky's longing for Marusia; it is not Marusia in a personal sense that he is pining for, but rather what she represents. On receiving the letter he realizes, if not at a fully conscious level, that the Marusia of his youthful memory belongs now to the irretrievable past. His longing for her thus has a symbolic and archetypal, rather than personal, quality.

Second, the motif of communication foregone may also be the author's way of signalling his belief that, at the time of writing in the 1950s (the novel is set circa 1950), the time was not yet ripe for a re-union or re-integration of the masculine and feminine, or, at the level of the political subtext, for a restoration of coherence and harmony to life in the Soviet Union; that Alexander's and Marusia's generation had no hope of effecting such a reconciliation, and could hope to achieve, at best, some awareness of the problem. In the context of such a reading the essential problematic of the novel is the onset of modernity. Modern industrial society, the novel argues, focuses exclusively on the material world of action and reason (in archetypal terms generally characterized as the masculine side of life) and neglects spiritual values and the feeling, non-rational side

Rudnytsky. For a discussion of the idea of Ukraine as archetypally feminine, and of the connection with the idea of rape, see George S. N. Luckyj, 'The Archetype of the Bastard in Shevchenko's Poetry', *Slavic and East European Journal*, 14(1970), 277–83.

16. It is a question for speculation whether the author introduces this coincidence simply out of necessity, to enable the plot and dramatic structure to move forward, or whether he may intuitively have held views similar to those of Jung on the subject of what the latter calls 'synchronicity'. See also the episode when Postolovsky, thinking about his childhood and dead brother, overhears his mother quite fortuitously talking about the same things (44, 58).

of the psyche (likewise characterized as feminine). Yet the novel does not advocate primitivism or rejection of the modern world – on the contrary, in numerous places it is critical of aspects of peasant life. In Chapter 20, for example, the inability, both technical and cultural, of Uzbek peasants to cope with a difficult childbirth is unsentimentally contrasted to the capabilities of a modern doctor. *Behind the Curtain* does not sow doubts concerning the benefits of modern medicine, science and rational thought properly applied. The plea is, rather, that inner life be given its due.

The portrayal of the two principal Uzbek characters is pertinent to the evolution of the novel's standpoint toward the question of modernity and tradition. Nazira, a woman of immense energy and commitment, is the director of a collective farm – an unusually responsible position for a woman in Soviet Central Asia. But she is strangely one-dimensional, having completely turned her back, it would seem, on her own spiritual and cultural traditions. It is noteworthy that she comes to Alexander for treatment of sores on her breasts – that is, of a disorder connected with her feminine, nurturing aspect. In counterpoint to her, Dr. Khodzhaev, the other major Uzbek character, while likewise energetic and effective (he is the head of the regional medical directorate, but continues to practise medicine in addition to performing conscientiously his administrative duties), nevertheless also retains a deeply compassionate commitment to people on a personal level; at the end of the novel it is he who gives emotional support to Alexander and helps him begin his inner healing process. He is a role-model for Alexander as someone who, while having a similar dedication to medicine and humanity, appears not to have turned his back on his culture and traditions.

The third crisis point of the novel is Alexander's discovery that his mother has been suffering from cancer. Her symptoms should have been apparent even to a novice doctor, but Alexander had completely failed to notice them until alerted by Khodzhaev. Our reading of the novel suggests that he does not notice precisely because it is his mother who is concerned: his blindness is consistent with the fact that she is the main symbol of the sphere of emotions which he has repressed. One might recall the episode, early in the novel, where he sees a neglected, dirty, one-eyed bitch near the clinic (15, 13). His preoccupation with the dog is obsessive, and the psychologically attentive reader might speculate that it is connected with his attitude to his mother and, through her, the repressed emotional world. Though Postolovsky is unaware of it, the dog's unwholesome, forlorn appearance is a reminder of his neglect of his mother – a neglect that is too painful at this stage for him to confront. To do so would involve him in a re-evaluation of his life for which he is not yet ready. Postolovsky's repressed feelings of guilt towards his mother are activated by the sight of the dog, though not to the point where he becomes consciously aware of them or of their origin.

The dog Zhuchka has a significance in the novel well beyond the mere evocation of a sentimental effect. By drawing a detailed psychological portrait of the dog, complete with attributed feelings and emotions, Antonenko-Davydovych, one might suggest, seeks to refute the notion that love is related to, or a product of, the rational faculties of the mind. By depicting an animal as the subject of feelings analogous to human love, Antonenko-Davydovych endeavours to demonstrate, on the contrary, that our deepest feelings, and love itself, well up from our animal depths. This is by no means an innocent position. It stands in opposition to Marx's Enlightenment-derived view that love would flourish once society had been organized along lines dictated or revealed by Reason or the science of dialectical materialism – that is, as an outcome of human rationality and at an advanced level of human social development.[17] By locating a pure feeling in an animal Antonenko-Davydovych advances a competing view of the 'noble' emotions and thus challenges, if only by implication, a tenet of the official Soviet image of humankind.

The theme of cancer, also connected to Odarka, is likewise fraught with subtextual import. The disease makes its appearance in the novel long before the reader learns that Odarka Pylypivna is suffering from it; indeed, the whole of Chapter 8 is devoted to this subject and Alexander's thoughts about it. There are suggestive analogies, perhaps intended by Antonenko-Davydovych as contributing to the meaning of the novel – between cancer and the repression of psychic contents. Cancer does much of its work of cell-destruction in secret before its symptoms become manifest; similarly, the destructive effects upon the personality of repressed thoughts and feelings become patent only when they break through into behaviour in the form of neuroses. Furthermore, neither cancer nor such repressed contents are readily susceptible to treatment based on rational scientific precepts.

Cancer, then, is emblematic of the psychic malady, brought on by

17. For a contemporary Soviet Marxist treatment of love, see the article in *Filosofskaia entsiklopediia*, Vol. 3, Moscow: Sovetskaia entsiklopedia, 1964, pp. 265–7. Love here is defined as a 'moral-aesthetic sentiment' ('nravstvenno-esteticheskoie chuvstvo'), and is seen as exclusively the product of a high level of social development.

false social values, from which Alexander suffers. His personality has been damaged by the repression of his emotional self and his links to his roots in his place of origin. The discovery of his mother's physical cancer triggers Postolovsky's coming to consciousness of his own psychic illness. His reaction to his mother's death is therapeutic. As the novel closes, he departs with his mother's coffin for Pereyaslav. Her interment in her birthplace and his, the reader may conclude, will be an attempt by Postolovsky to recover his original self.

It was not the intention of this study to examine a work by Borys Antonenko-Davydovych as an illustration of the author's tacit posture of cultural and political dissent. Yet the examination of one aspect of the structure of *Behind the Curtain* – the novel's management of character and therefore its implied psychology – could not but reveal the work as a vehicle for a scheme of values such as had, in effect, been proscribed in the Soviet Union.

It is the argument of the novel that an individual's sense of ease with self and society – the boon of the harmonious personality – depends in large part on that individual's unbroken relationship to his or her own origins. This relationship encompasses attitudes to the locality inhabited by one's ancestors, its past, its folklore, its customs and traditions – in brief, to the component parts of a national identity. Subtextual advocacy of national identity as an essential part of human identity is what sets *Behind the Curtain* in opposition to the orthodox theory of a beneficent and progressive 'internationalism', and to the orthodox practice of Russian cultural imperialism.

It was a measure of the genuineness of the Khrushchevian thaw that *Behind the Curtain* was published. Yet Antonenko-Davydovych, though formally rehabilitated, remained a *persona non grata*, and *Behind the Curtain* joined the ranks of undiscussable books. The ambivalence of its reception – published, but officially disapproved – serves to illustrate a feature of all thaws: as liberalizations granted from above by a power which remains in ultimate control, they provide only relative relief. The limits of the permissible, though widened, remain real, and the author who approaches them does so at personal risk.

-13-

Fiction as History: L. P. Beria in Thaw Fiction

KEVIN WINDLE

Only a short while ago, in the days before Fedor Burlatskii's and Arkadii Vaksberg's historical and biographical exposés in *Literaturnaia gazeta*, and before such films as Abuladze's *Pokaianie* (Repentance), Soviet readers seeking to fill in the 'blank pages' in their knowledge of past rulers had few sources of any kind to consult. Of those available, some provided little beyond oft-repeated inconsequential detail bordering on the mythic, such as Stalin's tastes in tobacco and wine. Given this paucity of authoritative factual material, fiction treating the same topics comes to occupy a special place. As so often in Soviet affairs, it is fiction that goes part of the way towards amplifying the historical picture, opening new insights, and occasionally even giving wider currency to factual information known only in restricted circles. A number of writers clearly felt that the novelist had a duty to step into those areas which the historian or biographer could enter only with difficulty, although even the fiction-writer's difficulties – of access to raw material, and to a publisher – must have seemed scarcely less daunting. The novelist Konstantin Simonov, describing his working method, once said that he, and all others who wrote about the Great Patriotic War, were historians.[1]

While some of his confrères might dissent from such a categorical statement, it is clear that writers of realistic works of literature dealing with past events of national importance must engage in historical research. Given that the term 'informatsionnyi roman' was once in vogue to describe some fiction with a highly specific period setting, and that it is writers of *belles-lettres* who have taken the lead in the current re-examination of Soviet history, it seems appro-

---

1. I. Zolotusskii, 'Kazhdyi den' - dlinnyi' [interview with Konstantin Simonov], *Literaturnaia gazeta*, 2 May 1966. I am grateful to Mr. P. R. Ireland for drawing my attention to this interview.

priate to examine the literary product as, in some sense, a historical source, while bearing in mind the difference in methodological constraints governing the work of academic historians and fiction writers.

In the now considerable body of post-Stalin literature dealing with the Stalin era, numerous works of fiction contribute to a composite portrait of Stalin himself which is, on the whole, consistent within itself, conforms to known, or at least near-certain historical fact, and is totally at variance with the legend propagated in Soviet publications during his lifetime.

Stalin's lieutenants, however, have been subjected to less searching examination in fiction. In *The First Circle*, particularly the definitive edition (Paris, 1978), Solzhenitsyn paints a detailed portrait of Stalin, and is informative about Abakumov and Poskrebyshev, but Beria receives no more than a few passing references. Anatolii Rybakov's *Deti Arbata* (Children of the Arbat) provides the fullest study of Stalin in fiction to date, as well as vivid portraits of numerous of his henchmen – Iagoda, Ezhov, Kirov, Ordzhonikidze, Enukidze, and others – but, being set mainly in Moscow in 1934, can say little about Beria, who did not have an important role in events in Moscow at that time.[2] I. Dombrovskii's *Fakul'tet nenuzhnykh veshchei* (Faculty of Unwanted Objects) includes Stalin in its cast of characters, but Beria is scarcely mentioned.

Nevertheless, Lavrentii Pavlovich Beria does figure, often only briefly, in a subsidiary role, alongside Stalin, in a number of works of fiction – perhaps more than is generally realized. Here it is proposed to consider the fictional portraits of Beria and attempt some correlation with the historical facts of his career. Consideration of the works in question will centre on the figure of Beria which they present, and its verisimilitude in the light of known historical fact, and will be accompanied by only minimal comment on the artistic merits or demerits of the work as a whole. However, since we are dealing with fiction, in which imagination must play some part, in the many cases where statements in the novel or story are not of a kind that can be readily verified, some appraisal of their 'artistic truth', or plausibility, may be offered. The picture of Beria which emerges reflects in some measure the circumstances of the period in which publication occurred, that is, by and large, the Khrushchev thaw and that following the introduction of *glasnost'* in 1986.

Broadly speaking, Russian fiction as a whole presents two distinct

2. Anatolii Rybakov, 'Deti Arbata', *Druzhba narodov*, 1987, Nos. 4, 5, 6. Presumably Beria will have a larger role in the forthcoming sequel to this novel.

Stalins, according to date (and place) of writing, but only one Beria. During his lifetime Stalin was well established as a character in Socialist Realist writing, making regular appearances and fulfilling a definite symbolic function, in addition to having his name ritually invoked. In the years following his death, a Stalin of a quite different kind began to appear in literature as the cultural climate changed.

The position with regard to his lieutenants is rather different. They could not, without considerable personal risk, allow themselves to be the subject of sycophantic works of art during the dictator's lifetime (assuming the availability of sycophants to create them). They could appear at Stalin's side in Stalinist literature, their glory enhanced by his presence, but as this does not appear to have happened in Beria's case, and as sycophantic literature soon fell into disrepute with the invention of the term 'cult of personality',[3] 'pro-Beria' writing is hard to find. Although his exemplary service to Stalin and the party earned him the famous article and full-page photograph in the *Great Soviet Encyclopedia*,[4] the small amount of fiction involving him began to appear only after his death, and was exclusively anti-Beria in spirit, in keeping with the tone set by Khrushchev himself in the 'secret speech' and later developed in his memoirs.

The pioneering work in this field in the official Soviet press (although, in all probability, not the first to be written) was Vera Ketlinskaia's novel *Inache zhit' ne stoit* (Life is Pointless Otherwise).[5] The novel is prefaced by a disclaimer, in which the reader is requested not to seek real people or events in it, but since the characters include Stalin and Beria, however briefly, under their own names, an exception begs to be made. The scene in which these two appear occupies no more than four out of over four hundred journal pages, and in this scene Beria receives no more than a few descriptive lines and utters one short, but significant, paragraph.

Brief though this scene is, Rosalind Marsh is doubtless right to infer that the burden of it is to support the contention that Beria, rather than Stalin, should be held responsible for the 'negative phenomena' of the period, including the stifling of scientific initiative. As Marsh points out, this view of Beria still found official favour at times during the period of uncertainty between the Twentieth and

---

3. As Abdurakhman Avtorkhanov points out, the term 'cult of personality' was coined as early as 10 June 1953, when it appeared in an unsigned article, possibly written by Beria, in *Pravda*. *Zagadka smerti Stalina*, Frankfurt/Main: Possev, 1976, p. 253.
4. 2nd ed., Vol. 5, 1950.
5. Vera Ketlinskaia, 'Inache zhit' ne stoit', *Znamia*, Nos. 6–10, 1963.

Twenty-Second Party Congresses, when the novel was published.[6]

In this novel a group of scientists working on the extraction of gas from coal are summoned to the Kremlin, following a number of setbacks and a serious accident. At the meeting, an unfavourable report on their work is delivered by Klinskii, a deputy people's commissar. Stalin's demeanour is severe, and he does not appear well-disposed towards the scientists, but having heard both sides, he adjudicates in their favour. Thus Stalin appears here as the voice of moderation, while Beria's role is to emphasize the scientists' errors and press for condign punishment.[7]

The physical features selected to identify Beria in minimal space are those found in other accounts: ice-cold eyes behind a pince-nez, a bald head, and a pampered face. (The adjectives 'cold', or 'icy', of his eyes, and 'pampered' – Russ.: *kholenyi* – of his face or hands, are favourites in other fictional descriptions.) If the image evoked is somewhat less loathsome than can be found elsewhere,[8] the chosen details do not add up to an appealing figure.

Ketlinskaia's novel was followed in 1962 by Daniil Granin's *Idu na grozu* (Into the Thunderstorm), which contains a brief but telling episode dealing with Beria's later years.[9] At the end of the war the scientist Anikeev is appointed to a key position on the atomic bomb development project, then code-named 'The Problem' and under the stewardship of Beria. After a particularly acrimonious exchange with his political master, Anikeev writes to the CPSU Central Committee complaining about Beria's meddling – an act tantamount to suicide. Only Anikeev's prestige in his field saves him from anything worse than demotion to a pedagogical institute in the North. However, he defies the removal order and remains in office, at great risk, to see the installations commissioned, and only then departs for the North.[10]

In this episode, which Granin offers as 'one of the legends' surrounding the name of Anikeev, there are points of contact with the career and personality of the well-known nuclear physicist Petr

6. Rosalind J. Marsh, *Soviet Fiction since Stalin: Science, Politics and Literature*, London: Croom Helm, 1986, pp. 41–2.
7. *Znamia*, 1960, No. 10, 20–3.
8. E.g. Igor Gouzenko, *The Fall of a Titan*, trans. by Mervyn Black, London: Cassell, 1954. It is planned to make the figure of Beria as shown in this novel, and in a number of others whose publication owed little to any thaws, the subject of a separate study, focussing on the exploitation of the *myth* of Beria, rather than the historical reality.
9. Daniil Granin, 'Idu na grozu', in *Sobranie sochinenii*, Leningrad: Khudozhestvennaia literatura, 1979, Vol. 2.
10. *Sobranie Sochinenii*, Vol. 2, pp. 124–5.

Kapitsa, although Kapitsa is also mentioned in the novel under his own name.[11] Kapitsa is reputed to have been at least as fearless and independent in his dealings with his political masters as Anikeev is shown to be.[12] But if Beria was thwarted in Ketlinskaia's novel, in Granin's the victim's defiance secures him only a precarious reprieve.

A glimpse of Beria in the very last days of Stalin's rule is provided by Nikolai Sizov in his novel *Trudnye gody* (Difficult Years).[13] The theme is the parlous condition of Soviet agriculture at the time, and unsanctioned efforts to improve it at the local level. In February 1953, Zagradin, an obkom first secretary and Central Committee member, is called to account at a session of the USSR Council of Ministers for his independent attempts to consolidate collective farms and improve efficiency in his *oblast'*.[14] Stalin is not present. Most of those present are hostile to Zagradin. Malenkov is implacable. Only Khrushchev offers some support for his initiatives. (This novel, published in Khrushchev's last year in office, is unusual in featuring not only Stalin and Beria, but also Malenkov and Khrushchev.) At this stage Beria's only contribution is to limit Zagradin to the presentation of the case of his own *oblast'*, and disallow generalizations about the state of agriculture in the nation as a whole.[15]

Zagradin succeeds in obtaining an audience with Stalin at the Kuntsevo *dacha* to present his case. He does not know how Beria has briefed Stalin for the interview. The reader, however, is made privy to the details of Beria's preliminary briefing, in a scene which makes an interesting study of the relations between the two men. Beria is formal and respectful, addressing Stalin by first name and patronymic, and using *vy*, while Stalin calls him Lavrentii and uses *ty*. However, when *à deux* with Stalin, Beria is not afraid to take the seat at the head of the table, where Stalin himself never sits, and which 'nobody else dares occupy'.[16]

As in other accounts, Beria is careful to maintain his flattering tone ('As usual, you've hit the nail on the head, Iosif Vissarionovich').[17] Lest he be accused of having shifty eyes, he fixes Stalin with

11. Ibid., p. 127.
12. A brief account of Kapitsa's relations with Beria was given in 'Risk-2', a Soviet television feature on 1 Aug. 1988. See BBC's *Summary of World Broadcasts*, SU/0227/C/1-5, 11 Aug. 1988.
13. Nikolai Sizov, 'Trudnye gody', *Oktiabr'* 1964, No. 4.
14. Ibid., 92–3.
15. Ibid., 97.
16. Ibid, 103. This curious detail, Stalin's avoiding the head of the table, may be drawn from Djilas's description, *Conversations with Stalin*, Harmondsworth: Penguin, 1963, p. 63.
17. *Oktiabr'*, 1964, No. 4, 103.

his 'bulging, yellow eyes'.[18] Beria describes Zagradin's views as 'ne nashi' (not ours), aimed at undermining the Central Committee's line and Stalin's own instructions concerning agriculture and rural life. Beria hints at a conspiracy, possibly backed by imperialist agents ('Delo ne bez ch'ikh-to sovetov').[19]

Stalin, however, seems unimpressed, and frowns at Beria's advice to act promptly. This may reflect the waning of Beria's influence on Stalin following the Slánský trial in Prague and the Doctors' Plot.[20]

Having put his case to Stalin, and uncertain whether Stalin's consideration of the matter will lead to endorsement or arrest, Zagradin returns home. His anxiety is terminated by the announcement of Stalin's death. Here Sizov ventures a few general observations on the feeling in the country at large regarding the new leadership of Malenkov, Molotov and Beria. There is little enthusiasm, he tells us, for the first two, and considerable antipathy towards Beria, who is 'disliked by all, or at least, an absolute majority'.[21] The narrative continues: 'His square, yellowish face, and cold, lacklustre, narrowed eyes behind the lenses of his pince-nez evoked an involuntary sense of unease. But nobody dared to mention this, even in a whisper.'[22] There are widespread doubts as to whether power has fallen into the right hands. However, in the closing pages, Khrushchev is shown leading the way to a more rational agrarian policy, and enjoying some success in the struggle against the dogmatists.

A novel of this nature could scarcely have been cleared for publication without approval at the highest level. Hence, perhaps, the author's feeling that there was a need to pander to the vanity of the then General Secretary, Khrushchev, who, it is claimed, had a less hidebound approach to the crisis in agriculture. The thrust of the novel is to justify the removal of Khrushchev's erstwhile rivals, and the arrest and execution of Beria, although no mention is made of these events. Nevertheless, all allowance being made for the political exigencies of the day, and for artistic licence in the handling of detail, Beria's behaviour and *modus operandi* as shown here are fully consistent with other descriptions of him.

18. This point tallies with what Khrushchev tells us of Stalin's close observation of the eye movements of others. N. S. Khrushchev, *The Secret Speech*, Nottingham: Spokesman Books, 1976, p. 46.
19. *Oktiabr'*, 1964, No. 4, 103.
20. Roy Medvedev mentions an estrangement ('otdalenie') between Stalin and Beria at this point: *K sudu istorii*, revised ed., New York: Knopf, 1974, p. 1121.
21. *Oktiabr'*, 1964, No. 4, 109.
22. Ibid.

A work which provides valuable insights into the workings of the Stalinist system of government, while remaining fundamentally within the sub-genre of the production novel, is Aleksandr Bek's *Novoe naznachenie* (New Appointment). This novel owes its genesis to the impetus provided by the Khrushchev thaw, and has much in common with the fiction of that period, but it came too late to benefit from the relatively liberal publishing policy of the early 1960s. Long after its first publication in the West, it became one of the first of the literary works 'exhumed' for Soviet publication in 1986.[23] Both Stalin and Beria have an important role to play in the life of the hero, Aleksandr Leont'evich Onisimov, the name given to a character based on the old Bolshevik, I. Tevosian, who served as USSR Minister of Ferrous Metallurgy before ending his career as ambassador to Japan after Stalin's death.[24]

Onisimov is a devoted Stalinist yes-man, whose advancement has been greatly aided by his humiliating betrayal of his mentor, Ordzhonikidze. Pressed by Stalin to say whether he agrees with him or Ordzhonikidze in a violent argument, in Georgian, which Onisimov does not understand, he takes Stalin's side against his friend, who then commits suicide. Dubbed by his son 'the Great Silent One', he epitomizes the type of Stalinist bureaucrat immortalized in the lines of the song by Aleksandr Galich: 'And the silent ones have become the chiefs, because silence is golden.'

In this novel, the paths of Onisimov and Beria first cross as early as the days of the Civil War, when Onisimov is checking the registry of party members in Baku, and Beria, aged twenty, is seeking a responsible Cheka assignment. Finding Beria's replies unsatisfactory, Onisimov withholds his party card, and thus makes a lifelong enemy.[25]

The two meet again in 1938, when Onisimov is summoned to Stalin's presence and finds 'the Georgian from Baku' there too, now a more dangerous adversary than ever, as he commands 'the vast machinery of arrests, interrogations, shootings, prisons, and camps'.[26] But Onisimov is protected by Stalin's trust in him.

Beria is seen again when Onisimov has another meeting with

23. Aleksandr Bek, *Novoe naznachenie*, Frankfurt/Main: Possev, 1971. References are to this edition. A Soviet edition, prepared by T. Bek, appeared in *Znamia*, 1986, Nos. 10, 11. There are some variations in the text, but no significant differences in the parts dealing with Beria.
24. See Grigorii Svirskii, *Na lobnom meste*, London: Overseas Publications Interchange, 1979, pp. 303–8, for background information about Bek's novel and the prototype of the hero.
25. Bek, *Novoe naznachenie*, pp. 34–5.
26. Ibid., p. 35.

Stalin in 1950. Beria, who is again present, now master of vast areas of the country through his control of Gulag, considers Onisimov with cold blue eyes (neither yellow – cf. Ketlinskaia and Gouzenko, nor green – cf. Djilas, in this version),[27] through his round, rimless spectacles.[28] Beria is biding his time, waiting for Onisimov to fall from grace, while working energetically to undermine his position. This he does by funding, through the Gulag system, an experimental smelting process which Onisimov has tried and dismissed as unworkable. Beria's aim is to demonstrate to Stalin that Onisimov has been placing obstacles in the way of inventive talent.[29]

On Stalin's death in March 1953, Beria's power is all the greater. Bek shows him chairing a meeting of the USSR Council of Ministers in June, at which a report by Onisimov is on the agenda: 'Preliminary Results in the Production of Heat-Resistant Steel for Jet Engines.'[30] Beria clearly has no inkling that 'within a few days, he – the chief accomplice, the chief perpetrator of the crimes of the past – will be publicly exposed'.[31] Bek clearly enjoys using the benefit of hindsight to stress the element of hubris in this. It is worth noting, however, that Bek is not of that school which finds in Beria a scapegoat for the iniquities of the period. Here Beria is a 'souchastnik' (accomplice) and 'ispolnitel'' (literally 'executor, implementer'), rather than the initiator of these crimes. (The phrase containing these words is not included in the *Znamia* text, but the tenor of this version, in so far as it concerns Beria, is affected but little.)

At this session of the Council of Ministers the animosity between Beria and Onisimov comes into the open, in connection with the Lesnykh smelting technique, which Onisimov has not backed. Beria calls his behaviour 'nepartiinoe' and 'negosudarstvennoe' (unworthy of the Party and the state) – and the narrator's voice interpolates, in a tone of indignation worthy of Solzhenitsyn, 'As before, Beria could give instruction in *partiinost'* without the slightest embarrassment'.[32] An unspoken charge of 'wrecking' hangs in the air. Onisimov, however, finds the courage to rebut the charges in

27. Gouzenko, *Fall of a Titan*, p. 230; Djilas, *Conversations with Stalin*, p. 124. It is noteworthy that yellow is the eye colour attributed to Stalin himself by Djilas, Rybakov, and Solzhenitsyn. The sinister connotations of yellow eyes have been emphasized by Vladimir Grebenschikov, who points out the similarity in colouring between Solzhenitsyn's Stalin and Dante's Satan: 'Les cercles infernaux chez Soljénitsyne et Dante', *Canadian Slavonic Papers*, 13(1971), 147–64, here 155–8.
28. Bek, *Novoe naznachenie*, p. 52.
29. Ibid., p. 97, p. 106.
30. Ibid., p. 103.
31. Ibid., p. 124.
32. Ibid., p. 125.

convincing detail, and his instinct tells him that, despite appearances, Beria's power is no longer so securely based now that Stalin is gone: 'Stalin had been the sole source of that man's immense, awesome power.'[33] (It seems clear from this that Bek has little time for those who would exonerate Stalin at Beria's expense.) A week or two later Beria has fallen, Onisimov is cleared, and the Lesnykh method condemned.

As Onisimov's terminal cancer takes hold, the doctor studying his medical record is able to read in it the recent history of Soviet society. From this record only the broad outlines are discernible, for the specifics are in no small measure related to the patient's dealings with, and fear of, Lavrentii Pavlovich Beria. It is true that the gastritis of 1937 seems to be associated with the great purge, when Onisimov feared for his life, in the days before Beria took control. But 1938, the year in which he started smoking, is also the year of his letter to Stalin in defence of his colleagues, and the year of the crucial audience with Stalin, in the presence of his old enemy, Beria – a time of great anxiety. The uncontrollable trembling of his hands dates from 1952, when he learned that Beria was actively working to promote Lesnykh – a time when the axe might have fallen at any moment.

In the absence of detailed biographical information about Tevosian, it is difficult to establish the degree of historical truth in Bek's novel. It is not clear whether Tevosian's widow reacted to the portrait with indignation because she found it excessively inaccurate, or excessively accurate.[34] However, Bek gives every impression of being extremely well informed, and of basing at least the essentials of his story on known facts. In the portrait of Beria, maximum credibility is his aim.

References to Beria, fleeting though they are, in another 'exhumed' novel, Vasilii Grossman's *Zhizn' i sud'ba* (Life and Fate), do impart a modicum of information about the man. Getmanov reports that in government circles only Beria and Molotov address Stalin as *ty*, a clear indication that by the war years he is perceived as having reached as close to Stalin as possible.[35]

33. Ibid.
34. Svirskii, *Na lobnom meste* (p. 307) gives details of the bar on publication in 1965, mentioning the role of Tevosian's widow. It is a pity that Beria's widow's reaction to this (and other) literary portraits of her husband does not appear to have been recorded.
35. Vasilii Grossman, *Zhizn' i sud'ba*, Lausanne: L'Age d'Homme, 1980, p. 228. At the time of writing, it has not been possible to check this text against the Soviet version, publication of which began in *Oktiabr'*, 1988, No. 1. Reports differ on Beria's pronominal usage in speaking to Stalin: Mikhail Shul'man, *Butyrskii*

An incident in the novel in which a boy of four adds a beard and ear-rings to a portrait of Stalin, thereby causing great consternation, is used to recall another case, in which a student fired an air-rifle at a picture of the leader. Mashuk, an NKVD officer, fearing denunciation to Beria for 'liberalism' if he fails to report it, deals with the offender with all severity: a confession is extracted, of being the son of a 'kulak whore', and we presume that appropriate punishment ensues.[36] Both incidents speak eloquently of the climate of the times, and, if the second of them appears improbable, it is worth noting that Gustaw Herling-Grudziński records an almost identical case in his prison memoirs. Here the malefactor, known as 'Stalin's murderer', received a sentence of ten years, and died in the Kargopol' camp.[37] In Grossman's novel the story makes the point that Beria is clearly established, at an early date, as the centre from which retribution for 'lack of vigilance' (and other misdemeanours) flows.

A quite different novel, containing portraits of Stalin and Beria as vivid and lifelike as any to be found in Russian literature, is Fazil' Iskander's *Sandro iz Chegema* (Sandro from Chegem).[38] Set some years before Grossman's novel, in the mid-1930s, it shows a Beria already close to Stalin and, at the one point where we are granted access to Stalin's private thoughts, offers the germ of an explanation for Beria's success. Witnessing and fuelling the antagonism between Beria and Nestor Lakoba, Chairman of the Central Executive Committee of Abkhazia, at a banquet for raikom secretaries, Stalin foresees that Beria will 'devour' Lakoba (whom he publicly calls his 'best friend') and he feels powerless to prevent this. The reason he can do nothing lies basically in his own wishes and his own nature:

Power means you can't be fond of anybody. Because no sooner do you grow fond of somebody than you begin to trust him. But once you start trusting somebody, sooner or later you get a knife in your back. Yes, yes, that he knew very well. People had been fond of him, and sooner or later been stabbed in the back for it. What a wretched thing was life and

dekameron, Tel Aviv: Effect Publications, 1979, Vol. 1, p. 320, has *vy*; Roy Medvedev, *All Stalin's Men*, Oxford: Blackwell, 1983, p. 21, says that only Molotov and Voroshilov used *ty* to Stalin; P. Logachev, as reported by A. T. Rybin, 'Riadom s I. V. Stalinym', *Sotsiologicheskie issledovaniia*, 1988, No. 3, 83–94, has *ty*.

36. Grossman, *Zhizn' i sud'ba*, p. 66.
37. Gustaw Herling-Grudziński, *Inny Świat*, London: Gryf Publications, 1953, p. 54.
38. F. Iskander, *Sandro iz Chegema*, Ann Arbor: Ardis, 1979. A later volume, *Sandro: novye glavy*, Ann Arbor: Ardis, 1981, adds nothing to the motif of Beria. The much shorter version published in *Novyi mir* 1973, Nos. 8–11, does not include the passages referred to here. Some of the missing chapters appeared in *Iunost'* and *Znamia* in 1988.

human nature! If only you could like somebody and mistrust him at the same time. But that was impossible.[39]

Thus Stalin is possessed of a tragic inability to change his own nature and allow himself to have friends and trust them. He himself, no less than those about him, is the victim of his own personality. Not only his many enemies, but also those friends whom he might begin to trust must be eliminated. Beria, into whose psychology we are granted no such intriguing insights, is adept at eliminating both categories indiscriminately, fulfilling Stalin's innermost wishes.

Neither figure can be said to emerge with much credit from another anecdotal scene at the same banquet, in the chapter entitled 'Belshazzar's Feasts'. Beria enquires what should be done about Tsulukidze, an old Bolshevik against whom he has harboured a grudge for a remark made at least a dozen years previously. Beria says merely that he 'talks too much', and has 'gone soft in the head'. Stalin, displeased at having such a matter raised while he is on holiday, on recalling that Tsulukidze has a brother, suggests, 'Make the blabbermouth regret for the rest of his days that he ruined his brother's life' – a solution that strikes Beria as inspired.[40]

There is nothing here to suggest that this conversation, occupying only one page, is anything more than an illustration of Beria's vengeful nature and Stalin's ingenuity in applying what he here calls 'the dialectic of punishment'. However, the choice of name is interesting, and presumably deliberate, since Aleksandr Tsulukidze (1879–1905) was a well-known revolutionary, active in the Caucasus in the 1890s. One cannot exclude the possibility that Iskander has inside information about Aleksandr Tsulukidze's relatives, information which is not recorded in the more accessible published sources. (Verification is complicated by the absence of forenames, patronymics, and even initials in Iskander's story.)

Beria proceeds to 'devour' Lakoba, as Stalin foresaw he would. Speaking of Lakoba and Trotskii at a later point, the narrative tells us: 'Beria poisoned one of them, and Bushy Whiskers' man did for the other with a crowbar.'[41] Non-fictional sources are few, but if Suren Gazarian and Roy Medvedev (the latter apparently relying on Gazarian's information) are correct, the poisoning story has a sound basis in historical fact.[42]

39. Iskander, *Sandro*, p. 220.
40. Ibid., p. 222.
41. Ibid., p. 553.
42. Suren Gazarian, 'O Berii i sude nad berievtsami v Gruzii', *SSSR: vnutrennye protivorechiia*, 6 (1982), 109–46, here 117; Medvedev, *K sudu istorii*, p. 515.

Iskander also holds Beria personally responsible for the death of Lakoba's son Rauf'. In this story, the boy is arrested, aged 14, in 1937, but then forgotten until in 1941 he writes to Beria, asking to be sent to the front. On realizing that Rauf' is still alive, and now old enough for a death sentence, Beria orders his execution.[43] Here again the resemblance to Gazarian's account is striking, differing only in the date and the boy's motive for requesting release. According to Gazarian, Rauf' and three friends, finding themselves in a camp and not knowing why, wrote to Beria, asking to be released to continue their studies. Though still schoolboys – Gazarian stresses that Rauf' was still a minor – all four were shot.[44]

Here Iskander demonstrates his knowledge of the Rukhadze trial (highly relevant to Beria's career), held in Tbilisi in 1955, at which the Lakoba case was examined. It is not clear whether Iskander used Gazarian's manuscript (unpublished when *Sandro* was written) as a source, or drew on other, unpublished sources.

It is plain that neither old Makhas, nor the first-person narrator of *Sandro of Chegem*, accepts the story that Stalin died a natural death, and their thoughts on this matter must implicate Beria, although at this point he is not mentioned by name. It was the 'Minders' (Russ.: *prismatrivaiushchie*) who 'toppled Bushy Whiskers', who was the 'Minder of all the Minders'. (Since it is known that Stalin died, the word 'toppled' – Russ.: *sverzili* – seems somewhat euphemistic.) Because of this, 'everybody felt better, but all the same the Minders would inevitably seize most of the benefits for themselves – that was the purpose of the whole exercise', the narrative tells us.[45] This is one of very few intimations in Russian fiction to date of the view that Stalin's rule was terminated not by natural death, but by a conspiracy to murder, of the type suggested by Avtorkhanov.[46] If the 'Minders' were involved, this cannot but implicate their leader, Beria.

Iskander's novel may well be the only work of fiction yet published to say anything at all about Beria's wife. An indication is given of Beria's discomfiture as Stalin needles him by making his reluctant wife dance, and then drawing invidious comparisons with Lakoba's wife, who is a graceful dancer. As Beria urges his wife to

43. Iskander, *Sandro*, p. 306.
44. Gazarian, *SSSR: vnutrennie protivorechiia*, pp. 141–2.
45. Iskander, *Sandro*, p. 228.
46. A. Avtorkhanov, *Zagadka smerti Stalina*, Frankfurt/Main: Possev, 1976. In his *Zheltyi dom*, Vol. 1, Lausanne: L'Age d'Homme, 1980, A. Zinov'ev makes a brief reference to 'the killing of Stalin', but merely as one item in a list of political assassinations (p. 327).

begin dancing, Sandro notices his 'twisted lips whispering unprint-able words to her.'[47] This brief vignette of Beria's family life con-forms with what little is known of it from other sources. It also accords with Khrushchev's well-known account of Stalin's banquets and the entertainment he compelled his guests to provide. Allilueva states that Beria, alone among Stalin's henchmen, was immune to the worst humiliations and practical jokes, though he still had to accept a certain amount of mischievous provocation from Stalin.[48]

Beria's well-known sexual preference for adolescent schoolgirls is alluded to in a somewhat cryptic aside (but even this is more than most Soviet fiction writers will say on the subject).[49] Beria is said to be the author of a Soviet-style slogan aimed at encouraging diligent study: 'A pupil's heroism and valour is to study for top marks.' As for schoolgirls, we are told in parentheses, after his arrest it emerged that he had his own 'highly individual view of the nature of heroism and valour of schoolgirls, or of some of them, at least'.[50] (An anecdotal episode in a short story by Iskander, 'Malen'kii gigant bol'shogo seksa', (The Very Sexy Little Giant) probes a related theme. In it the hero, on learning that he is sharing his mistress with Beria, is stricken with impotence.)[51]

Perhaps the most striking feature of *Sandro* in its treatment of figures such as Beria, Stalin, and Lakoba is that, although the author's preface speaks of his humorous and parodic intent, and despite the free rein given to his creative imagination, the material dealing with these historical personae appears to be closely based on fact, some of it little known, and does much to bring them to life as credible fictional figures, even though little space is allotted to them.

It will not escape notice that in the place filled by Beria in at least the more orthodox Soviet-style fiction, i.e. that written in conformity with the norms of acceptability as perceived during the Khrushchev

---

47. Iskander, *Sandro*, p. 211.
48. S. Allilueva, *Only One Year*, New York: Harper & Row, 1969, p. 386.
49. It is left to an English novelist to be more explicit on this point: Alan Williams, *The Beria Papers*, London: Blond & Briggs, 1976. Some non-fictional detail was supplied by the lawyer G. A. Terekhov in a television feature on 29 April 1988. See *Summary of World Broadcasts*, SU/0140 B/4. See also *Khrushchev Remembers*, Boston: Little, Brown & Co., 1970, p. 338; the recollections of Svetlana Vas-il'evna Sh. and Maiia Ivanovna Koneva (daughter of the late Marshal, who presided at Beria's trial), in Nikolai Zhusenin, 'Beriia: neskol'ko epizodov odnoi prestupnoi zhizni', *Nedelia*, 22–8 Feb. 1988, 11–12; and A. Skorokhodov, 'Kak nas gotovili na voinu s Beriei', *Literaturnaia gazeta*, 27 July 1988, 13.
50. Iskander, *Sandro*, p. 390.
51. Fazil' Iskander, 'Malen'kii gigant bol'shogo seksa', in *Metropol': literaturnyi al'manakh*, Ann Arbor: Ardis, 1979, pp. 381–424. I am grateful to Dr Michael Ulman for pointing this out to me.

decade, a certain pattern emerges. The hero, an upstanding, patriotic official or scientist, encounters Beria and/or Stalin at a meeting or conference in the Kremlin, having been summoned to explain shortcomings in his work. This is the case with the works of Ketlinskaia, Bek and Sizov. Granin presents a variation of the pattern. (The verisimilitude of these scenes has recently been borne out by Simonov's description in his memoirs of just such an encounter with Beria.)[52] In each case, Beria appears as an opponent, and a dangerous one, questioning the hero's honesty and his patriotism. The threat of arrest, and even death, looms large if Beria is allowed to win the arguments.

This is not to imply that these writers – most of them beneficiaries of the first thaw – contrast a 'hard-line' Beria with a 'liberal' or 'moderate' Stalin. In fact, few of them are concerned to apportion blame between these two. Only one work, Ketlinskaia's novel, reflects a political view, briefly in favour during a moment of reaction in the Khrushchev thaw, that Beria was more culpable than Stalin. Sizov's novel, showing Beria conspiring to bring down an enemy by giving Stalin an adverse report on him, is aimed less at blackening Beria in comparison with Stalin than at comparing these two with Khrushchev, and suggesting what might have been, but for the speedy elimination of Beria in 1953 in a conspiracy led by Khrushchev. This support for Khrushchev is implied in most of the works of the period, but is most explicitly stated by Sizov, the only one to introduce Khrushchev by name. The works proscribed in the earlier period, but published in the thaw of the 1980s, do not differ substantially in their approach to Beria, but add to the detail.

Treatment of Beria is fragmentary, at best, in the few works published during the Khrushchev decade, and only slightly fuller in one of those suppressed until Gorbachev's *glasnost'* (Bek's). Thus to suggest any connection between these factors would be to overestimate the importance assigned by Glavlit to the memory of Beria. To the Stalinists, such as Vsevolod Kochetov, who once described a thaw as 'a rotten, slushy season',[53] it was extensive critiques of Stalin himself and his legacy that gave offence. While even Kochetov had little interest in defending Beria's reputation *per se*, excessive detail surfacing in the 'slush' would reflect badly on the period as a whole.

If political considerations exerted an influence on the fiction

<hr>

52. Konstantin Simonov, 'Glazami cheloveka moego pokoleniia' (Part 2), *Znamia*, 1988, No. 3, 49–121, here 81–2.
53. Quoted by Anatol Goldberg, in *Ilya Ehrenburg*, New York: Viking, 1984, p. 260.

published in 1960–4, no such constraints are visible in those 'exhumed' in the late 1980s. The novels by Grossman and Iskander share a publishing history similar to that of Bek's novel, and all present a picture of Beria compiled with little apparent regard for the political exigencies of the time of writing.[54] While clearly writing in the hope that the Khrushchev thaw would continue, the authors were to be disappointed. The Kochetovs regained the ascendancy.

Most of the works of fiction reviewed here start from the premise that the times under scrutiny were dominated by a thoroughly malign spirit, and Beria clearly plays a central role in maintaining it. Few supporters can be found for him. If Stalin had admirers and apologists in plenty, Beria has been less fortunate. Nor is the view that he was 'only obeying orders' in evidence in any of the works under consideration. Most writers implicitly accept that he was a willing participant in Stalin's repressions, while some, such as Sizov and Iskander, suggest that he was adept at manipulating Stalin to suit his own fell designs.

Allilueva expresses surprise at how 'helpless' her father seemed in the face of Beria's machinations, and tells how Beria played on Stalin's weaknesses,[55] but elsewhere finds them 'jointly to blame for many things', and 'spiritually inseparable'.[56] The majority of the fiction-writers tend towards the latter view.

In most accounts, the two figures complement each other. Beria owes his power and prestige to Stalin, and his position is the weaker (according to Bek) after Stalin's death. Stalin finds in Beria a reliable assistant, with an unerring ability to pinpoint and act on his most villainous wishes without having to be told.[57] Stalin does not emerge as Beria's moral superior, any more than the reverse would be true.

It is noteworthy that Russian fiction to date offers no account of Beria's arrest and death, several 'factual' versions of which have circulated at various times. Referring to this event in his novel, Bek

54. Vladimir Voinovich's story of Ivan Chonkin, shortly to be published in *Iunost'*, has had a similar history. The second volume, *Pretendent na prestol*, Paris: YMCA Press, 1979, contains a charming scene featuring Stalin and Beria (with *ty* used mutually). Since the author terms his novel a 'roman-anekdot', it is hardly appropriate to consider it under the heading 'Fiction as History'.

55. Svetlana Allilueva, *Dvadtsat' pisem k drugu*, New York: Harper & Row, 1967, p. 75; 'Perepiska Svetlany Alliluevoi i Ol'gi i Romana Gulia', *Novyi zhurnal*, 1986, No. 164, 168.

56. Allilueva, *Dvadtsat' pisem*, p. 131.

57. Stalin's preference for precisely such assistants is noted by (*inter alia*) Anatolii Butenko, 'Stalinskoe okruzhenie', *Nedelia*, 12–18 Sept. 1988, 9, and Marshal Tolubko, in Zhusenin, *Nedelia*, 22–8 Feb. 1988, 11–12.

has this to say: 'One truly auspicious day Beria was overthrown. Some day historians, and perhaps writers too, will recreate the details of this gripping episode.'[58]

As it happens, in filling this particular 'blank page' it is the journalists who have taken the lead. At least some of the articles published in the Soviet press under *glasnost'*, giving details of Beria's arrest, imprisonment, and execution, appear to bear the stamp of authority.[59]

The pace of recent revelations about this period gives rise to hope that a serious exploration in fiction of the circumstances surrounding another death, that of Stalin himself, and of Beria's role in events at that time, may not be long in coming. Already there are indications that Avtorkhanov's theory of a conspiracy by Beria to hasten Stalin's death is not regarded as totally fanciful.[60] At least three well-publicized current projects by Soviet authors appear likely to treat this episode and contribute to the way in which Beria is seen by future generations.[61] While a general reappraisal would seem an unlikely outcome, such publications do suggest that the current thaw will do much to lay the ghost of Beria once and for all, in a way that the Khrushchev thaw, being too close to the events, could not.

58. Bek, *Novoe naznachenie*, p. 127.
59. See especially the aforementioned articles by Zhusenin and Skorokhodov, and S. Bystrov, 'Zadanie osobogo svoistva', *Sovetskaia Estoniia*, 31 Mar., 1 and 2 Apr. 1988. Cf. Tadeusz Wittlin, *Commissar*, New York: Macmillan, 1972, p. 395, and A. Antonov-Ovseenko, 'Konets Berii', *Strana i mir*, 1987, No. 2, pp. 43–51, for the several versions put about by Khrushchev. (Antonov-Ovseenko's *Kar'era palacha*, in *Zvezda*, came too late to be considered here.) The version set forth by Karlo Stajner in his *7000 dana u Sibiru*, Zagreb: Globus, 1971, p. 455, according to which Beria was killed only twenty minutes after his arrest, must now be discounted, but this memoir remains notable for the reported sighting of some (unspecified) members of Beria's family in exile in Maklakov, Krasnoiarsk krai, in 1955 (p. 464).
60. Oleg Moroz, in an aside in his article 'Poslednii analiz', *Literaturnaia gazeta*, 28 Sept. 1988, p. 12, mentions the 'fully plausible' theory that Beria poisoned Stalin. Konstantin Simonov also raises the possibility of murder by Beria: 'Glazami cheloveka moego pokoleniia' (Part 2), p. 94.
61. Publication of the following is imminent: in fiction, the aforementioned sequel to Rybakov's *Deti Arbata*, and Vladimir Amlinskii's *V marte 53-ego*; among historical studies, Dmitrii Volkogonov's *Triumf i tragediia (Politicheskii portret I.V. Stalina)*.

Select Bibliography

I General Works

Alexeyeva, Ludmilla, *Soviet Dissent: Contemporary Movements for National, Religious and Human Rights*, Middletown, Connecticut: Wesleyan University Press, 1985

Ash, Timothy Garton, *The Polish Revolution: Solidarity, 1980–82*, New York: Scribner, 1984

Eattle, John M., '*Uskorenie, Glasnost'* and *Perestroika*: The Pattern of Reform Under Gorbachev', *Soviet Studies*, 40(1988), 367–84

Bialer, Seweryn, *Stalin's Successors: Leadership, Stability and Change in the Soviet Union*, Cambridge: Cambridge University Press, 1980

—— (ed.), *Politics, Society, and Nationality: Inside Gorbachev's Russia*, Boulder: Westview, 1988

Bielasiak, Jack, 'Modernization and Elite Cooptation in Eastern Europe, 1954–1971', *East European Quarterly*, 14(1980–1), 345–69

Brown, Archie, and Michael Kaser (eds.), *Soviet Policy for the 1980s*, Oxford: St Anthony's College, 1982

Cracraft, James (ed.), *The Soviet Union Today: An Interpretive Guide*, 2nd ed., Chicago: University of Chicago Press, 1988

Crankshaw, Edward, *Khrushchev: A Career*, New York: Viking, 1966

Dawisha, Karen, *Eastern Europe, Gorbachev and Reform: The Great Challenge*, Cambridge: Cambridge University Press, 1988

——, *The Kremlin and the Prague Spring*, Berkeley: University of California Press, 1984

Disard, Wilson P., and S. Blake Swensrud, *Gorbachev's Information Revolution: Controlling Glasnost in the New Electronic Era*, Center for Strategic and International Studies, Significant Issues Series, Vol. IX, No. 8, Boulder: Westview, 1987

Dmytryshyn, Basil, *USSR: A Concise History*, 4th ed., New York: Macmillan, 1984

Drachkovitch, Milorad M. (ed.), *East Central Europe: Yesterday, Today, Tomorrow*, Stanford, California: Hoover Institution Press, Stanford University, 1982

Dyker, David A. (ed.), *The Soviet Union under Gorbachev: Prospects for Reform*, London: Croom Helm, 1987

Eklof, Ben, *Soviet Briefing: Gorbachev and the Reform Period*, Boulder: Westview, 1988

Fehér, Ferenc, and Agnes Heller, *Hungary 1956 Revisited: The Message of a Revolution – A Quarter of a Century After*, London: Allen and Unwin, 1983

Fischer-Galati, Stephen (ed.), *Eastern Europe in the 1980s*, Boulder: Westview, London: Croom Helm, 1981

Friedberg, Maurice, and Heyward Isham (eds.), *Soviet Society under Gorbachev: Current Trends and Prospects for Reform*, Armonk, NY: Sharpe, 1987

García Alvarez, Manuel B., 'Political Clubs in People's Democracies', *East European Quarterly*, 11(1977), 477–92

Gibian, George, 'Ferment and Reaction: 1956–57'. *Problems of Communism*, 7(1958), No. 1, 21–7

Goble, Paul A., 'Gorbachev and the Nationality Problem', in Maurice Friedberg and Heyward Isham (eds.), *Soviet Society under Gorbachev: Current Trends and Prospects for Reform*, Armonk, NY: Sharpe, 1987, pp. 76–100

Goldfarb, Jeffrey C., *On Cultural Freedom: An Exploration of Public Life in Poland and America*, Chicago: University of Chicago Press, 1982

Goudoever, Albert P. van, *The Limits of Destalinization in the Soviet Union*, trans. Franz Hijkoop, London: Croom Helm, 1986

Havel, Václav, et al., *The Power of the Powerless: Citizens Against the State in Central-Eastern Europe*, ed. John Keane, intro. Steven Lukes, London: Hutchinson, 1985

Hughes, H. Stuart, *Sophisticated Rebels: The Political Culture of European Dissent, 1968–1987*, Cambridge, Massachussetts: Harvard University Press, 1988

Jancar, Barbara Wolfe, 'Modernity and the Character of Dissent', in Charles Gati (ed.), *The Politics of Modernization in Eastern Europe: Testing the Soviet Model*, Studies of the Institute on East Central Europe, Columbia University, New York: Praeger, 1974, pp. 338–57

Johnson, Chalmers (ed.), *Change in Communist Systems*, Stanford, California: Stanford University Press, 1970

Johnson, Paul M., 'Modernization as an Explanation of Political Change in East European States', in Jan F. Triska and Paul M. Cocks (eds.), *Political Development in Eastern Europe*, New York: Praeger, 1977, pp. 30–50

Kaplan, Frank L., *Winter into Spring: The Czechoslovak Press and the Reform Movement 1963–68*, East European Monographs, 29, Boulder: East European Quarterly, 1977 (distributed by Columbia University Press).

Kautsky, John H., 'Revolutionary and Managerial Elites in Modernizing Regimes', *Comparative Politics*, 1(1969), 441–67

Kelley, Donald R., *Soviet Politics from Brezhnev to Gorbachev*, New York: Praeger, 1987

Lewin, Mosche, *The Gorbachev Phenomenon: A Historical Interpretation*, Berkeley: University of California Press, 1988

Lewystzkyj, Borys, *Politics and Society in Soviet Ukraine 1953–80*, Edmonton: Canadian Institute of Ukrainian Studies, 1984

London, Kurt (ed.), *Eastern Europe in Transition*, Baltimore: Johns Hopkins University Press, 1966

Lovenduski, Joni, and Jean Woodall, *Politics and Society in Eastern Europe*, Bloomington: Indiana University Press, 1987

McCauley, Martin (ed.), *Khrushchev and Khrushchevism*, London: Macmillan, 1987

—— (ed.), *The Soviet Union under Gorbachev*, New York: St Martin's Press, 1987

Martin, Jay, *Fin de Siècle Socialism and Other Essays*, New York: Routlege, 1988

Mason, David S., *Public Opinion and Political Change in Poland 1980–1982*, New York: Cambridge University Press, 1985

Miller, R. F., and Ferenc Féhér (eds.), *Khrushchev and the Communist World*, London: Croom Helm, 1984

Miller, R. F., J. H. Miller and T. H. Rigby, *Gorbachev at the Helm: A New Era in Soviet Politics?*, London: Croom Helm, 1987

Motyl, Alexander J., *Will the Non-Russians Rebel? State, Ethnicity, and Stability in the U.S.S.R.*, Studies in Soviet History and Society. Ithaca, NY: Cornell University Press, 1987

Nove, Alec, *Stalinism and After*, New York: Crane, 1975

——, 'The USSR after the Death of Stalin. Some Comments on Mr. Miller's Article', *Soviet Studies*, 6(1954–5), 41–52

Ramet, Pedro (ed.), *Yugoslavia in the 1980s*, Boulder: Westview, 1985

Rigby, T. H., 'Conclusion: The Gorbachev Era Launched', in R. F. Miller, J. H. Miller and T. H. Rigby, *Gorbachev at the Helm: A New Era in Soviet Politics?*, London: Croom Helm, 1987, pp. 235–46.

Rothberg, Abraham, *The Heirs of Stalin: Dissidence and the Soviet Regime 1953–70* Ithaca, NY: Cornell University Press, 1972

Ryan, Michael, and Richard Prentice, *Social Trends in the Soviet Union since 1950*, New York: St Martin's Press, 1987

Shlapentokh, Vladimir, *Soviet Ideologies in the Period of Glasnost: Responses to Brezhnev's Stagnation*, New York: Praeger, 1988

——, 'The XXVII Congress: A Case Study of the Shaping of a New Party Ideology', *Soviet Studies*, 40(1988), 1–20

Skilling, H. Gordon, *Charter 77 and Human Rights in Czechoslovakia*, London: Allen and Unwin, 1981

Stojanović, Svetozar, *Perestroika: From Marxism and Bolshevism to Gorbachev*, Buffalo, NY: Prometheus, 1988

'Summary of the XX Party Congress', *Soviet Studies*, 8(1956–7), 82–166, 185–203

Taubman, William, 'The Change to Change in Communist Systems: Modernization, Postmodernization, and Soviet Politics', in Henry W. Morton and Rudolf L. Tökés, *Soviet Politics and Society in the 1970's*, New York: Free Press, 1974, pp. 369–94

Tökes, Rudolf L. (ed.), *Opposition in Eastern Europe*, Baltimore: Johns Hopkins University Press, 1979

Touraine, Alain, et al. *Solidarity: Poland 1980–81*, Cambridge: Cambridge

University Press, 1983

Tucker, Robert C., *Political Culture and Leadership in Soviet Russia: From Lenin to Gorbachev*, Brighton, Sussex: Wheatsheaf, 1987, esp. 'To Change a Political Culture: Gorbachev and the Fight for Soviet Reform', pp. 140–98

Ulč, Otto, *Politics in Czechoslovakia*, San Francisco: Freeman, 1974

Wildman, Allan (ed.), *Gorbachev Reforms*, Special issue of *The Russian Review*, 48(1989), No. 3

Wilson, Andrew, and Nina Bachkatov, *Living with Glasnost: Youth and Society in a Changing Russia*, Harmondsworth: Penguin, 1988

Yanov, Alexander, *The Drama of the Soviet 1960s: A Lost Reform*, Berkeley: Institute of International Studies, University of California, 1984

Zaslawsky, Victor, 'Soviet Reforms in the 1980's: Current Debate', in R. F. Miler, J. H. Miller and T. H. Rigby, *Gorbachev at the Helm: A New Era in Soviet Politics?*, London: Croom Helm, 1987, pp. 136–60

II   Thaws, Literature, Culture, the Arts

1.   General

Bernard, Paul P., *The Limits of Enlightenment: Joseph II and the Law*, Urbana: University of Illinois Press, 1979

Birnbaum, Henrik, and Thomas Eekman (eds.), *Fiction and Drama in Eastern and Southeastern Europe: Evolution and Experiment in the Postwar Period*, Columbus, Ohio: Slavica Publishers, 1980

Blumenfeld, Yorick, *Seesaw: Cultural Life in Eastern Europe*, New York: Harcourt, 1968

Bodi, Leslie, 'Tauwetter', in E. W. Herd and August Obermayer (eds.), *A Glossary of German Literary Terms*, Dunedin: University of Otago, 1983, p. 219

——, *Tauwetter in Wien: zur Prosa der österreichischen Aufklärung 1781–95*, Frankfurt: Fischer, 1977

Brown, Deming, *Soviet Russian Literature Since Stalin*, Cambridge: Cambridge University Press, 1978

Carden, Patricia, 'The New Russian Literature', in K. Brostrom (ed.), *Russian Literature and American Critics*, Papers in Slavic Philology, 4, Ann Arbor: Michigan University Press, 1984, pp. 11–22

Clark, Katerina, 'Political History and Literary Chronotope: Some Soviet Case Studies', in Gary Saul Morson (ed.), *Literature and History: Theoretical Problems and Russian Case Studies*, Stanford, California: Stanford University Press, 1986, pp. 230–46

——, *The Soviet Novel: History as Ritual*, Chicago: University of Chicago Press, 1981

Crouch, Martin, and Robert Porter (eds.), *Understanding Soviet Politics Through Literature: A Book of Readings*, London: Allen and Unwin, 1984

Curry, Jane Leftwich (ed. and trans.), *The Black Book of Polish Censorship*, New York: Random House, 1983

Davis, Ossie, 'Film and Human Liberation: Some Thoughts on the Moscow Film Festival', *New World Review*, 40(1972), No. 1, 34–47

Dewhirst, Martin, 'Soviet Russian Literature and Literary Policy', in Archie Brown and Michael Kaser (eds.), *The Soviet Union Since the Fall of Khrushchev*, London: Macmillan, 1975, pp. 181–95

—— and Robert Farrell, *The Soviet Censorship*, Metuchen, N. J.: Scarecrow, 1973, esp. 'Evading the Censor', pp. 130–48

Dodge, Norton, and Alison Hilton (eds.), *New Art from the Soviet Union: The Known and the Unknown*, Washington: Acropolis, 1979

Findlay, Robert, et al. (eds.), *Contemporary Russian and Polish Theater and Drama*, Theater Perspectives, 2, New York: American Theater Association, 1982

French, Alfred, 'The Art and Politics of East European Film', *Southern Review* (Adelaide), 11(1977), No. 1, 94–101

——, *Czech Writers and Politics 1945–1969*, East European Monographs, No. 94, Boulder: East European Monographs, 1982

Gella, Aleksander (ed.), *The Intelligentsia and the Intellectuals: Theory, Method, and Case Study*, Beverly Hills, California: Sage, 1976

Gibian, George, 'New Aspects of Soviet Russian Literature', in Stephen F. Cohen et al. (eds.), *The Soviet Union Since Stalin*, Bloomington: Indiana University Press, 1980, pp. 252–75

Gladilin, Anatoly, *The Making and Unmaking of a Soviet Writer: My Story of the 'Young Prose' of the Sixties and After*, trans. David Lapeza, Ann Arbor: Ardis, 1979

Glazov, Yuri, *The Russian Mind Since Stalin's Death*, Sovietica, Vol. 47. Dordrecht: Reidel, 1985

Golan, Galia, 'Czechoslovak Marxism in the Reform Period', *Studies in Soviet Thought*, 16(1976), No. 1–2, 67–82

Golomshtok, Igor, 'The History and Organization of Artistic Life in the Soviet Union', in Marilyn Rueschmeyer et al. (eds.), *Soviet Émigré Artists: Life and Work in the USSR and the United States*, Armonk, NY: Sharpe, 1985, pp. 16–59

——, 'The Mechanism of Control: Unofficial Art in the USSR', *Studio International*, December 1974, 239–44

——, 'Unofficial Art in the Soviet Union', in Igor Golomshtok and Alexander Glezer, *Soviet Art in Exile*, New York: Random House, 1977, pp. 81–106

Gömöri, George, 'The Cultural Intelligentsia in Poland: The Writers', in Bernard L. Faber (ed.), *The Social Structure of Eastern Europe: Transition and Process in Czechoslovakia, Hungary, Poland, Romania and Yugoslavia*, New York: Praeger, 1976, pp. 167–94

——, 'The Political and Social Setting of the Contemporary Arts', in George Schöpflin (ed.), *The Soviet Union and Eastern Europe*, rev. and updated ed., New York: Facts on File, 1986, pp. 547–64

Goulding, Daniel J., *Liberated Cinema: The Yugoslav Experience*, Bloomington: Indiana University Press, 1985

Hanhardt, Arthur M., Jr., and Gregory P. Swint, 'Literature and Political Culture', in Lyman H. Legters (ed.), *The German Democratic Republic: A Developed Socialist Society*, Boulder: Westview, 1978, pp. 155–78

Haraszti, Miklos, 'The Seduction of Censorship: The Common Interests of Artists and Censors', *New Republic*, 23 November 1987, 32–4

Hayward, Max, 'The Decline of Socialist Realism', *Survey*, 18(1972), 73–97

Heller, Agnes, Ferenc Fehér, '"Thaw" as Promesse de Bonheur', in Walter Veit et al. (eds.), *Antipodische Aufklärungen. Antipodean Enlightenments: Festschrift für Leslie Bodi*, Frankfurt: Lang, 1988, pp. 133–9

Hingley, Ronald, *Russian Writers and Soviet Society 1917–1978*, New York: Random House, 1979

Hirszowicz, Maria, 'Intelligentsia versus Bureaucracy? The Revival of a Myth in Poland', *Soviet Studies*, 30(1978), 336–61

Hollander, Paul, 'The Subordination of Literature to Politics: Socialist Realism in a Historical and Comparative Perspective', *Studies in Comparative Communism*, 11(1976), 215–25

Hosking, Geoffrey, *Beyond Socialist Realism. Soviet Fiction Since Ivan Denisovich*, London: Granada, 1980

Hrubý, Peter, *Fools and Heroes: The Changing Role of Communist Intellectuals in Czechoslovakia*, Oxford: Pergamon, 1980

Kaplan, Frank L., 'The Writer as Political Actor in Czechoslovak Society: A Historical Perspective', *East European Quarterly*, 7(1973–4), 199–220

Kliche, Dieter, and Rosemarie Lenzer, 'The Function of Literature in Socialist Society', in Arthur W. McCardle et al. (eds.), *East Germany: A New Nation Under Socialism?*, Lanham, Maryland: University Press of America, 1984, pp. 346–64

Labedz, Leopold, 'The Destiny of Writers in Revolutionary Movements', *Survey*, 18(1972), No. 1, 8–46

Lakshin, Vladimir, *Solzhenitsyn, Tvardovsky and 'Novy Mir'*, trans. and ed. Michael Glenny, Cambridge, Massachussetts: MIT Press, 1980

Leyda, Jay, *Kino: A History of the Russian and Soviet Film*, 3rd ed. Princeton, N.J.: Princeton University Press, 1983

Liehm, Mira, and Antonin J. Liehm, *The Most Important Art: Soviet and East European Film after 1945*, Berkeley: University of California Press, 1980

Loseff, Lev, *On the Beneficence of Censorship: Aesopian Language in Modern Russian Literature*, Arbeiten und Texte zur Slavistik, 31, Munich: Otto Sagner, 1984

Lowe, David, *Russian Writing since 1953: A Critical Survey*. New York: Ungar, 1987

Luckyj, George S. N. (ed.), *Discordant Voices: The Non-Russian Soviet Literatures 1953–1973* Oakville, Ontario: Mosaic Press, 1975

——, 'Polarity in Ukrainian Intellectual Dissent', *Canadian Slavonic Papers*,

Select Bibliography

14(1972), 269–79

——, 'The Ukrainian Literary Scene Today', *Slavic Review*, 31(1972), 863–75

Marković, Mihailo, 'Marxist Philosophy in Yugoslavia: The *Praxis* Group', in Richard T. De George and James P. Scanlan (eds.), *Marxism and Religion in Eastern Europe*, First International Slavic Conference, Banff. Dordrecht: Reidel, 1975, pp. 63–89

Marsh, Rosalind J., *Soviet Fiction Since Stalin: Science, Politics and Literature*, London: Croom Helm, 1985

Mead, Igor, and Paul Sjeklocha, *Unofficial Art in the Soviet Union*, Berkeley: University of California Press, 1967

Milner-Gulland, Robin, and Martin Dewhirst (eds.), *Russian Writing Today*, Harmondsworth: Penguin, 1977

Mlikotin, Anthony M., 'Yugoslav Literary Criticism: The Crucial Decade, 1955–1965', *East European Quarterly*, 10(1976), 273–307

Rühle, Jürgen, *Literature and Revolution: A Critical Study of the Writer and Communism in the Twentieth Century*, trans. and ed. Jean Steinberg, New York: Praeger, 1969

Sashegyi, Oskar, *Zensur und Geistesfreiheit unter Joseph II*, Budapest: Akadémíai Kiadó, 1958

Schwarz, Boris, *Music and Musical Life in Soviet Russia, 1917–1981*, Bloomington: Indiana University Press, 1983

Schwarz, Walter Friedrich, and Nina Gütter, *Sowjetrussisches und tschechisches Drama von 1964 bis in dis siebziger Jahre. Materialien zur Produktion und Rezeption (Situationsanalyse und Bibliographie)*, Slavische Sprachen und Literaturen, 3, Munich: Hieronymus, 1984

Shandor, Donald, R., *Behind the Lines: The Private War against Soviet Censorship*, New York: St Martin's Press, 1985

Sher, Gerson S., *Praxis: Marxist Criticism and Dissent in Socialist Yugoslavia*, Bloomington: Indiana University Press, 1977

Shneidman, N. Norman, *Soviet Literature in the 1970s: Artistic Diversity and Ideological Conformity*, Toronto: University of Toronto Press, 1979

——, 'Soviet Prose in the 1970s: Evolution or Stagnation?', *Canadian Slavonic Papers*, 20(1978), 63–77

Simmons, E. J., 'The Writers', in H. Gordon Skilling and F. Griffiths (eds.), *Interest Groups in Soviet Politics*, Princeton, NJ: Princeton University Press, 1971, pp. 253–90

Siniavskii, Andrei, *For Freedom of Imagination*, trans. Laszlo Tikos and Murray Peppard, New York: Rinehart and Winston, 1971

Škvorecký, Josef, 'A Cabaret of Censorship', *Index on Censorship*, 13(1984), No. 5, 38–40

Slonim, Marc, *Soviet Russian Literature: Writers and Problems 1917–77*, 2nd, rev. ed., New York: Oxford University Press, 1977, esp. 'The Thaw', pp. 320–37

Solzhenitsyn, Aleksandr, *The Oak and the Calf: Sketches of Literary Life in the*

Select Bibliography

Soviet Union, trans. Harry T. Willetts, New York: Harper and Row, 1980

Součková, Milada, *A Literary Satellite: Czechoslovak–Russian Literary Relations*, Chicago: University of Chicago Press, 1970

Southard, Andrea Castle, 'The Effects of Politics and Censorship upon Soviet Dramatic Literature', *Slavic and East European Arts*, 3(1985), No. 1, 127–39

Spechler, Dina R., *Permitted Dissent in the USSR. Novy mir and the Soviet Regime*, New York: Praeger, 1982

Sverstiuk, Ievhen, *Clandestine Essays*, trans. and intro. George S. N. Luckyj, Harvard Ukrainian Research Institute Monograph Series, Littleton, Colorado: Ukrainian Academic Press, 1976

Svirskii, Grigori, *A History of Post-War Soviet Writing: The Literature of Moral Opposition*, trans. and ed. Robert Dessaix and Michael Ulman, Ann Arbor: Ardis, 1981

Sviták, Ivan, 'Marxist Philosophy in Czechoslovakia: The Lesson from Prague', in Richard T. De George and James P. Scanlan (eds.), *Marxism and Religion in Eastern Europe*, First International Slavic Conference, Banff. Dordrecht: Reidel, 1975, pp. 45–62

Vladimirov, Leonid, 'Glavlit: How the Soviet Censor Works', *Index on Censorship*, 1(1972), No. 3–4, 31–43

Walker, Gregory, *Soviet Book Publishing Policy*, New York: Cambridge University Press, 1978

Whyte, Alistair, *New Cinema in Eastern Europe*, New York: Dutton, 1971

Zaitsev, Mark, 'Soviet Theater Censorship', *The Drama Review*, 19(1975), No. 2, 119–28

2.   1950s and 1960s

Aczél, Tamás, and Tibor Méray, *The Revolt of the Mind: A Case History of Intellectual Resistance Behind the Iron Curtain*, New York: Praeger, 1959

Balmashov, Michael, 'Soviet Drama: A Commentary', *Studies on the Soviet Union*, 8(1968–9), No. 3, 45–53

Benno, Peter, 'The Political Aspect', in Max Hayward and Edward L. Crowley (eds.), *Soviet Literature in the Sixties: An International Symposium*, New York: Praeger, 1964, pp. 178–202

——, 'The Politics of Current Literature', *Studies on the Soviet Union*, 3(1963), No. 2, 20–41

Berger, John, *Art and Revolution. Ernst Neizvestny and the Role of the Artist in the USSR*, London: Weidenfeld and Nicolson, 1969

Besançon, Alain, 'Painting [in the USSR]: Tradition and Experiment', *Survey*, No. 46(1963), 83–93

Blackwell, Vera, 'Literature and the Drama [in Czechoslovakia]', *Survey*, No. 59(1966), 41–7

Brown, Deming, and Mark E. Suino, 'Soviet Russian Poetry: A Study', *Studies on the Soviet Union*, 8(1964), No. 3, 24–44

Select Bibliography

Brown, Edward James, *Russian Literature Since the Revolution*, rev. and enl. ed., Cambridge, Massachusetts: Harvard University Press, 1982, esp. 'After Stalin: The First Two Thaws', pp. 190–221

Burg, David, 'The "Cold War" on the Literary Front', *Problems of Communism*, 11(1962), No. 4, 1–14, and No. 5, 33–46

Cousins, Norman, 'Readers and Writers in Russia: A Conversation with Ilya Ehrenburg in Moscow', *Saturday Review*, 3 October 1959, 15–17, 44

'The Cultural Front', *Survey*, No. 48(1943), 3–51

De Mauny, Erik, 'Current Trends in the Soviet Theatre', *Survey*, No. 57(1965), 73–80

De Vinzenz, A., 'Recent Ukrainian Writing', *Survey*, No. 59(1966), 102–12

Fedenko, Panas, 'The Principle of Selective Rehabilitation', *Bulletin of the Institute for the Study of the USSR*, 9(1962), No. 4, 23–8

Forgues, Pierre, 'Russian Poetry 1963–65', *Survey*, No. 56(1965), 54–70

——, 'The Young Poets', *Survey*, No. 46(1963), 31–52

Frank, Victor S., 'The [Soviet] Literary Climate', *Survey*, No. 56(1965), 46–53

Frankel, Edith Rogovin, *'Novy Mir': A Case Study in the Politics of Literature 1952–1958*, Cambridge: Cambridge University Press, 1981

Friedberg, Maurice, *A Decade of Euphoria: Western Literature in Post-Stalin Russia, 1954–64*, Bloomington: Indiana University Press, 1977

——, 'Literary Output: 1956–62', in Max Hayward and Edward L. Crowley (eds.), *Soviet Literature in the Sixties: An International Symposium*, New York: Praeger, 1964, pp. 150–77

——, 'Soviet Writers and the Red Pencil', *Midway*, 8(1967), No. 3, 39–58

Gaev, Arkady, 'The Decade Since Stalin', in Max Hayward and Edward L. Crowley (eds.), *Soviet Literature in the Sixties: An International Symposium*, New York: Praeger, 1964, pp. 18–54

Gibian, George, *Interval of Freedom: Soviet Literature During the Thaw, 1954–1957*, Minneapolis: University of Minnesota Press, 1960

——, 'Soviet Literature During the Thaw', in Max Hayward and Leopold Labedz (eds.), *Literature and Revolution in Soviet Russia 1917–62*, London: Oxford University Press, 1963, pp. 125–49

Gorchakov, Nikolai A., 'The Soviet Theatre Since the Twenty-Second Congress', *Bulletin of the Institute for the Study of the USSR*, 9(1962), No. 3, 39–44

Hayward, Max, 'Conflict and Change in Literature', *Survey*, No. 46(1963), 9–23

——, 'A Note on Recent Developments in the Soviet Theater', *Cahiers du Monde Russe et Soviétique*, 7(1966), No. 3, 408–13

——, and Edward L. Crowley (eds.), *Soviet Literature in the Sixties: An International Symposium*, New York: Praeger, 1964

Hoffmann, Hilmar, 'Revival of the Cinema [in the USSR and Eastern Europe]', *Survey*, No. 46(1963), 102–11

Horbatch, Anna-Halya, 'The Young Generation of Ukrainian Poets', *Ukrai-*

nian Review, 12(1965), No. 4, 23–34

Ignotus, Paul, '[Hungary:] Literature Before and After', *Survey*, No. 40(1962), 94–104

Ireland, P. R., 'Soviet Writing: Towards a New Situation', in J. D. B. Miller and T. H. Rigby (eds.), *The Disintegrating Monolith: Pluralist Trends in the Communist World. Papers from a Conference at the Research School of Pacific Studies, Australian National University, August 1964*, Canberra: Australian National University, 1965, pp. 96–108

Johnson, Priscilla, and Leopold Labedz (eds.), *Khrushchev and the Arts: The Politics of Soviet Culture, 1962–64*, Cambridge, Massachusetts: MIT Press, 1965

Kadić, Ante, 'Socialist Realism and Modernism in Present-Day Yugoslavia', *Books Abroad*, 33(1959), 139–43

Kagarlitsky, Boris, *The Thinking Reed: Intellectuals and the Soviet State 1917 to the Present*, 'trans. Brian Pearce. London: Verso, 1988, esp. 'The Thaw', pp. 128–87

Khrushchev Speaks. Selected Speeches, Articles, and Press Conferences, 1949–1961, ed., with a commentary, by Thomas P. Whitney, Ann Arbor: University of Michigan Press, 1963

Kusin, Vladimir V., *The Intellectual Origins of the Prague Spring: The Development of Reformist Ideas in Czechoslovakia 1956–1967*, Cambridge: Cambridge University Press, 1971

Laqueur, Walter Z., 'The "Thaw" and After', *Problems of Communism*, 5(1956), No. 1, 20–5

——, and George Lichtheim (eds.), *The Soviet Cultural Scene: 1956–1957*, New York: Praeger, 1958

Liehm, Antonin J., 'Some Observations on Czech Culture and Politics in the 1960's', in William E. Harkins and Paul I. Trensky (eds.), *Czech Literature Since 1956: A Symposium*, New York: Bohemica, 1980, pp. 134–59

——, 'The Mosaic of Czech Culture in the Late 1960's: The Inheritors of the Kafka–Hašek Dialectics', *Mosaic*, 1(1968), No. 3, 12–28

Luckyj, George S. N., 'Literary Ferment in the Ukraine', *Problems of Communism*, 11(1962), No. 6, 51–7

McClure, Timothy, 'The Politics of Soviet Culture, 1964–1967', *Problems of Communism*, 16(1967), No. 2, 26–43

McLean, Hugh, and Walter N. Vickery, *The Year of Protest 1956: An Anthology of Soviet Literary Materials*, New York: Random House, 1961

Malnick, Bertha, 'Current Problems of Soviet Literature', *Soviet Studies*, 7(1955–6), 1–13

——, 'The Soviet Theatre, 1957', *Soviet Studies*, 9(1958), 245–55

Mayer, Hans, 'DDR 1956: Tauwetter, das keines war', *Frankfurter Hefte*, 31(1976), No. 11, 15–23 and No. 12, 29–38

Mikhantyev, B., 'The Changes in Intellectual Life: A Provincial Aspect', trans. in *Soviet Studies*, 8(1956–7), 321–5

M[iller], J. (ed.), 'The Argument on *The Thaw*', *Soviet Studies*, 6 (1954–5), 289–302

—— (ed.), 'A Difficult Spring Follows the Thaw', *Soviet Studies*, 8(1956–7), 279–98

—— (ed.), 'A Practical Note in the Literary Discussion', *Soviet Studies*, 6(1954–5), 302–7

Monas, Sidney, 'The Private Muse: Some Notes on Recent Russian Literature', *Hudson Review*, 11(1958), 101–9

Mond, Jerzy, and Robert Richter, 'Writers and Journalists as a Pressure Group in Eastern Europe', *Polish Review*, 11(1966), No. 1, 92–108

Padtra, Jiri, 'Current Trends in Czechoslovak Painting', *Survey*, No. 59(1966), 21–9

Pelenski, Jaroslaw, 'Recent Ukrainian Writing', *Survey*, No. 59(1966), 102–12

Perina, Rudolf V., 'Intellectuals and Political Change in Czechoslovakia: A History of *Literarni Noviny* and Its Contributors, 1952–1969', PhD diss., Columbia, 1977

Prieberg, Fred K., 'The Sound of New Music [in the USSR]', *Survey*, No. 46(1963), 94–101

Reichman, Edgar, 'The Literary Scene in Rumania', *Survey*, No. 55(1965), 38–51

Rubin, Burton, 'Highlights of the 1962–1963 Thaw', in Max Hayward and Edward L. Crowley (eds.), *Soviet Literature in the Sixties: An International Symposium*, New York: Praeger, 1964, pp. 81–99

Rubinstein, Joshua. 'Refreezing the Thaw', *Artnews*, No. 68(1970), 34–7

Rudy, Peter, 'The Soviet Russian Literary Scene in 1961: A Mild Permafrost Thaw', *Modern Language Journal*, 46(1962), 245–54

Schwarz, Boris, 'The Vicissitudes of Soviet Music', *Problems of Communism*, 14(1965), No. 6, 67–82

Segel, H. B., 'Censorship and Literature: Russia, Poland and the Ukraine', *Slavic and East European Journal*, 16(1958), 3–21

Seton-Watson, Hugh, 'The Role of the Intelligentsia', *Survey*, No. 43(1962), 23–30

Shapiro, Jane P., 'Rehabilitation Policy and Political Conflict in the Soviet Union, 1953–64', PhD diss, Columbia, 1967

Slavov, Atanas, *The 'Thaw' in Bulgarian Literature*, East European Monographs, Boulder, New York: Columbia Univesity Press, 1981

Smith, D., 'Soviet Film in the Sixties', *Russian Literature Triquarterly*, No. 7(1973), 321–41

Soviet Literature: A Reappraisal, Special issue of *Studies on the Soviet Union*, 8(1968–9), No. 3

'Soviet Russian Prose [a discussion]', *Studies on the Soviet Union*, 8(1968–9), No. 3, 6–23

'Soviet Underground Literature [a discussion]', *Studies on the Soviet Union*, 8(1968–9), No. 3, 67–85

Stillman, Edmund O., 'The Beginning of the Thaw, 1953–55', *Annals of the American Academy of Political and Social Science*, No. 317(1958), 12–21
—— (ed.), *Bitter Harvest: The Intellectual Revolt Behind the Iron Curtain*, New York: Praeger, 1959
Swayze, Harold, *Political Control of Literature in the USSR, 1946–1959*, Cambridge, Massachusetts: Harvard University Press, 1962
Taborsky, Eduard, 'The Revolt of the Communist Intellectuals', *Review of Politics*, 19(1957), 308–39
Thomas, Lawrence L., 'Polish Literature and the Thaw', *American Slavic and East European Review*, 18(1959), 394–416
Trumpa, Vincas, 'Dawn of Free Criticism in Soviet Lithuanian Literature', *Lituanus*, 4(1958), 126–9
Vickery, Walter N., *The Cult of Optimism: Political and Ideological Problems of Recent Soviet Literature*, Bloomington: Indiana University Press, 1963
——, 'Some Critical Trends in 1956 Soviet Literature', *Indiana Slavic Studies*, 2(1958), 181–211
Zaporowski, Bogdan, 'The Young Generation of Post-Stalin East Europe', *Central European Federalist*, 14(1966), No. 2, 21–5

3. 1980s

Aksyonov, Vassily, 'Through the Glasnost, Darkly: A Cool Reaction to Gorbachev's Thaw', *Harper's Magazine*, 274(1987), No. 1643, 65–7
Alt, Noamy, 'Is there a Cultural Thaw?', *Index on Censorship*, 15(1986), No. 8, 11–13
Bowlt, John E., 'How "Glasnost" Is It?', *Artnews*, February 1989, 117–19
Boym, Constantin, 'Notes From the Underground', *International Design*, May–June 1989, 29–41
Brown, Deming, 'Literature and Perestroika', in Jane Burbank and William G. Rosenberg (eds.), *Perestroika and Soviet Culture*, special issue of *Michigan Quarterly Review*, 28(1989), No. 4, pp. 761–70
Buhks, Nora, 'Journalism or Literature? Influence of the Journalistic Forms of Expression upon the Soviet Prose of the 1980's' (Resume), *Cahiers du Monde Russe et Soviétique*, 28(1987), 209–19
Burbank, Jane, and William G. Rosenberg (eds.), *Perestroika and Soviet Culture*, special issue of *Michigan Quarterly Review*, 28(1989), No. 4
Christie, Ian, 'The Cinema', in James Cracraft (ed.), *The Soviet Union Today: An Interpretive Guide*, 2nd ed., Chicago: University of Chicago Press, 1988
Condee, Nancy P., and Vladimir Padunov, 'Reforming Soviet Culture Retrieving Soviet History', *Nation*, 13 June 1987, 817–20
Eagle, Herbert, 'Soviet Cinema Today: On the Semantic Potential of a Discredited Canon', in Jane Burbank and William G. Rosenberg (eds.), *Perestroika and Soviet Culture*, special issue of *Michigan Quarterly Review*, 28(1989), No. 4, 743–60
Gillespie, David C., 'Art, Politics and *Glasnost*': The Eighth Soviet Writers'

Congress and Soviet Literature 1986–7', in Michael Scriven and Dennis Tate (eds.), *European Socialist Realism*. Oxford: Berg, 1988, pp. 149–70

Goldfarb, Jeffrey C., *Beyond Glasnost: The Post-Totalitarian Mind*, Chicago: University of Chicago Press, 1989

'History and Literature: A Symposium', in Jane Burbank and William G. Rosenberg (eds.), *Perestroika and Soviet Culture*, special issue of *Michigan Quarterly Review*, 28(1989), No. 4, 553–79

Hochfield, Sylvia, 'Soviet Art: New Freedom, New Directions', *Artnews*, October 1987, 102–7

Hosking, Geoffrey, 'The Politics of Literature', in James Cracraft (ed.), *The Soviet Union Today: An Interpretive Guide*, 2nd ed., Chicago: University of Chicago Press, 1988, pp. 272–83

Laber, Jeri, 'The Moscow Book Fair: Glasnost Has Its Limits', *New York Times Book Review*, 11 October 1987, 13–14

Laird, Sally, 'Soviet Literature – What Has Changed?' *Index on Censorship*, 16(1987), 8–13

Marsh, Rosalind J., 'Soviet Fiction and the Nuclear Debate', *Soviet Studies*, 38(1986), 248–70

Morgan, Patrick, 'Inside the Leviathan: The New Novelists of Russia and Eastern Europe', *Quadrant*, 29 September 1985, 15–20

Nemec-Ignashev, Diane, 'Soviet Russian and East European Post-Modernism', *Slavic and East European Journal*, 31(1987), 110–26

Olcott, Anthony, 'Glasnost' and Soviet Culture', in Maurice Friedberg and Heyward Isham (eds.), *Soviet Society under Gorbachev: Current Trends and Prospects for Reform*, Armonk, NY: Sharpe, 1987, pp. 101–30

Recent Polish and Soviet Theatre and Drama, special issue of *Slavic and East European Arts*, 3(1985), No. 1

Romanenko, Alla, 'Perestroika, Glasnost and Theatre', *Soviet Literature*, 1988, No. 9, 184–9

Rumens, Carol, 'Unthawed Ice', *Poetry Review*, 77(1987), No. 3, 11–12

Seton-Watson, Mary, *Scenes from Soviet Life: Soviet Life Through Official Literature*, London: BBC Publications, 1986

Taubman, William, and Jane Taubman, *Moscow Spring*, New York: Summit, 1989

Volkov, Oleg, 'It's Hard To Be Optimistic', *Index on Censorship*, 16(1987), No. 2, 7–8

Weil, Irwin, 'Soviet Culture: New Attitudes toward the Arts', in *The Soviet Union under Gorbachev: Assessing the First Year*, New York: Praeger, 1987, pp. 121–35

Ziolkowski, Margaret, '*Glasnost*' in Soviet Literature: An Introduction to Two Stories', in Jane Burbank and William G. Rosenberg (eds.), *Perestroika and Soviet Culture*, special issue of *Michigan Quarterly Review*, 28(1989), No. 4, 639–47

Notes on Contributors

Judith Armstrong, MA PhD (Melbourne), is a Senior Lecturer in the Department of Russian at the University of Melbourne. She is the author of *The Novel of Adultery* (London: Macmillan, 1978) and *The Unsaid Anna Karenina* (London: Macmillan, 1988). She has published a translation from the French, *In the Land of Kangaroos and Goldmines* (Adelaide: Rigby, 1981) and co-edited a Festschrift, *Essays to Honour Nina Christesen* (Melbourne: Australian International Press, 1981). She also publishes in literary theory, and is at present working on the comparative semiotics of the fin-de-siècle. She is director of the programme in European Studies at the University of Melbourne.

Leslie Bodi, Dr Phil. (Budapest, 1948), is Emeritus Professor at Monash University in Melbourne. Having been a lecturer in Hungary, he came to Australia in 1957 and was Chairman of Monash University's Department of German from 1963 to 1987. He has published extensively on the relationship between literature, politics and society in German-language writing. His main field of research is Austrian literature, concentrating on the eighteenth century and the survival of enlightenment traditions in Austrian culture. He is the author of *Tauwetter in Wien. Zur Prosa der österreichischen Aufklärung* (Frankfurt: Fischer Verlag, 1977). In 1989 the Academy for German Language and Literature (Darmstadt) awarded him the Friedrich Gundolf Prize for German studies abroad.

Katerina Clark, MA (ANU, 1967), M. Phil. (Yale, 1969), PhD (Yale, 1971), is Associate Professor of Comparative Literature and Slavic at Yale University. She is the author of *The Soviet Novel: History as Ritual* (Chicago: Chicago UP, 1981) and with Michael Holquist of *Mikhail Bakhtin* (Cambridge, Mass.: Harvard UP, 1985). She is at present working on an interpretive cultural history of Petersburg/Petrograd/Leningrad from 1913 to 1931.

Zhanna Dolgopolova, PhD (Melbourne, 1983), is Assistant Professor of Russian at Washington and Lee University in Lexington, Virginia. She is the author of numerous articles published in the USSR, USA and Australia on the stylistics and structure of Russian prose. She compiled *Russia Dies Laughing: Jokes from Soviet Russia* (1st ed. London: André Deutsch, 1982), which has since been translated into Dutch, German, Finnish and Japanese. At present she is working on Russian anti-utopian literature of the late 1970s and the 1980s.

David Farrer is the Slavic languages cataloguer at the Monash University Library, and an early graduate of Monash's (then) Russian Department. The paper in this collection is his first published work.

Rosh Ireland, MA (Cantab.) is Senior Lecturer in Russian in the Department of Modern European Languages at the Australian National University and is the author of articles in classical and modern Russian literature.

Amanda Metcalf, MA (ANU, 1977), PhD (Hull, 1985), formerly a member of the Russian Section of the Department of Modern European Languages at the Australian National University, now works in that University's administration. She is the author of *Evgenii Shvarts and His Fairy-Tales For Adults* (Birmingham: Birmingham Slavonic Monographs, 1979), the editor of an annotated edition of E. Shvarts' *Drakon* (Canberra: Department of Slavonic Languages, ANU, 1984) and the translator of A. Vampilov's play *Proshchanie v iune* (in: A. Vampilov, *Farewell in June*, trans. by K. Windle and A. Metcalf, Brisbane: University of Queensland Press, 1983).

Janet Neville, BA (ANU, 1977), is a former research assistant in the Russian Section of the Australian National University's Department of Modern European Languages. She is currently engaged in freelance scientific translation.

Aleksandar Pavković, Senior Lecturer in Slavonic Studies at Macquarie University in Sydney, was previously Docent at the University of Beograd. The author of *Razlozi za sumnju* (Reasons for Doubt), (Beograd: Istraživačkõizdavački centar, SSO Srbije, 1988) and the editor of *Contemporary Yugoslav Philosophy: The Analytic Approach* (Dordrecht: Kluwer, 1988), he is currently working on the political philosophy of Slobodan Jovanović, the leading Serbian political theorist in pre-war Yugoslavia.

Pavel Petr, Dr Phil. (Leipzig, 1960), CSc (Prague) teaches German literature at Monash University. His areas of interest include Marxist literary theory, the theory of the comic and the German literature of Prague. He has also published on Kafka, Brecht, Stefan Heym, Anna Seghers, GDR literature, Czech literature and Marxist dialectic.

Marko Pavlyshyn, MA (Monash, 1979), PhD (Monash, 1983) is the Mykola Zerov Lecturer in Ukrainian at Monash University in Melbourne. He co-edited *Slavic Themes: Papers from Two Hemispheres* (Neuried: Hieronymus, 1988) and is the author of articles on nineteenth- and twentieth-century Ukrainian literature, as well as Ukrainian writing in Australia. At present he is researching contemporary Ukrainian prose.

Peter Stupples, BA Hons (Leeds, 1963), M. Phil. (Leeds, 1977), is an Associate Professor in the Department of Russian and Soviet Studies at the University of Otago, New Zealand. He is the author of a number of articles on modern Russian literature and the visual arts, and has recently published a monograph on *Pavel Kuznetsov: His Life and Art* (Cambridge: Cambridge University Press, 1989). He is at present working on a study of the Russian avant-garde at the turn of the century.

David Wells, D. Phil. (Oxford, 1988), has written several articles on the poetry of Anna Akhmatova. His doctoral thesis, 'Akhmatova and Pushkin: A Study of a Literary Relationship', concentrates particularly on the functions of literary borrowing in Akhmatova's work. He is currently working in the Department of Politics at La Trobe University, Melbourne, on a project to create a database on Soviet political personnel.

Kevin Windle, BA (Liverpool, 1968), MA (McMaster, 1969), PhD (McGill, 1974), is a Lecturer in the Department of Modern European Languages at the Australian National University in Canberra. He has translated, *inter alia*, works by Sergei Zalygin, Valentin Rasputin and Alexander Vampilov (University of Queensland Press), as well as Ireneusz Iredyński and Jerzy Lutowski (BBC Radio Three, ABC Radio). A translation of Vasyl' Sokil's novel *Taka dovha nich* (A Night So Long) has recently been completed.

Index

Abakumov, Viktor, 45, 168
Abuladze, Tengiz: *Repentance*, 11, 13, 167
Acta Analytica (Ljubljana), 78
'Aesopian language'
  ambiguity of, 36, 66
  as vehicle for subversive political messages, 21, 64, 143
  in the Habsburg Empire, 32, 34
  Loseff on, 19, 42
Aitmatov, Chingiz, 9
  The Executioner's Block, 11, 14, 62
Akhmatova, Anna, 84, 119, 128, 144–5
  Anno Domini, 144–5
  From Six Books, 119, 124, 144–6
  Poem Without a Hero, 143–56
  Requiem, 85, 87, 127, 144–6
  Selected Poems, 145
  White Flock, 144
  'And the Word Fell Like a Stone', 146
  'July 1914', 145
Akimov, Nikolai, 113, 121
Akopian, Akop, 102
Aksenov, Vasilii, 2, 16
Aleksandrov, G. F., 71
Allilueva, Svetlana, 181
Alpatov, Mikhail, 96, 101
Alxinger, Johann Baptist von, 35
analytic philosophy: in Yugoslavia, 78, 80–1
Andronov, Nikolai, 98, 101
Andropov, Iurii, 103
Antonenko-Davydovych, Borys, 157
  Behind the Curtain, 157–66
    Jungian perspective on, 158, 160, 162–3
    national issues in, 159–61, 166
    repression in, 158, 166
Antonov, Sergei: *Vas'ka*, 88
apartment Art (Apt Art), 103, 107
Apollo's Lute, 55
Astaf'ev, Viktor: *The Sad Detective*, 62

autumn open air exhibitions, 100, 107
Avtorkhanov, Abdurakhman, 178, 182

Baines, Jennifer, 133
Bakhtin, Mikhail, ix, 140
  'Discourse in the Novel', 5–6
  see also reaccentuation
Balter, Boris, 88
Barachnaia shkola, 97–8
Baratynskii, Evgenii, 151
Beaumarchais, Pierre: *The Marriage of Figaro*, 30
Bek, Aleksandr, 84
  New Appointment, 86, 173–5, 180–2
Belinskii, Vissarion, 15
Berdiaev, Nikolai, 12, 79
Berghofer, Armand, 31
Beria (Beriia), Lavrentii, 45
  as depicted in literature, 168–82
Bezdukhovnost' (lack of spiritual values), 3–4, 12
Biebl, Konstantin, 40
Birger, Boris, 98
Bitov, Andrei, 4, 15
  Pushkin's Photo, 91–2
  'Flight With a Hero', 15
Bitt, Galina, 97
Bloch, Ernst, 45
Blok, Aleksandr, 148
Blumauer, Aloys: *The Adventures of the Hero Aeneas*, 27
Bondarev, Iurii: *The Game*, 4, 12
Brezhnev, Leonid, 99, 103, 107
Brezhnev period
  as literary theme, 86
  as time of stagnation, 3, 107
  culture and the arts during, ix, 4, 14
  partial approval of Stalin during, 2
Brissot, Jean-Pierre, 31
Brodskii, Iosif, 15
Bukharin, Nikolai, 10
Bulgakov, Mikhail, 11–12, 84, 114
  Molière, 121

Index

Index

Index

Meyern, Friedrich Wilhelm von: *Abdul Erzerum's New Persian letters*, 32
Mikhoels, Solomon, 118
Milanov, Kajica, 71
Mitin, M. B., 71
Mlynář, Zdeněk, 47
modernization: *see* Thaws, modernization as objective of
Molotov, Viacheslav, 172, 175
Montherlant, Henry de, 42
Moroz, Valentyn, 60
Moscow Archive of the New Art, 103
Moscow Club of Avant-Gardists, 107
Mozart, Wolfgang Amadeus, 30
Mukařovský, Jan, 40
'Mukhomor', 103
Mushketyk, Iurii, 56
  Standpoint, 56
  The Boundary, 56
myths
  of the origins of the USSR, 4–5, 7–8, 11
  of Persephone, 129–30
  of Petersburg, 15, 147
  of Psyche, 129–30
  questioning of, ix, 9
  of Russia's benign colonialism, 66

Nabokov, Vladimir, 11, 15, 83, 150
Nagibin, Iurii: *Get Up and Be On Your Way*, 87
nationalism
  Hungarian, 45
  Polish, 45
  Russian, 8, 14, 52, 102–3
  Ukrainian, 52, 67
nationality issues
  Aitmatov's defence of Kirghiz ethnicity, 12
  in Czechoslovakia, 39
  in Shevchuk's *House on the Hill*, 57
  in Shevchuk's *Three Leaves Beyond the Window*, 64–6
  in the Habsburg Empire, 28–9, 33
  in the USSR, 49–50
  in Ukraine, 51–2, 55, 61–4, 157–8, 166
  see also Antonenko-Davydovych
  in Yugoslav philosophy, 78
  quest for a European identity, 14–15
  revived during thaws, ix, 9, 19
  Russian cultural imperialism, 12, 52, 57

Russification, 50, 58
Russophilia in Czechoslovakia, 40, 45
Russophobia, 45
  see also language policy, nationalism, themes of thaw literature
Nedeljković, Dušan, 71, 72, 74, 76
Nedobrovo, Nikolai, in Akhmatova's verse, 153–6
Neizvestnyi, Ernst, 100
Nemirovich-Danchenko, Vladimir, 118
Nemukhin, Vladimir, 101
Neva (Leningrad), 85
New Economic Policy, 2, 10, 86
Nezval, Vítězslav, 40
Nicolai, Friedrich, 35
Nilin, Pavel: *Cruelty*, 88
Novotný, Antonín, 44, 45
Novychenko, Leonid, 62
Novyi mir (Moscow), 14, 43

Ogonek (Moscow), 9, 51, 63, 83, 85
Oktiabr' (Moscow), 85
Oliinyk, Borys, 58, 59
Ordzhonikidze, Grigorii, 3, 168, 173
Orlov, Igor', 102
Osadchyi, Mykhailo, 54
  Cataract, 60
Ovid, 131

parody, 20, 32, 34
  see also satire
Pasternak, Boris: *Doctor Zhivago*, 2, 11, 128
Pavlychko, Dmytro, 58, 62
Perestroika, 17, 57, 83
Pertsov, Viktor, 119
Petronijević, Branislav, 71
Petrović, Gajo, 74
Petrov-Vodkin, Kuz'ma, 95
Pezzl, Johann: *Faustin*, 27
Pidmohyl'nyi, Valer''ian, 60
Pil'niak, Boris, 84
Platonov, Andrei, 84
Pogodin, Nikolai, 118
Polevoi, Nikolai, 150
Polishchuk, Valer''ian, 58
Pomerantsev, Vladimir, 110
Popović, Nikola, 71
Poskrebyshev, Aleksandr, 3, 168
Praxis (Zagreb), 76, 79
Praxis Marxism
  as dominant force in Yugoslav philosophy, 76–7

Index

12, The Esplanade, 53
Shistdesiatnyky, 51, 157
Shkvarkin, Vasilii: The Last Judgement, 121
Shmelev, Nikolai, The Pashkov Home, 92–4
Shterenberg, David, 96
Shukshin, Vasilii, 14
Shvarts, Evgenii, 114
    The Shadow, 121, 124
Simonov, Konstantin, 167
Sizov, Nikolai: Difficult Years, 171–3, 180
Skilling, H. Gordon, 44
Skovoroda, Hryhorii, 55, 64
Slánský, Rudolf, 44, 172
Slovo o polku Igoreve, see Lay of Igor's Campaign, The
Socialist Realism
    and Soviet visual arts, 96, 97, 99, 101, 103, 104, 106, 108
    calls for transformation of, 51
    decline of, ix, 61
    emergence of, 2
    in Honchar, 52
    in Mushketyk, 56
Solchanyk, Roman, 55
Solzhenitsyn, Aleksandr, 38, 43, 99, 179
    Matriona's House, 8
    The First Circle, 168
    The Gulag Archipelago, 3
Sosiura, Volodymyr, 52
Stalin, Joseph, 40, 69
    criticism and demythicizing of, ix, 8
    in literature, 3, 86, 167–82
Stalin period and Stalinism
    as depicted in literature, 4, 86–91, 146
    impact on philosophy, 37–8
    in Czechoslovakia, 44–5
    Kundera on, 42
    reaction against in Ukrainian literature, 51
    see also Stalin, Joseph, and de-Stalinization
Sterligov group, 97
Sterne, Laurence, 56
Stojanović, Svetozar, 74
Stozharov, Vladimir, 102
Stus, Vasyl', 54, 60
Subbi, Olav, 102
Sukhovo-Kobylin, Aleksandr, 113
    The Lawsuit, 113, 120–1

Sundukov, A.
    'The Endless Train', 106
    'When in a Queue', 106
Surov, Anatolii: Decent People, 110
Sverdlov, Iakov, in Shatrov's Thus We Shall Triumph, 10–11
Sverstiuk, Ievhen, 60
Svitlychnyi, Ivan, 60
Symonenko, Vasyl', 51

Tadić, Ljubomir, 78
Tairov, Aleksandr, 122
Tatlin, Vladimir, 16, 101
thaws
    as metaphor of political and cultural liberalization, vii–ix, 6–7, 18, 37–8, 69
    as transitional period in culture, 1–2, 6–7
    change in perceptions of time during, 4–7, 8, 9–10
    see also Reaccentuation
    complaints and demands during, 1, 50, 58–9, 61–2, 83–4, 118
    criticism of Stalinism during, 2, 3, 9, 49, 58, 60
    cultural change during, ix, 6–7, 16
    general features of, vii–ix, 1–2, 6–7, 9, 19–22, 37–8, 66, 69–70
    history rewritten during, ix, 7, 10, 58
    illusory quality of, 47
    in Czechoslovakia, 43–4, 46, 47
    in the German Democratic Republic, 45
    in the Habsburg Empire, 23–34
    in the USSR in 1940, 117–26
    in the USSR under Gorbachev, vii, 49, 57–64, 103–8
    in the USSR under Khrushchev, viii, i, 2, 43, 91, 95–9, 146, 182
    in the Soviet theatre, 109–16, 118, 120–3
    in the Soviet visual arts, 95–108
    in Ukraine, 49–53, 58–9, 67, 119, 157
    increased freedom of expression during, viii, 2, 19–20, 21, 26–7, 46, 50
    intelligentsia and, ix, 17–18
    interest in the 1920s during, 9–10, 11–13, 58
    limitations of, viii–ix, 20–1, 182
    'liquidation of blank spaces' during, 83, 84